Printing Statement:

Due to the very old age and scarcity of this book, many of the pages may be hard to read due to the blurring of the original text, possible missing pages, missing text and other issues beyond our control.

Because this is such an important and rare work, we believe it is best to reproduce this book regardless of its original condition.

Thank you for your understanding.

THE SECRET HISTORY

OF THE

COURT OF FRANCE

UNDER LOUIS XV.

EDITED, FROM RARE AND UNPUBLISHED DOCUMENTS,

BY

DR. CHALLICE.

IN TWO VOLUMES.

VOL. II.

LONDON:

HURST AND BLACKETT, PUBLISHERS,

SUCCESSORS TO HENRY COLBURN,

13, GREAT MARLBOROUGH STREET.

1861.

JOHN CHILDS AND SON, PRINTERS.

CONTENTS

CHAPTER II.

CHAPTER III.

CHAPTER IV.

CHAPTER V.

CHAPTER VI.

CHAPTER VII.

THE SECRET HISTORY

OF THE

COURT OF FRANCE.

CHAPTER I.

Liberality of Frederic of Prussia — Potsdam Philosophy —
Voltaire, the enemy—Madame de Châtelet—Voltaire's Price
— What he did in Prussia—Letter of King Frederic to
Voltaire—Letter of Madame de Pompadour to Madame de
Châtelet—Transfer of Voltaire—Judas—The Empress and
the Marquise—Prussian Pamphlets—Royal Suppers at Pots-
dam—Royal Suppers at Choisy—Frederic outwitted—The
manufactory of *Sèvres*—The Palace of Work—*Belle Vue*—
Fête at Belle Vue—Sèvres Flowers—Belle Vue Retreat of
Capuchin Friars—King's Temptation—Priest's Picture—
State Cabinet — Threats — Importunities — Royal visit to
the Camp at Compiégne—Grenadiers of France—Soldiers'
Children—Military Nobility—Royal visit to the Arsenal at
Havre—Suspicious uneasiness of England—Daring pro-
posal to increase the French Navy—Marshal Belleisle's
Bureau—English "Bills"—Foundation of Naval School in

THE Pope's Nunzio at Versailles informed King Louis XV. that the King of Prussia, under the tutelage of Voltaire, (who still enjoyed French pensions and sinecures,) had grown so liberal as to offer the free exercise of the Roman Catholic religion at Berlin.

Jansenists and Jesuits were welcome to the " Solomon of the North," who had turned his palace into a barrack, and who only tolerated the wives of his subjects as machines to manufacture good soldiers.   With a view to increase his kingdom he could not afford to restrict his religion.   So a French courtier said to King Louis, "Sire, this sovereign wants a taste of all things; formerly, he had only soldiers, now he invites monks.   I advise your Majesty to make him a present of all the Jesuits in France." " No," said another, " we will keep them for the first article of a new peace, when we

can change six *Loyalists* against one soldier."
France suspected Prussia in every movement, for at
Venice the Abbé de Bernis had been informed by
the envoy of Poland that Frederic was in treaty with
England, and that the preliminaries of an agreement
had been signed with the Whigs as to subsidies.*

Frederic found the limits prescribed by the
treaty of Aix-la-Chapelle too narrow for him.
He had but one real vocation, that of a soldier,
(though he affected that of author and philosopher,) and he must tear the world to tatters
wherewith to drapery his own ambition. It
was necessary that he should conciliate the
Court of Rome, because, although the Pope
was nothing but a shadow to him, there were elements beneath that shadow which were portentous
in the growth of a military power, to say nothing
of a desirable influx of prolific subjects.

As to the *Philosophes*, and the Pamphleteer-
ing Jansenists, who had been exiled from France,
they were drawn from London, Amsterdam,

* Correspondence de Bernis, 1752.

At Versailles it was also believed that the death of
Marshal Saxe had been one cause of these movements on
the part of Prussia. " Marshal Lowendhal," it was said,
" has lost his counsel, the King his general, and Prussia her
check."

and elsewhere, into Berlin by the magnetic presence there of Voltaire.

Frederic had betrayed France twice. He had compromised the campaigns of France. " But what matter ? Voltaire flatters him. The French are not yet philosophic enough to relish Voltaire entirely. Prussia suits him. A circle of atheists surround Frederic. They are the anti-nationalities of France. True, they mock at Frederic as at other things. But what matter? He serves their purpose, and they his. Voltaire, for a season, is hailed their chief. It is in Prussia that he really verifies his Jesuit tutor's prediction that he would become ' the leader of French Deism.' "

The men (Anti-Jesuits) if left to themselves would have extolled the power of the Marquise in France as opposed to their common foe, the Jesuits; but encouraged by King Frederic and banded together by Voltaire, for his own personal motives, they formed a faction against the representative of the liberty they had advocated in the land from which they were driven.

The voice of the people, the voice of God! It is often but the servile echo to that of one man, who, the chances are, is a monomaniac.

To King Frederic himself, surnamed the Great, this faction was personally and politically agreeable. He scorned women, and he knew that the power he had to contend with in France was that of a woman who bade fair to ally herself with that other woman, Maria Theresa of Austria. " Neither priest nor woman ever entered the palace of Frederic the Great. In a word, he lived without a court, without a council, and without worship."

Voltaire was enraged against the Marquise, (who, by his own account, had originally showered down upon him all his honours,) because she had not found him a place in the ministry. This was impossible, he being the leader of the proscribed Encyclopédistes. He was Historiographer and Editor of State Documents, but he wanted, as before said, a post for which he was unfitted by antecedent and even by his genius.

Louis XV. objected to poets as statesmen. " No," said he to the Marquise, " let your poets remain poets; not even your faithful secretary, Marmontel, could assist *us* in such work as this."

Voltaire's friend and late companion, that somewhat pedantic and didactic Marquise Emilie

de Châtelet, was not well pleased at his trans-
plantation to Prussia. Even his queen was not
tolerated by Frederic, king of soldiers and prince
of philosophers.*

Of Madame de Châtelet Voltaire tells us :—

" I found in 1733 a young lady who thought
much in the same way as I did, and who took
the resolution of passing several years in the
country, there to cultivate her mind far from the
tumult of the world. It was Madame de Châtelet,
the woman who in all France had the greatest
disposition for all the sciences. . . . She knew by
heart the finest pieces from Horace, Virgil, and
Lucretius ; all the philosophic works of Cicero
were familiar to her. Her predominant taste was
for mathematics and metaphysics. So much
accuracy of judgment and taste have seldom
been united with ardour for instruction. She
did not the less love the world and all the amuse-
ments of her age and of her sex.

" I taught English to Madame de Châtelet ;
who at the end of three months read, equally,
Locke, Newton, and Pope... Madame de Châtelet
attached herself at first to Leibnitz, and developed

---

* See Appendix, Vol. 2. Original Letter from the King of
England to the Queen of Prussia.

a part of his system in a very well written book, entitled 'Institutions of Physic.' But born for the truth, she soon abandoned systems and attached herself to the discoveries of the great Newton. She translated into French all the book of Mathematical Principles."

Madame du Châtelet had to take refuge in 1749 at the Court of Ex-King Stanislas (father to the Queen of France), that " Beneficent Philosopher " who once had starved out Voltaire.

Versailles might have been preferable to the Châtelet, in spite of Madame Pompadour there, who abhorred straight lines and angles, and who was clothing all Paris in forms of artistic beauty, even to the very chairs, tables, and costume of the population.

But there the Châtelet could not go when Voltaire was meditating, under Frederic's protection, scurrilous verses against his former friend and patroness. Her home, Cirey, was a desert to the Châtelet without Voltaire, although with Voltaire she had declared to Marshal Richelieu that Cirey was a terrestrial paradise. But that was long ago.

If Voltaire would rather spend the income

he derived from the favour of his patroness, the
Pompadour, at the Court of that Prince who
most delighted in her defamation, the senti-
mentalism of his beloved Châtelet must be regulated by those studies in which she most excelled. Euclid is not a bad whipping-post for
Cupid.

She had shown extreme repugnance to
Voltaire's residence at the Court-Barrack of
Frederic. When she died, this must have been
a remembrance to Voltaire, which, like his misfortunes, was only good to forget. " She would not,
at any price, that I should leave her for the King of
Prussia," says he : " she found nothing so cowardly
and abominable in the world as to separate one's self
from a woman to go and seek a monarch." But
Voltaire persuaded her, or tried to do so, that
the welfare of the human race depended on his
alliance with Frederic the Great. Whatever was
her feeling on the subject, Madame du Châtelet
was philosopher enough now to yield to " le
Roi Voltaire." Years before, he confesses, " She
would have made a horrible tumult."

After her death Voltaire completely passed
into the service of the King of Prussia, on con-

dition that he should receive the grand cross of
the Order of Merit, the key of Chamberlain,
and the promise of a Barony, with £20,000 attached to his title. It has been declared in his
own words how all his former elevation was
owing to " three civil words he said to a King's
mistress," and now that he sold himself to a
king who reviled her, he bound himself to
adopt Prussian prejudices as his own to a
degree that, as says one of his outraged countrymen, " The French were no more to him than
the Welsh." In fact, from Voltaire's own account of himself he must have submerged his
existence with his independence. He whom
the King delighted to honour is scarcely
recognisable as the clear-headed Encyclopédiste
when he asks : * " The means to resist a victori-
ous King, a poet, musician, and philosopher,
who appeared to love me ! I believed that I
loved him. At last I again took the road to
Potsdam in the month of June, 1750. To be
lodged in the same apartment that had had the

* The satire lurking beneath Voltaire's Brandebourg Mémoires was the birth of his after disappointment. After Frederic
had " squeezed him dry," he wrote flattering letters to him with
one hand and these Memoires with the other, as will be seen.

Marshal Saxe! To have at my orders all the King's cooks when I wished to eat at home, and King's coachmen when I wished to go out, were the least of the favours accorded to me. The suppers were very agreeable.... I worked two hours a day with his Majesty; I corrected all his works, never failing to praise strongly all in them that was good, while I scratched out all that was worthless. I gave him my reason for everything in writing, which composed a rhetoric and a poetry for his use; he profited by this, and his genius served him still better than my lessons. I had no court to make, no visit to return, no duty to fulfil. I made for myself a free life, than which I can conceive nothing more agreeable.

" *Alcine Frédéric,* who saw that my head was already a little turned, redoubled his enchanted potions to inebriate me quite. The last seduction was a letter that he wrote to me from his apartment to mine. A mistress cannot express herself more tenderly. . . . This is it:

" ' How could I ever cause the misfortune of a man whom I esteem, whom I love, and who sacrifices to me his country, and all that humanity has the most dear? . . . I respect you as my master in eloquence. I love you as a virtuous friend. What slavery, what misfortune, what change is there to fear in a country where you are esteemed as much as in your own country, and with a friend who has a grateful heart! I have respected the friendship that bound you to Madame de Châtelet,* but after her I was one of your oldest friends. I promise you that you shall be happy here as long as I shall live.' "

* There was another who had respected this friendship in the person of Madame de Châtelet herself, and that was the Marquise de Pompadour; to wit, the following extracts from a letter written by Pompadour in answer to some favour begged by Madame de Châtelet. The favour is gracefully conferred, and then is added :—"Permit me at the same time to compliment my sex which you honour by your talents, of which men ought to be jealous. When Newton astonished Europe by his sublime discoveries, he could never have imagined that a Frenchwoman, celebrated by her rank and beauty, would be not only capable of understanding him, but of interpreting him. Whilst the talented Voltaire sings your praise, and France admires you, permit that a woman who knows nothing," (a slight satire this on pedantry,) "but who is full of esteem for learning, present to the charming and illustrious '*Emilie*' the sincere homage that all Europe will soon render to her."

When Madame de Châtelet died in the palace of Stanislas, after two days' illness, "We were all so troubled," says Voltaire, "that nobody thought of fetching either Curé, Jesuit, or Sacrament. She had none of the horrors of death. We only felt them." Immediately afterwards he speaks with self-adulation of the attention King Stanislas paid him.

"There was a letter," continues Voltaire, "that few Majesties would write! It was the last glass that intoxicated me. The protestations by mouth were still stronger than those in writing. He was accustomed to singular demonstrations of tenderness with favourites younger than myself; and forgetting for a moment that I was not of their age, and that I had not a beautiful hand, he took mine to kiss it. I kissed his, and made myself his slave. It needed a permission of the King of France to belong to two masters. The King of Prussia undertook all.

"He wrote to beg me of the King, my master. . . I did not imagine that they would be shocked at Versailles, that an ordinary gentleman of the bed-chamber, who is of the most useless species to the Court, had become an useless chamberlain at Berlin. They gave me permission. But they were very vexed, and they did not forgive me for it."

Forgive you for what, Voltaire? for transferring your allegiance from one master to another, just as the one by the loss of his brave General and faithful friend was threatened by that other? You say you were placed in the room once occupied by Saxe, whose victories you had helped to celebrate in France; did you ever dream of that hero? Did you feel the weight of that Versailles sinecure, you speak of so lightly, when retaining it in the court of another master, with whose sine-cures you were also burdened? To that and other favours lavished on you by the " elevation" of one you formerly flattered as the centre of " all acts, all tastes, all talent to please, the charm of all hearts, and treasure of one mortal," you were welcome. But when, having sold yourself, your King, and country, to the enemy of that object of your time-serving adulation, you so pandered to him who was " great" enough to buy you, as to write, under his tutelage, your filthiest book to please the traditional foes of France whom he wanted for his allies instead of her, you were not forgiven.

In that book you betray your country's honour by a kiss. And by it you forfeit your own.*

---

* " Voltaire," says Capefigue, " welcomed and *fêté* at Berlin by Frederic who wished to use his great popularity to his service, finished there the indecent Poem, Anti-French, of the *Pucelle d'Orleans*, written in honour of the English. In this poem, where all is delivered to the impure kisses of the Englishman, John Chandos, Voltaire, to serve the policy of Prussia which desired

Voltaire, in time, had his Judas reward. He found out, when too late, how he himself had been betrayed, and confesses:

" I strongly displeased the King of France without pleasing the King of Prussia more, who mocked at me in the bottom of his heart."

But, while blinded by Frederic's flattery, he made it a fashion at Berlin to insult his own King and the woman who was toiling for the welfare of that King. France became a bye-word in those little suppers at Potsdam, where, in the presence of the Great Frederic, impiety usurped the place of wit, and profanity of philosophy. At these suppers where the exiled discontent of France had access, and was nurtured, the Marquise was served up under coarse soubriquets; especially when it was whispered that a suspected alliance between France and Austria was due to the good understanding that had arisen between Maria Theresa and Madame de Pompadour.

When it was told to Frederic the Great that the Prince de Kaunitz (who had met the Abbé de Bernis and the Duc de Choiseul at Venice)

the debasement of Madame de Pompadour, wrote those shameful verses (too shameful for quotation) against the protectress he had formerly so servilely praised."

was sent by his Imperial Mistress as Ambassador to Versailles, and that the Queen-Empress wrote to the Marquise as " dear Cousin," the King's rage against women in general, and these two in particular, knew no bounds.

He employed the wounded self-love of the refugees he had collected round him to spawn forth libellous pamphlets and foul pasquinades. To those are due some few lies by which the memory of the Marquise de Pompadour and French Monarchy have been degraded. No assertion is too monstrous for the digestion of Revolutionary fury.

The pamphlets, exported from Prussia, and imported in England for political motives, were afterwards circulated in France for the furtherance of ends which were supposed to justify the means.* It was impossible, by all the laws of epidemic malevolence, that the plague would stop until it had sealed with a death-spot the fame of one who, by her peculiar position, was exposed to its mortal influence.

A hundred years afterwards the disease can be

* Many of these pamphlets, the scum of Revolutionary literature, have lately been cast out of the Bibliothéque Impériale, though they still find a place in the British Museum.

tracked without fear.   It leads us behind a
curtain where sits a hero surrounded by parasites,
and at his right hand the Judas-Voltaire; a
hero on the battle-field, with his enemy face to
face, an absolute monarch in his own kingdom,
where he openly legislates with a hand of iron
justice, but a pitiful man who scorns not to forge
false weapons, to dip his arrows in poison, and to
shoot at an enemy who is weaker than himself, in
the dark.   Let great kings bow their heads and
scatter thereon dust and ashes.

It was a little room in which this great king
supped, discussing infidelity and manufacturing
lies; he loved not women, and before him was
placed what his slave Voltaire calls, " a singular
ornament," in the form of an indescribable
picture.   This picture (which the King had
ordered to be painted by one of the best
colourists—Pêne—and for which he had given
the design) was a gross satire on love and
marriage.   But Voltaire declares : " a chance
guest who could have listened to us, seeing this
picture, would have thought to hear the seven
Sages of Greece."

If corrective, it is a pity this " singular ornament " was not, instead of being paraded before his

guests, kept in the back-ground for his own use, like the monk's instruments of self-torture or the hidden sackcloth next the skin.

Voltaire had long ago adopted this picture with other Prussian singularities, albeit some were startling to the now experienced courtier of Choisy and Versailles. The suppers of Frederic, penurious of fare, cynical in ornament, and ' where only the name of God was spared,' though no creature or motive was respected,—were a contrast to those at Choisy, with their refined profusion, their graceful adornment, and that goodly company of which the King of France was the head and the Marquise the soul : where, asserts their chronicler, " the choicest wines flowed without drunkenness, where wit conversed without licentiousness, where business was banished, and yet where the young and most brilliant gentlemen of France showed their genius to the King in sprightly discourse without revelry, and in a moment of relaxation without debauchery."

For a moment, the " *stérile abondance* " of the lively de Bernis was too much for the Anti-Machiavel Frederic, and his French Mephistophiles, Voltaire. Their fears were precipitate as to the alliance between the women of France

and Austria. The Prince de Kaunitz was sent
Ambassador to Paris in 1750, and his mistress
called the Pompadour " Cousin," in acknowledg-
ment of her power, and for other reasons, hereafter
to be divulged ; but the absolute alliance was the
result of an elaborated and long-studied policy on
both sides.   It was only thoroughly accomplished
after the hostilities of the English, and subsequently to the treaty of alliance and subsidies of
Frederic with the Whigs. Frederic seems to have
mistaken friendly overtures, attributable to the
meeting between de Bernis and Kaunitz in Venice, for negotiations of a more severe importance.

So say the French.   The terms of the treaty,
between France and Austria, will appear in their
proper place and time.

In the mean while Paris was like a hive of bees
for industry.   If Frederic invited and cherished
unpatriotic discontent in Prussia, the woman he
was doing his worst to injure invited and cherished everybody and everything competent and favourable to the plans she was executing for the
good and glory of France.   Not contented with
those vast buildings which have survived the
storm of the Revolution, and stand as monuments

to her zeal and genius, she elaborated even the *fantaisies* of art so as to give employment to hundreds, to carry the adornment of taste into the homes of thousands, and to afford a fresh source of revenue to the State.   The French government, at her instigation, had for some time past encouraged attempts to rival the celebrated Dresden China.   These attempts had succeeded so far as to justify her recommending to the King to establish a manufactory, or school, for this delicate branch of art at the Château of Vincennes.   The choice of place was in itself a fine tribute to peace and the progress of civilization.   Afterwards, when the plan of this manufactory was developed by a lucrative result, it was transferred to Sèvres.   The Marquise there bought a building which belonged to the company of the farmers-general, who, truth to say, were generally at the head of industrial improvement.   This building, situated above the village of Sèvres, and towering above the woods of Meudon, she caused to be reconstructed on a comprehensive plan of her own, for which she, as usual, drew the appropriate designs.   Considering that the manufacture, which she desired should equal that of China and Japan, would employ not only

2 *

workmen, but artists, she caused this vast building at Sèvres to represent under a palace-like exterior a grand republic, where each, from the highest to the lowest engaged in the work, co-operated according to his capacity for the glory of the general result.

This important branch of ornamental manufacture was attempted, and had failed, in the reign of Louis XIII., but under the direction of the Marquise de Pompadour in that of Louis XV. it succeeded, and that at a time when the people had most need of employment, and the King of wholesome distraction from his gloomy thoughts, sensual temptations, and the petty dissensions of his kingdom of which he was the victim.

To this work-palace of Sèvres she often went, accompanied by Louis the " well beloved."

The manufactory had its fine gardens, its cascades, fountains, groves, woods, and a small chase for the artists, who enjoyed to hunt the stag and wild-boar in the forest, none the less for their sedentary lives in the art-palace.

No wonder that the works were carried on there with what a Frenchman, in speaking of them, calls " incomparable ardour," with the King himself frequently present to approve them, and the Queen of artistes adding to their perfection, as she often did, by the delicacy of her touch in moulding the soft wax, or tinting it. She frequently, also, designed the forms and subjects for this plastic art with infinite perfection.

In art she sought a refuge from a suffering body, an aching heart, and a sore conscience. Her most earnest desire was that the King she revered, and the man she loved too well, should participate in the solace it afforded her.

Her fear of a rival no doubt spurred on her zeal in thus beneficially amusing him, for his own glory and the good of his people.

Every year Louis XV. ordered an importation of these works of Sèvres to Versailles, where he invited his courtiers to buy them. Who is not familiar with the anecdote of the young Abbé de Pernon standing in mute admiration before a fine Sèvres ornament in the gallery of Versailles, when the King came up to him, and said, "Very well, Abbé, take it ; it is fine?" "Sire," replied the Abbé, "I am neither great enough nor rich enough to possess anything so magnificent." "Take it all the same," said the King, "a good abbey will pay for all ;" and forthwith his Majesty found the great Almoner, and

ordered him to confer on the Abbé de Pernon,
who was modest and of good taste, the best vacant
benefice.

One fine day in the month of May, when the
Marquise was driving from Sèvres with the King
to the Château de Meudon, where they were staying, to be in the vicinity of the works, she caught
sight of a wooded height crowned by a heath.
Having ascended, she clapped her hands, and
with the spontaneousness of quick appreciation
that was part of her artistic nature, cried out,
" Oh ! the beautiful view ! " This view extended
over the Seine, St Cloud, Versailles, and even to
St Germaïn's. The King marked her delight, and
was not slow to execute a plan that placed the
" beautiful view " at her own disposal ; and upon
the upland heath there soon arose that fairy-palace
which was known, before the Revolution, as
" *Belle Vue.*" It need not be said how, to do justice to the King's chivalric gift, the Marquise
convoked the best of those architects, painters,
decorators, and landscape gardeners she had assembled in France. The King himself had never
shown such enthusiasm in any work as in this he
designed to her honour, and she as the chef-
d'œuvre of his kingdom. The building com-

menced the 30th of June, 1748, and was finished, under royal auspices, in 1750. The interior of the Château was wonderful for its marbles, pictures, and statues, its music-gallery, &c. When finished, the Marquise invited the King to visit her there. She prepared a fête for his reception. He had often breakfasted there among the workmen, but he had been excluded during the latter days of interior decoration. The King came. A special apartment was prepared for him. It was a cold day in winter, and at night it hailed and snowed. The King was unable to leave, the weather being inclement, but he found himself the centre of one of those refined and brilliant suppers before described, which rose, as if by magic, from the floor. There were flowers on the table, and the only thing the King felt wanting was, that none had been presented to him, as usual, by the Marquise.

After supper, she conducted the King into a magnificent conservatory, brilliantly illuminated, where innumerable flowers, exotic and indigenous, emitted a delicious perfume. The King contemplated their beautiful hues with delight, but involuntarily stretched forth his hand, as if in deprecation that none of these, so choice at that

season, had been offered to him. The Marquise
told him to feel them, and then, for the first time,
he discovered that they were cold and lifeless, although in each were dropped essences that per-
fumed the air. The King was delighted at the
progress that the art of Sèvres had made under
the patronage of his beautiful hostess, but the
man understood too well the metaphor it afforded
to their mutual life.

Behind her Château, Madame de Pompadour
built a retreat for Capuchin friars, as if to recall
to herself perpetually the idea of death and repentance.

The King often came to Belle Vue; for some
time it was his favourite residence. It was there
that the Marquise proposed to him some of the
noblest plans for France, and introduced Genius to his notice. It was there that she showed
the King how the faithful servants of religion,
the poor Capuchins, dwelt beneath the shadow of
her protection, even at her gate;—she, the excommunicant and enemy of the Jesuits ! * It was
there he learned to know her best, and obtained
an insight not only into the realms of art, of which

* In the revolutionary storm that levelled Belle Vue to
the ground, the "retreat for the poor Capuchins" was also

his kingdom had insensibly to him become the centre, but into those feuds of party which he mistook for religion.

This latter insight was soon eclipsed by the traditions that were too strong for him, having been born and bred in them. Custom was omnipotent to the King in matters of faith as in morals. For the latter he found a tempter in every courtier, who was disaffected by envy or disappointment to the Marquise, and a bait in every valet-de-chambre about his palace who had a pretty sister or cousin. He seems to have gained absolution for everything but his friendship for Madame de Pompadour. Having exhausted all other means, the priests tried to frighten the King into her dismissal from his confidence. A picture was painted, representing the infernal regions, wherein were several crowned heads in various stages of torture, whose awful contortions proved the fiery reality of their sufferings. The King's confessor, who was a Jesuit, placed this before his Majesty. Louis frowned as he looked at it, and demanded an explanation.

swept away. The plans of both are still preserved in the Archives of France and the accounts of it in the "Chroniques Artistiques." Bib. Imp.

The Priest then pointed out one who was in agony, because he had been an ambitious and self-aggrandizing King. Another who was a miser; another who had allowed his Parliament to govern for him; but the worst-tortured King of all, was the one who publicly worshipped a woman, and who set her up on high in the face of his kingdom.

The allegory was as clumsy as the picture was coarse. The King's worship was not now sensual: but gloom again overspread the mind of Louis, though it was impossible for him to divest himself or his people of the woman who was set on high to the advantage of the latter, and on whom it was habitual for him to lean in every case of difficulty and emergency.* It was his custom to work with his Ministers and Secretaries of State in her salon. This tribute, however, to the necessity of her presence entailed on the Marquise

---

* In 1748 a fanatic had stopped the King in his way from his carriage, and declared that France would be destroyed if he did not send away Madame de Pompadour. Unto which the King only answered: "You are mad, go and get bled." — When Madame de Pompadour heard of this, she said: "The man was not mad, neither was he sent by Heaven, but by men whom I despise and fear not."

much inconvenience, as her ante-chambers became thronged with supplicants for royal favour ; so that there was not a grievance, public or private, but was thrust upon her notice. This served to increase the number of her enemies within the kingdom, as the majority of the cases were not remediable by a monarch not possessed of absolute authority, and some exemplified domestic feuds and disappointments that were below his notice. Those which were in her power to relieve only provoked the jealousy of double their number that were beyond, or beneath, her control.

The King, in spite of Jesuits and parasites, was nevertheless so anxious to associate the Marquise with his good works in the eyes of his people, that he desired she should accompany him on his visits to the Camp, by which, from time to time, he renewed the loyal enthusiasm of his troops. She no longer followed him, as in former days, in the disguise of a young musketeer, and in the "elegant baggage" of the Duc de Richelieu, but openly, as became one who had laid the first corner-stone of the military school, and who had benevolently enlarged and adorned the military hospital. Together they went to the Camp at

Compiegne, to review a new troop, the " Grenadiers of France."   " It was an excellent idea,"
confesses one of the bitterest anonymous enemies
of the Marquise, " of the ministry which, not to
lose what was most precious in each reformed regiment, that is to say the Grenadiers, in whom
were generally the soul and spirit of the body, to
preserve and re-unite them under a generic deno-
mination."

M. de Crémile, who had been Marshal General of army homes in 1744 and 1745, and who,
having contributed to the success of those campaigns, was afterwards appointed Inspector of Cavalry, Infantry, and Dragoons, asked the King as
a favour to be permitted to exhibit his tactics.
The King introduced to his soldiers, their friend.
It was therefore she went to Compiegne, where
athwart the chasm of a hundred years filled with
the refuse of public revolution and much personal
slander, the Marquise has a claim to be remembered.

She deserves to be so, by a military power ;
for, encouraged by the tribute paid to her by the
Inspector of Cavalry, she suggested to the King
of France one of the noblest projects that ever
did honour to the Kingdom, viz. — a provision

for the orphan children of those who had died in their country's service, and a patent of nobility which should be hereditary, " so that those who had secured the throne and its privileges should be remembered in after-generations, by the names that had distinguished them from the rest of the people." *

Who, in France, does not appreciate this aristocracy of courage now ?

Louis XV. issued a decree conferring different degrees of nobility according to the previous rank of the officer and his deeds of valour. This was scoffed at, spurned, more or less, under the old régime, but, surviving the Revolution, it came out in full practical force under the military rule of the first Napoléon, and is cherished as one of the chief incitements to France to support the present imperial dynasty. In fact, by it the Emperor Louis lays best claim to his throne and title.

But while the Marquise thus helped to raise France highest in the scale of military power, she did not forget the navy, which M. de Rouillé was doing his best to re-construct. She went with the King to the Arsenal at Havre, where royalty gave every encouragement in the new attempt to

* Arrêts de Louis XV.

strengthen this, the most feeble part of the administration.   To this encouragement it was due
that England, ever suspicious and watchful of her
neighbour's doings, grew uneasy.   Lord Albemarle, her Ambassador in Paris, demanded an
explanation.

France only laughs at this, and declares that
directly " she thinks of her ships, her neighbour
is sleepless."

Lord Albemarle insists, "What is the use of
these vessels ? "

M. de Puisieux, Minister of Foreign Affairs,
replies, " Milord Albemarle, my master the King
of France is not bound to render an account of his
actions to any power in Europe.   France is at
peace with Great Britain, consequently these ships
cannot be destined for war with England."

But England, though seemingly satisfied, was
not the less watchful.

What would England have said if she knew
that at that very time it was proposed and seriously
considered in France, to escape prying observation in building ships, by buying them ready-
built from every maritime power, except England,
in the world ?

" And," says a memorial, " if Holland, Den-

mark, Genoa, and Venice, have not enough to
sell, let France look to Malta, Algiers, Tripoli,
Constantinople, and elsewhere, to supply her
wants. What matters it from whence come the
vessels and how they are, in form, constructed, if
they can contain men and cannon! . . . . . . As to
sailors, recourse must also be had to foreigners. . .
It is but to offer to idle and underpaid sailors certain advantages. Sailors, like common soldiers,
decide for the State that pays them most. Their
natural Prince is money!"

This proposal, which was anonymous, was
seriously debated in the Cabinet of Versailles.
There was wisdom in it, on the same proverb-
ial ground of " Let foolish men build houses, and
wise ones live in them." France would have
done anything just then to evade the lynx-eyed
watchfulness of England, but she wanted the essential—money!

For lack of this, many fine projects were laid
aside in France, exhausted by war, to be re-con-
sidered by her in a more prosperous after-gener-
ation.* Many a seed was sown in the 18th

* The memorial was, however, acted on in the matter of
sailors. De Belleisle, it will be remembered, had told the
King that, though soldiers would never be wanting in France,

century which has sprung up in the 19th. Politics, like the aloe, flower once in about 100 years.

Marshal Belleisle had a Memorial bureau, which he labelled, " A collection of very fine projects, just now useless to France." *But he did not destroy them.* Some of these have turned out more useful than the waste paper of the English House of Commons.

Louis XV., though afraid of the British Navy, was not afraid of the British Parliament. One day, when he was discussing politics, he said :

" It is a great question if the English are more powerful or happier for the volumes of ' Bills ' that are always being brought in for her reform. England herself is not agreed about it. There is

she found, and ever would find, a comparative difficulty in generating sailors. De Rouillé, therefore, the new Minister of Marine, successor to Maurepas, laid his hands on them wherever he could find them ready-made and willing to transfer their allegiance. He instigated France to carry her flag into the Northern Seas, to sift the East India Company, to test piratical practices, not only for men, but instruction. " In a word, he adopted the best, the most prompt, and the most multifarious means, of re-establishing that almost obsolete class of men."

This was a sign that peace was transitory.

a party in England which declares that the government is entirely ruined, that the State is in debt beyond remedy, &c. I presume, nevertheless, that England's strength increases, but this must be attributable to the inadvertence of other powers rather than to internal reform, which would have produced but small results if other States had followed her example."*

In 1754, the naval school was established in France, " a centre of communication for intelligence on a subject which most needed light." M. de Rouillé had the credit of this establishment; the fact that the *Marine* under his rule was being re-constructed rapidly and successfully, justified his appointment, at which many had cavilled because it came through the direct intervention of Madame de Pompadour.

She was consulted, necessarily, as " part and parcel of the King," concerning this naval school, the idea of which she had pondered, it will be remembered, when the military school was founded. " Such an establishment as a Marine Academy,"

* Mems. Politiques, published at Liege, 1762. Requiring authentication on some points by comparison with more authentic works, &c..&c., but valuable as expressing the contemporary views of France concerning England.

writes an anonymous observer, " was at first derided, because it partly consisted of officers who many of them could not hold a pen to sign their name; but it was a link of fraternity between the different parts of a great whole. . . . . It was a centre of emulation, from which some day would spring all the best of those who have some function to fulfil in the arsenals of the navy."

Incorporated into this *Académie de Marine* were scientific members, who introduced into it the studies essential for naval superiority and per- fection. It was subsequently developed into a departmental system, courses, apprenticeship, examinations, &c., which eventually educated France to compete with her enemies, and for which, in the progress of a century, she has now much to be grateful.

These naval plans and projects in time of peace were chiefly owing to that often-quoted clause in the treaty of Aix-la-Chapelle, which was defective towards France respecting the limits of Canada.

The Duc de Mirepoix was ambassador in Lon- don. " A good appointment," said Marshal Saxe, " because he has a good leg and can teach the English how to dance."* To him Madame de Pompadour wrote in 1751.

"Your despatches, M. le duc, appear to us more important than you seem to imagine. We fear that this chicanery on the subject of Canada may eventually produce a rupture. Your King George is a German, and he seeks with us a quarrel which is patriotic. The English, who are treated as defective politicians, have nevertheless had the cleverness to leave this Canadian point undecided in the treaty of Aix, and to put off its discussion on irresponsible commissioners; in consequence of which this famous peace, which seemed to assure repose to Europe for a long time, is in fact only a suspension of arms, during which there is leisure to breathe and to prepare for another war.

"M. de Montesquieu says that the 'English do not understand the art of negotiation!' . . . . . but the oversight of our plenipotentiaries is unpardonable. The snare was so evident, and yet they fell into it like children.

"As it is, we must keep a good countenance and not seem afraid. Is it possible that an English-

Appendix 2.

3 *

man has said in open parliament that we dare not fire a cannon at sea without the consent of Great Britain?

" This is ridiculous and insolent; but it shows the spirit of the nation, and that English justice, like religion there, is ex parte. . . . .

" Milord Albemarle passes his time agreeably here. The King of England, who loves him—though I know not why—sends him his lesson all ready, and he comes to repeat it, like a schoolboy, to the Minister of Foreign Affairs. . . . As for you, M. le duc, it is hoped that you will do honour to your nation, by your vigilance and your talents. It is especially necessary at present that you have the hundred eyes of Argus, to see all and observe all.

" Albemarle amuses himself here by drinking, &c. Pray amuse yourself by zealously serving your King and country. Good-night, M. l'Ambassadeur. Love your friends faithfully, and reckon on their support."

The people of France, unconscious how they were threatened from without by the machinations of Frederic of Prussia, and the ambition of England in America, went on blindly quarrelling among themselves about the Bull Unigenitus.

The Abbé de Bernis, as seen, had been in Italy, and the Duc de Choiseul was sent to Rome expressly to confer with the Pope concerning this bone of contention.*

Pope Benedict XIV. was a man who, like Cardinal Fleuri, loved peace above all things, though he could not ensure it. Voltaire describes him † as "beloved by all Christianity for the gentleness and gaiety of his character, and regretted more and more after his death." "It was his secretary," goes on Voltaire, "the Cardinal Passionei, who did everything. This Cardinal, the only one at that time in the Sacred College who was a man of letters, was of a genius exalted enough to despise these disputes. . . He hated the Jesuits who had fabriated the Bull ; he could not

---

* The wrangling over this bone was the vindication of philosophy. The Encyclopédiste school proclaimed all intimate thought, prejudice ; the sensualists cried : "Touch, compare, and judge." Meanwhile, Emmanuel Kant (born at Kœnigsberg, 1724) brought out one work after another. To proscribed French writers, who had fled to Germany, there was fascination in Kant's declaration of a "revelation of the conscience independent of the senses, and that idea could result from reflection on one's self, *à priori*, foreign to all teaching." But Kant gleaned his views from his predecessor, Descartes, and Descartes his logic from the Jesuits.

† Siècle de Louis XV. Voltaire, Vol. ii. p. 184.

hold his tongue on the false step they had made at
Rome, of condemning in that Bull virtuous
maxims, of a Truth Eternal, which belong to all
times and to all nations ; this, for example : " *The
fear of an unjust excommunication ought not to prevent the performance of duty !* * This maxim is
in all the earth the safeguard of virtue. All
the ancients, all the moderns have said that
duty ought to rise above the fear of punishment." But, strange as it may appear, neither
the Cardinal Passionei, nor the Pope, could re-
tract an edict such as was this Bull, which was
regarded as one of the Laws of the (Infallible)
Church.

The Pope sent a circular letter in 1756 to the
Bishops of France, which recognised the Bull as
an irresistible law, to which nobody dare resist
without eternal peril, but deciding that the dying
suspected of Jansenism should be warned that they
will be *damnés*, and their risks and perils communicated to them. The Pope, in his particular
letter to the King, recommended to him the rights
of the Episcopate.

" When," says Voltaire, " a Pope is consulted,

* Proverb 100 years old. " *Les miracles du jour m'em-
péchent de croire à ceux de la veille.*"

be he whom he may, it ought to be expected that he will write as a Pope ought to write."

The feud was accepted as an inevitable evil, sometimes lulled, and sometimes stimulated in the course of events.   It would be impossible to track its wearisome course here, where its history is glanced at in advance as showing its strength as an element in the Palace, in which were to be found the strongest partisans of the Jesuits and their Bull Unigenitus.

The King desired that all the honours of a "lady of the Palace" with the "Tabouret" should be accorded to her who was his best friend, and the most trustworthy adviser for his welfare and the glory of his nation. The Queen, who had years before, according to precedent, awarded all outward honour to ladies who were her dishonour, and who, when there was real ground of jealousy against Madame de Pompadour, had favourably received her, resisted this wish of the King by the instigation of her spiritual advisers.

Once more it must be recalled to the reader what custom had sanctioned in the Court of France in the earlier part of the reign of Louis XV. before his connection with Madame de Pompadour, and in the reigns of his predecessors.

The case under immediate notice was, however, unprecedented as yielding the palm to friendship.

The special favours conferred by those "honours of the Louvre," ycleped " Lady of the Queen's Palace and the Tabouret," consisted principally in being seated in the presence of the Queen, and being qualified to receive her kiss. Also, the rank of Duchesse. These could be no matter of any consequence to the Marquise de Pompadour, who had long been the centre of the Court, and who, in the King's Council, was more powerful than the Queen herself in all matters of State, but she desired to avail herself of the etiquette, not only to confirm that power (which she exercised for the good of the King), but to prove to the world at large that her life had ceased to be a scandal to her King, her country, and herself. The same motives justified Louis in the demand, especially when he felt himself to be on the eve of a new war, which would necessitate the concentration of all the fidelity and ability he could command in his own kingdom, of which fidelity and ability this woman was the brightest example and leader.

For some time past, as often hinted, Madame de Pompadour knew herself to be stricken by a

disease which, though slow, was mortal. As was
natural in such a case, her mind, always ardent
and impulsive, turned to religion; but a religion
opposed, in its aspirations for spiritual liberty,
to the miserable juggling of party feuds by which
she was environed, and from which she vainly
strove to deliver the King. Frequently she took
refuge from this discord that disgraced the name
of Christianity, and from other State anxieties, with
her daughter in the Convent of the Assumption.
She was notorious among the sisterhood for the
rigour of her ascetic observances. During the
Jubilee in 1750 she had, either from conscientious
scruples or ill health, declined to take an open
part in public rejoicings, and lived at the Convent
in the society of the Nuns, and that daughter who
was the cherished object of her life. She had
also affiliated herself to the third order of St
François.

Although these facts might not at the time be
publicly proclaimed to the Court and world, the
observation of the former had noted that the Father
de Sacy who, though a Jesuit, was a gentle and
enlightened man, confessed the Marquise, and
was in the habit of holding long and serious con-
versations with her.

The directors of the Queen were Father Griffet, the Cardinal de Luynes, the Bishop of Verdun, and M. de Nicolay. These, under the inspiration of the Archbishop of Paris, who openly expressed his hatred of the Marquise, and his wish for her destruction as an enemy of the Church (i. e. the Bull Unigenitus), banded together with other bigots of their order in condemning Father de Sacy for holding converse with his penitent. He received orders from his Superiors to cease to visit her, " to expose to Madame de Pompadour the duties of a conscientious confessor," and to " excuse himself, as best he might, for having so long a time *amused* her."

What this meant will presently be seen. In the meanwhile, for the first time in her life, the Queen, who had no will of her own, disobeyed her husband, and, repeating the words that had been put into her mouth, declared to him :

" There would be too much indecency for me to grant honours to a person who lives in a fraudulent separation from her husband; who dare not approach the altar to receive the communion there. I have nothing to say against the innocence of her life, nor the tie which binds her to your Majesty. But that innocence does not repair the reputation of Madame de Pompadour, since, although she is married, she lives as though she were not, without fulfilling any of a wife's duties in the house of her husband," &c.

The King was outraged by this duplicity, although he held the Queen guiltless of it. The position in which it placed him was certainly unpleasant, for on the other hand he knew the proud spirit ("l'humeur lucifer," as she herself called it) of the Marquise, and had reason to dread that this mocking insult would drive her away from him altogether, just as he had most need of her. He must throw himself upon her mercy. He complained to her of his unhappy position, thus :

. . . . " All love favour, but none love the King. . . . I see around me a number of people whom I suspect have no honour, but my rank prevents my piercing the veil that covers them. To me they are impenetrable, nevertheless I am compelled to employ them for the service of the State, and from thence spring public troubles for which, with my reign, I am responsible to posterity. . . . . When I have a choice to make, and decide in favour of one of my subjects, it seems as if all France had agreed to deceive me ; they vaunt to

me the talents, the merit, and the virtue of the
man I am about to honour. I cannot find one
honest man in my kingdom who, at the time, can
tell me of his vices; for everybody is afraid to
displease the one who bids fair to obtain my favour;
and it is to this fear that I am sacrificed with the
State.

"If, on the contrary, I withdraw my confidence
from a Minister or some one in place, he is de-
picted as a man without capacity or genius. . . . .
I am then told of faults, and dishonest means that
he has employed during the time of his administration. . . . A patriotic King is the most unhappy
mortal existing under the roof of heaven. He
wishes to render his people happy, and everywhere he finds those who prevent his doing so."

The King's gloom drew the Marquise more
closely to him; she believed him, in spite of his
weakness, and the vices of his century, to be
worthy of all happiness and glory. She herself
was pitiable for many things, not only as sharer of
those troubles he had referred to, but chiefly in
finding herself a subject of discord between the
Monarch and his family. She wanted to be in
charity with all men, and she had done much to
serve royalty, especially the Dauphin (who owed

all his power to her intercession for him with his father *), who now, acting under the same party-priest advice as his mother, took every occasion of insulting the Marquise as the pretended enemy of religion.

In a letter to a female friend the Marquise (after having assisted at some intimate réunion at Versailles) writes : " Nothing touches me more than to see the King in the midst of his family. His love for his children is remarkable ; his gentle manners towards them, beautiful."

It was as long ago as 1747 that, in writing to Madame de Noailles, she repeated :

" The pomp, the grandeur, the pleasures of this world enchant me no longer. . . . The charm is broken, and I find in my heart nothing but an immense void which cannot be filled.   The world is a liar ; it promises a happiness it is incapable of giving. . . Sometimes it seems as though I thought otherwise, and I am gay. . . . One would say that in the heart are two measures, the one of pleasure and the other of grief, which are alternately emptied and filled."

But to return.   The King was at bay.   The

---

* The Dauphin's seat in the Council was due to the advice of the Marquise.

Jesuits thought they had triumphed in excluding
Madame de Pompadour not only from the honours
of the Tabouret, but from the privileges of the
Sacrament.

Such artifices, which, to further party-
spirit, prevented a penitent from returning to
the bosom of the Mother-Church, must have
been contemptible in the estimation of a suffering
woman already tired of the earth, and who
wanted to learn the way to heaven. But they
attacked her vulnerable point—her pride. How
could she remain about the Court with this stigma
attached to her? They assailed, likewise, her purest
instinct. She loved her daughter and desired
honour in her eyes, as she was now advancing to
womanhood. How endure this notorious excommunication before her, and how sustain the
consciousness that she was the means of alienating
the King whom she loved from his own children?
The kingdom, under the Marquise's auspices, was
filled with noble works. Paris, under her direction, was teeming with industry and growing in
beauty. To her, alone, the King looked for
support and happiness. She, alone, had the power
to drive the demon of hypochondria away from
him, and to allure him from the temptation to

degrading pleasures that everywhere beset his path. But, how continue to do all this in defiance of the power he mistook for religion, in defiance of his family, and of his people who, worked upon by the machination that beset herself, would be taught to look upon her as a cause of execration to the King! Yet how desert him in the hour of coming need!

Either she or the Jesuits must triumph. In the meanwhile, they were preparing a test for her the most painful and humiliating that could be devised, never thinking in their condensed hatred of the Marquise how they were playing into the hands of Frederic of Prussia.

CHAPTER II.

The Prince de Kaunitz at Versailles—M. d'Etioles—What her confessor said to the Marquise—What she said to him —What said the Duc de Choiseul, and why—What said the Prince de Soubise, and why—Doubts of the King of Prussia —What Madame de Pompadour wrote to her husband— What King Frederic the Great did and said in Prussia— What King Louis did in France—Bargain between King and Husband—Forgotten fact of Royal Epistolary etiquette —What the Queen of France said—What the Dauphin and Dauphiness thought—What the Dauphin and the Marquise did — Autograph letter of the Queen's first lady to the Marquise — Autograph letter of the Marquise to the Queen's first lady—Fête of the Duc de Richelieu—His treatment by the mystic Count de St Germain—the Court dislike of de Richelieu's intrigues — Letter of the Marquise to an ambitious lady—Dedication of "Esprit des Loix" to the Marquise—Academic tribute to the Author —Letter of Madame la Marquise to M. de Montesquieu— Threat of poisoning the King—Police Records of Latude—

The Prince de Kaunitz, whom the Abbé de Bernis had met at Venice, was in 1752 the Austrian Ambassador at Versailles. He wrote to his Imperial Mistress what he saw in France, not the scandal but the glory of France ; and Maria Theresa, fired with emulation, essayed the foundation of a military school for Austria. At home, the Marquise, assailed on every side, one day received a letter from her husband, which presumed to insult and threaten the King.

The King found her in tears, and insisted on knowing the reason. She showed him the letter, although she had tried to conceal it, so as to screen the offender. The King read it, and said : " I forgive him, for he is much to be pitied." * They

* In 1750, when the people were opposed to Madame la Marquise (instigated by the priests concerning the Bull Unigenitus), her husband tried to turn their favour in his direction by venturing to sit in a box facing hers at the Opera.

neither of them suspected the probable cause of
this sudden resurrection of M. d'Etioles ; and the
answer of the King, intended as a compliment to
herself, no doubt helped to soften the heart of the
Marquise towards one against whom she had
sinned.   In vain she entreated absolution at the
hands of her confessor, Father de Sacy.   He had,
as recorded, received his instructions from his
superiors, and could in nowise disobey.*   At last,

There were *claqueurs* (paid clappers) about, who instigated
the bourgeoisie of the audience to applaud d'Etioles. Madame,
says an eye-witness, bore the trial firmly, although she bit her
lip as if in pain. " *Elle a soutenu l'insulte comme elle eût
soutenu une belle harangue ou bien une longue flatterie.*" Nevertheless, M. d'Etioles received royal orders not to repeat the
experiment. Sometimes he wanted the Marquise to gain
some favour for him (which, says his advocate, was "*extra-
ordinairement rare, et toujours d'une indispensable justice*"),
and then he employed the Abbé Bayle as his envoy, although
once he charged him with this threat in case it was not granted :
" Tell my wife that I will go to the Château (Choisy), that I
have resolved to go, and that there I will make the roof ring
with the equity of the things I require and demand." Surely
it was originally a mésalliance !

  * The account of this Court and Church cabal is principally taken from the work of a writer, who professes to
have compiled it from the unpublished documents found in the
portfolio of a Court Lady opposed to Madame de Pompadour.
Pub. Paris, 1802, under title of "Mems. de la Cour de France."

when the Marquise was worn by the conflict, and
her strength exhausted by it, the Father said to
her :

" Madame, the absolution you crave cannot be
granted; your abode at the Court away from your
husband, the murmurs of the public relative to
the favours granted you by the King, do not permit you to approach the holy table, nor consequently to receive absolution. The priest who
might grant it to you, instead of absolving you,
would pronounce a double condemnation, yours
and his own, whilst the public, accustomed to
criticize the conduct of the great, would confirm
that condemnation without appeal. You desire,
Madame, you have proved to me, to fulfil the
duties of a good Christian ; but among these, example is the first. Therefore, to obtain an absolution, and to deserve it, the first step consists in
re-uniting yourself to M. d'Etioles, or at least in
quitting the Court, and edifying your neighbour
whom you scandalize by your separation from your
husband."

She saw through the shallow pretence and
scorned it, but she was helpless.

That she flew into a violent passion and insulted her confessor is a false assertion, disproved

4 *

by her subsequently becoming spiritually affiliated to Father de Sacy, who had hitherto been her friend, and to whom she was too much of a politician to impute the blame of this step.

The words that are put into her mouth by one of her bitterest anonymous enemies, recording this scene, are rather those of fine irony than vulgar rage. They are these:

"You are, my father, an ignoramus,* and a true Jesuit.† Do you understand me well? You have played on the embarrassment and need in which you imagine I find myself. You would wish, I know well, to see me far from the King. But I am on this point as powerful as you think me weak and uncertain; and, in spite of all the Jesuits in the world, I will remain at the Court."

The irony, the reproach, the love, and its consequent determination conveyed in these few words, that have been inverted by contemporary rancour against their speaker, authenticate them. They must have been uttered with majesty; for the Jesuit, it is recorded, was frightened and hastily took his leave.

* Ignorant as to what game he was playing as the tool of others.

† In abnegation of his own will and obedience to authority.

Neither Father de Sacy, his superiors, nor Queen, nor Dauphin, knew the need of the King and country at that moment. They none of them knew how the King had thrown himself on the mercy of the Marquise, nor her secret contempt for the world, in which her only ambition was to serve the King faithfully to the end. All these facts successively unveiled themselves afterwards. But at the moment they afforded no vindication to the Marquise.

It was not, however, in the chivalry of France to behold a beautiful woman, the best friend of France, so oppressed, without stepping forth to her rescue. The Duc de Choiseul had returned from Rome, where, in conversation with Pope Benedict, he had learned how little the Bull Unigenitus, the origin of this cabal, was esteemed by the enlightened holy Father himself, although he could not annul it. He had, also, when at Rome made acquaintance with the general of the Jesuits, who impressed him (de Choiseul) with his power as a something to be guarded against in his own political career, although it was evinced by a wish to oblige him. The Duke mentioned to the general of the Jesuits that, for State purposes, he wished to know more of some man (one of the company) in France, when the next day, to his astonishment, the most minute particulars were rendered to him of the individual in question. This despatch and exactitude of detail were so incomprehensible to de Choiseul, that he expressed more surprise than gratitude or admiration ; whereupon he was informed that a system of espionnage was established which enabled them at head quarters, at Rome, to render an account of each of the company's members at a moment's notice. However much de Choiseul appreciated the strength of such union he dreaded it for himself, hoping some day to become first Minister of France. He taught the King to dread it too.

In offering to serve his friend and patroness Madame de Pompadour in her emergency, he was, therefore, contributing to his own interest in a possible future.

Then there was the Prince de Soubise, who openly professed a profound contempt for the turpitude of Prussia in the matter of Frederic's private arrangement with Austria.* He knew that a

---

* About this time the philosophic party in France lost one of their champions, in that Prince whose studious life France remembered when the King rode forth with his eldest son to Fontenoy.

The Duc d'Orleans died the 4th February, 1752. "He

storm was brooding over Europe, and that the alliance of Austria would be desirable for France against Frederic, who had lost the confidence and won the fear of nations since making his " particular peace with Maria Theresa." The Prince de Soubise knew how urgent it was that all Frenchmen, let their creed be what it might, should rally round the standard of France ;—that to restrict her forces to those who believed in the Bull Unigenitus was a deadly absurdity. Frederic bribed and enticed into Prussia all whom France drove out from herself. The case was imminent. If the Jesuits remained within the walls, the kingdom must bid farewell to inward liberty; from which alone could result outward glory. If the King gave up Madame de Pompadour, he would become their slave and tool. She alone stood between priests and liberty. By her alone could France be enfranchised.*

died at St Genevieve,—this serious Benedictine, this erudite, Jansenist. His studious life had passed without noise, but it left a long ray of light. . . . What a contrast to the agitated and libertine life of the Regent was that of the Duc d'Orleans, his son! The Benedictine of St Genevieve had for his successor, the Duc de Chartres, who had married a daughter of the Prince de Conti."

* The Prince de Soubise was a partisan of the Encyclopédistes,—an "enthusiastic philosopher."

It was, therefore, not only for love of her, but for their King and country, that the Duc de Choiseul and the Prince de Soubise heard with alarm that she had determined to make the amende to her husband, so as to be admitted to the Sacrament. Her motives have been, in this matter, perverted with all the acrimony that the most malignant enmity could dictate, and it is singularly observable, that by none has she been so aspersed for her determination as by writers of the party which instigated her to take this step. This, because the result outwitted that party, and defeated its intention,—a defeat which eventuated in its destruction.

It is also observable that the only letter which authenticates the Marquise having written to her husband in the style (as said her enemies and advisers) " of a penitent Magdalene," has been preserved by her enemies. It therefore needs to be carefully received.

Here it is.

" I confess my fault, and I wish to repair it. I have deplored the injustice of which I have been guilty towards you, and I repent sincerely. . . . . . Already my fault, in fact, exists no longer ; it but remains for me to cause all appearance of

evil to cease, which I ardently desire. I am resolved to efface by my future conduct all that has
been irregular in my past life. Reconcile yourself
to me ; you will only see me occupied in edifying
the world by the unity in which I will live with
you, equally as I scandalize it by my separation."

It is not extraordinary that to a woman, dying
by inches, it was unendurable to live any longer
without the pale of recognised religion. As to
the coarse perversion of her wish for marital reconciliation, that is refuted not only by the physical sufferings which caused her peculiar position
and made her eager for peace with heaven, but
also by her determination declared to Father
Sacy, "that in spite of all the Jesuits in the
world," she would remain at the Court; which
is recorded by the same adverse hand as her letter to her husband.

With her numerous abodes, and the Court
open to her, she might " live with her husband,"
in one sense, and be at peace with him and the
world, without involving herself with his habits
of life that were distasteful to her.

Accepting this letter, preserved by her enemies, as authentic, the pain that stung her into
repentance is proved by others that are indubitably

so, in the choice autograph collections of France and England. These will be produced in their proper place.

The words of the King, " he is much to be pitied," no doubt weighed with the Marquise in her desire for her husband's forgiveness.

If King Louis XV. had taken example by his late ally and about-to-be enemy, Frederic of Prussia, he would long ago have cut the knot of his present difficulty by making a new law of divorce, which would have freed the Marquise from the thraldom of matrimony. " Frederic," boasts Voltaire, " governed the Church as despotically as the State. It was he who pronounced divorces when a husband or wife chose to marry elsewhere. A minister one day cited the Old Testament to him, concerning one of these divorces; " Moses," said the King, " led the Jews as he willed, and I govern my Prussians as I will." One day, also relates Voltaire, some judges wanted to burn some peasant who had been accused of a great crime; but, as nobody could be executed without the King's seal, the case was laid before Frederic for his sanction of the sentence.

But, to the horror and consternation of the judges, the august monarch, instead of signing

the death-warrant of his offending subject, endorsed it with " Frederic gives liberty of conscience in his kingdom, and of other things into the
bargain." A priest who was scandalized by such
indulgence, preached a sermon upon wicked
rulers, citing Herod. The priest was hauled up
to Potsdam before the King. The Great Frederic arrayed himself in a preacher's robe and
bands, and d'Argens, Author of "Jewish Letters,"
and Baron de Pöllnitz, who had changed his religion three times, clothed themselves in the same
habit. They took the dictionary of Bayle, and
placed it on the table, in guise of a Bible, and the
culprit was brought before these three ministers
of the Lord. " ' My brother,' said the King to
him, ' I ask you in the name of God upon what
Herod you have preached.' ' Upon Herod who
killed the little children,' said the good man. ' I
demand of you,' continued the King, ' whether it
was Herod the first of that name, for you ought
to know there were several so called.' The village priest could not answer. ' How ! ' said the
King, ' you dare to preach about a Herod, and
you are ignorant of his family ! You are unworthy of the holy ministry. We forgive you this time,
but we will excommunicate you if ever again you

dare to preach about somebody you don't know.'
They then delivered to him his sentence and his
pardon, signing three ridiculous names invented
at pleasure. ' We go to-morrow to Berlin,' added
the King, ' we will beg your pardon of our reverend brothers. Do not fail to meet us there.'
The priest went to Berlin to seek the three holy
ministers ; they mocked at him. The King, who
was more funny than liberal, did not think of paying the poor priest's journey."

Let the reader judge for himself whether it
is best to have a King with a bad digestion
under Jesuit tyranny, who is not at all funny
but generous, or a King whose digestion is strong
enough to digest every obstacle to his own ambition, who is remarkably funny, but profane and
stingy. As to the woman one King loved and
the other hated, of course she was contemptibly
weak in body and mind not to like to live and die
an excommunicant.

Louis concerted with the Prince de Soubise
and the Duc de Choiseul to neutralize the Marquise's letter to her husband. He sent the
former to M. d'Etioles to warn that farmer-ge-
neral against compliance with a single word that
the letter of the Marquise might contain. And

not only was the Prince de Soubise commissioned
to threaten M. d'Etioles against encroachment
on the royal prerogative of companionship with
the Marquise de Pompadour, but, to give weight
to his counsel and warning, he was authorized
by the King to promise d'Etioles a large augmentation of his " rights of finance."

M. d'Etioles' refusal of open reconciliation
with the mother of his child was well paid.
It is to be hoped that he had dignity enough left
to let the fact of that child's existence convince
him of the mother's sincerity in her penitence
and friendly overtures. He wrote a letter to the
Marquise which sounded very magnanimous,
took the King's money, kept mistresses, and
was never more openly mentioned at Court.

Nevertheless he kept himself alive in the
memory of the Marquise (as observed in the first
note of this chapter), whenever he had favours to
ask. The Abbé Bayle, who tells these anecdotes,
was his envoy, and the Prince de Soubise the representative of the Marquise on these occasions.
" My wife ! " This title was reserved by the worthy d'Etioles as a threat. Her earlier life must have
been wretched in the company of a man capable
of the following, as asserted by the Abbé Bayle :

She one day wanted to see a picture of herself by Latour, which d'Etioles still possessed. " Go, and tell my wife," said he to Bayle, " to come and fetch it away herself."

Henceforth the ties of friendship between the Marquise, the Duc de Choiseul, and the Prince de Soubise, were stronger than ever. But it was before their personal services to her in delivering her from the Jesuit snare, that she had recognised their merit as loyal subjects of the King, and their capabilities to serve him in the Cabinet.

The King re-demanded the honours of the " Tabouret," and now, that her husband was bribed to decline her overtures, she could not be excluded from the privileges of religion, nor denied all the honours of the Queen's court. She was acquitted. She became Lady (Duchess) of the palace, and daughter of the Church, but the rage of those who ruled in both was boundless.*

---

* The historians who have alluded to the caressing letters of Maria Theresa to Madame de Pompadour, and have blamed her for styling her, in the language of royalty, " cousin," forget, or are ignorant of, the etiquette which, after she had the *Tabouret* conferred upon her, entitled her to be so addressed. By letter patent of the 5th of January, 1753, the Marquise de Pompadour received the rights and prerogatives of *Duchesse*.

The Queen only laughed, as she withdrew the opposition to which she had been incited. " It did not suit me," she said, " to allege all my reasons ; now, my silence authorizes that the pretext be removed."

" It must be confessed," says the chronicler who dwells longest on this Court or Church intrigue, " that the Marquise always conducted herself towards the Queen with all the respect and submission she owed to her ;" and then, determined that she should not have the credit of this, adds : " but it was not possible for her to act otherwise, knowing the sentiments of the King, and how he would take umbrage at the least shade of insult offered to her Majesty."

But the Dauphin, whose reticence was not so great as his mother's, was goaded by his Jesuit advisers to an act of indecent insult towards the Marquise. It has been shown, in the earlier pages of this work, that she had been his best friend, and

Even the sovereigns of France, themselves, under the old regime, gave to the *Duchesses* the title of " *Cousine.*" The Queen-Empress, putting aside her private respect for the Pompadour, dared not infringe this etiquette. It is strange that some even among French authors are ignorant or oblivious of this fact.

that she rendered the tribute of a just appreciation
to the new Dauphiness, when the latter was suffering from contrast with her predecessor, and the
consequent coldness of her bridegroom. The Dauphiness had justified the opinion formed of her by
the Marquise. She was learned and gentle, not
devoid of wit, and manifested the nameless charm,
the " Je ne sais quoi," which the Marquise was
the first to discover. She was passionately devoted to her husband. She had won his tender
esteem, although she had never rivalled his love
for his first wife. But her love for him induced
her to submit herself entirely to the Church party
to which he was subject. They lived retired from
the Court, and their opinions were entirely guided
by those about them who were the most strongly
opposed to the Marquise. They were taught to
look upon her as the enemy of religion, because
she was the sworn foe of the Jesuits.* So it came
to pass that when she was presented to him (according to the etiquette of ceremonial in taking
the Tabouret for the first time) to be kissed, with

* The King, still temporizing, issued Letters Patent in
1753, forbidding Parliament to take cognizance of ecclesiastical
proceedings. "He was like the Roman Emperors between the
blues and greens."

the rest of the royal family, he treated her with "gross indignity." The King was outraged by this proceeding, and feared its effect on the Marquise, of whose loss he lived in perpetual dread. He declared that to be wanting in respect to her was to insult himself; and the next day he ordered that the Dauphin should quit the Court and retire to the Château at Meudon. In vain the Queen, the ministers, and the Court interceded. The King was inflexible. At last the Marquise herself entreated as a favour that the insult should be forgiven, representing her unhappy position at being the subject of dissension in the royal family. The King then relented, on condition that the Dauphin should go in person to the Duchesse de Pompadour, and publicly apologize to her, in presence of several witnesses. The Dauphin submitted.

"The Pompadour received," says the Court chronicler, "his apology and declaration of it, being altogether a mistake, like a gracious Princess." Not only so. "A better understanding than had subsisted lately sprang up between them, and she carried her courtesy so far as to engrave the portrait of the Dauphin."*

* The medal of the Dauphin (Bib. Imp.) is pronounced by artistic connoisseurs beyond all price as a work of exquisite art.

The King was satisfied by this outward concord, but the heart of the Marquise could not recover from the insult. She forgave it, but the torture to her pride and the torments to which she had previously been subjected, were almost fatal to her constitution, which was enfeebled by nervous disease.

She had said to the Queen long ago: "Madame, my passionate desire is to serve you." She had never lost an occasion of doing so. The following letter, written by dictation of the Queen, but not dated, proves this, confounds the malice of enemies, and is a triumph to the Queen and the religion she professed, over the party politics of which that religion was made a cloak. Especially as the Duchesse de Luynes (a relative of the Cardinal de Luynes, one of her Majesty's spiritual advisers) was the Queen's amanuensis.*

"Madame, the Queen desires me to tell you that she has nothing against you, and that she is very sensible of the attention you have to please her on every occasion; she has desired me to assure you of this, and I do so with pleasure, knowing your sentiments, Madame, and loving your person, which you will permit me to say.

"Duchesse de Luynes."

* Autographe, Bib. Imp.

Madame de Pompadour hastened to reply:

"You restore to me my life, Madame, for since three days I have been in unequalled grief. They have blackly calumniated me to M. le Dauphin and Madame la Dauphine. These have kindness enough towards me to permit me to prove the falsehood. I am told that they had indisposed the Queen towards me. Judge of my despair. I who would give my life for her! It is certain that the more kindness she may have towards me, the more jealousy will be occupied in fabricating a thousand calumnies. Believe me, Madame, in all sincerity,

"De Pompadour." *

The Duc de Richelieu gave a grand fête to the King and Madame la Marquise (Duchesse) de Pompadour. The Duc has not been seen a long while in these pages, because he has been renewing his youth at Montpellier. He had placed himself under the care of the Count de St Germain, (the precursor, in mysticism, to the spirit-rappers of to-day,) who will hereafter re-appear at Choisy. Whether St Germain exorcised old age, being himself celebrated for eternal youth, or whether, as was supposed by simple folk, he

* Autographe.
5 *

gave de Richelieu an elixir, or golden water
of life, to drink, it is impossible to say. The
only thing certain was a " virulent eruption all
over the Duke's body, which, under treatment
of raw veal, gradually disappeared, left his skin
smoother than before, and was supposed, by
his renewed youth and beauty, to be the poi-
sonous effects of time that had thus escaped from
him." There were other reasons that prescribed
the Duke's absence from Court. They belong
particularly to the *Chroniques Scandaleuses* of the
time, and yet they cannot be altogether omitted
here. He had had an intrigue with the wife of
M. de Popelinière, the banker, who had formerly supplied Marshal Saxe with money. Richelieu
flattered this woman's vanity until she fancied
her intellect and beauty made her a worthy rival
of the Marquise de Pompadour.* This was told

* Saxe had advised the banker to ignore the Richelieu
scandal; the banker, preferring his honour to his interest, put
away his wife. The Marquise wrote:

" A Madame de la Popelinière,

"I could never have imagined, Madame, that we
should ever have had anything to say to each other. You
have written me a violent letter, and I will make you a moderate answer. I know that for some time past you have been
at the head of certain beautiful women who have designs on the

the Marquise, who only laughed, though she was
annoyed by the vulgar presumption and its pas-
quinade consequences; but she took an opportunity one day, when the Marshal came to Versailles and found the King with her, to compliment
the former on his zeal for the service of the latter
in a way so cutting, though brilliant, that de
Richelieu could only make a very wry face in
attempting to smile as he answered. The King
inquired the jest; and then, for the first time
heard—though all Paris had gossipped about it—
the true story of the banker's wife and the
" *cheminée tournante.*" * His Majesty laughed,

King, and that you follow him everywhere. It is a folly,
perhaps, to pity more than laugh at. But, to-day you insult
me by a violent letter which has neither sense nor justice,
since it pre-supposes that I am the obstacle to your ambition.
I have the misfortune, Madame, to know none of your merits,
and although you have done your best to represent them to
the King, he knows of them no more than I do. You are
the wife of a rich and respectable man; try to please but
him. . . . . This is the first time that I take the liberty of
writing to you, and it will be the last.

"I am, Madame, &c."

* By which the military tactics of the Marshal had insinuated him into the house of the Banker through the chimney.
The affair was more annoying to the Court, because the Financier was necessary to its supplies, and de Richelieu was
known to be the friend of the King. The affair was notorious;

too, and forgot all about it. The Marquise laughed, now that she had frankly told it, in presence
of the original offender—and forgave it. The
Marshal Duke laughed at the joke against himself,
but he neither forgot nor forgave it.

Noblesse oblige. Courtiers cannot afford to
indulge themselves in open enmity, any more
than Kings; and de Richelieu gave, as before
said, a grand fête to the King and the " Duchesse."
It was the way to regain royal favour; and the
presence of Madame de Pompadour was a sign of
her pardon of the annoyances to which his gallantries had subjected her.

About this time Montesquieu dedicated his (new
edition, or defence) " Esprit des Loix" to the
Marquise. Nothing could be more consoling to
her than this tribute at a time when Voltaire was
degrading himself and her by his pen in Prussia.
" M. de Montesquieu," says a contemporary, " was

the Court compromised. The disgraced wife was becoming
openly impatient to achieve royal dishonour. It was therefore
best for all concerned (herself included) that the Marquise informed the King in the culprit's presence. But her letters to
de Richelieu (published in Paris, 1757, with others to de
Soubise, Broglie, and d'Estrées) prove that, instead of retaining malice against him, she was more inclined to remember his
protection at Fontenoy, and the days of the elegant baggage.

always esteemed, sought, and beloved by all in the Church who were really great and respectable.'' By associating Madame de Pompadour with this his greatest work, he paid the highest tribute that genius could render to her. Montesquieu was not seeking Court favour nor royal patronage when dedicating his work to her. He was on the brink of the grave, and had always been elevated by birth, wealth, and position, above the need of favour or patronage. For a brief season the book was attacked, as were all works that breathed the philosophic necessity of good constitutional government, and aspired to the liberty of the subject. Short as was the time, Montesquieu outlived this attack, and, before his death, (in the words of his friend d'Alembert in his elegiac address to the Academy,) he had the satisfaction of seeing the effects that his book had begun to produce among us. The natural love of the French for their country turned towards its true object; the taste for commerce, for agriculture, and for useful arts, these spread insensibly in our nation: that enlightenment on the principles of government, which attaches people more firmly to what they ought to love. Those who have indecently attacked this book, owe to it more than they know or imagine. . . . The book, the glory of M. de Montesquieu and the triumph of true philosophy, is of too much importance to be passed in silence. May the opprobrium which covers its enemies become salutary to them ! "

Madame de Pompadour, who shared the glory of the author, who had already practically illustrated his views in the arts of peace and industry, and who likewise bore her part in the attack it received from her enemies at Court, wrote thus to him :*

" I have received your book : it is admirable, and I give it the first place in my little library, which only contains authors who, like you, are an honour to France, and excite the envy of foreigners. . . . You deserve the title of Legislator of Europe, and I doubt not it will be accorded to you unanimously. . . . . The Christian religion is true, holy, and consoling. Let it not be a question of destroying it, but of reforming its abuses. Cut off the useless branches, but maim

---

* This letter, published about 90 years ago, in Holland, has been handed down to the compiler, with others, as explained in the preface of this work. Dutch editions of French subjects need the authentication of private and unprejudiced contemporary testimony.

not the tree. I have sometimes heard speak of
the Quakers in England; I like not that they
believe themselves inspired by the Holy Spirit to
utter folly in their assemblies; but I admire
their wisdom in dispensing with priestcraft. . . .
Religion is good, but its ministers are often bad.
Some say it will soon be ridiculous to be a Christian'; if that happen, it will be the fault of these.
Elsewhere, I perceive how religion makes bad
subjects, in recognising a superior temporal power
to that of their country. Our Bishops are not
Frenchmen, but subjects of the Pope."

For such sayings as this, the Marquise was
often anonymously threatened with poison and
assassination. Of such threats to herself she took
no heed, but at last her attention was painfully
roused to lurking danger by receiving a packet of
white powder, by post, with an unsigned letter
which affirmed that this (the powder) was a violent and subtle poison, which was intended to be
administered to the King. Added to this warning was a list of accomplices, some of them holding high posts about the Court.*

---

* It may be as well here to observe that *Lettres de Cachet*
were beyond the control of individual enmity, except as repre-

This denunciation, true or false, was the sign of serious times. The Marquise ordered an inquiry to be made. The Lieutenant-General of Police was charged to seek the author of the letter, and to sift the details of the declared conspiracy. Was it really a plot? Or, was it a skilful calumny to turn attention from some conspiracy or danger that was brooding elsewhere? The head of Police (Berryer) instituted the most searching inquiries, but the innocence of all whose names were denounced as accomplices resisted these inquiries. Suspicion then fell on the author of the calumny, who turned out to be a Gascon gentleman of small fortune, of the name of Latude. Destined by his family for the army, he had studied at Beropzoom, and had subsequently become mixed up with some of those Protestant refugees and discontented pamphleteers who were encouraged by Frederic in Prussia.

He was asked by the Lieutenant-General of Police what motive he had for his alarming invention, and he replied that sooner than not be noticed, he would compel the attention of the

sented at petty theatres. Each one had to pass a regular process among grave men, and was regularly examined and tested.

Court to him by fear or gratitude for imaginary
services.

Every reign has shown instances of this love
of notoriety, and whether springing from mischief
or monomania, the safety of a State compels in-
carceration. Latude was imprisoned at the fortress of Vincennes, but he escaped.* Government took no trouble to find him, hoping that he
had been sufficiently punished for his folly, but,
true to his love of notoriety, he again thrust himself on its notice by seditious pamphlets and false
accusations ; so that this time he was caught and
caged in the Bastille, where a particular hint was
given to the Governor that he had a slippery pri-

* For a Jansenist's imprisonment the Dauphin might, with
more reason, have been suspected than the Pompadour. Yet
none in private life were more estimable than the Dauphin's
family. The Dauphiness especially so. When (in 1752) the
Dauphin was attacked with the small pox, the Dauphiness insisted on attending to him personally. The celebrated physician, Dr Pousse, who, until then, was a stranger to the
Court, mistook the royal nurse for a hireling. "There," said
he, "is a sick attendant beyond all price ! What is her
name? " Being informed who she was, Dr Pousse was alarmed at his own recent familiarity, and was full of fear lest the
Dauphiness should suffer from over-exertion and contagion,—
" What matters it if I die ! " cried the noble-hearted Princess,
" provided my husband lives ! France will never be in want
of a Dauphiness." She had then two children.

soner. There he allied himself with another Gascon, of the name of Alégre, and, by some extraordinary means, they both escaped, and rejoined their discontented countrymen in Holland, and elsewhere.

It was for amnesty that Madame de Pompadour had been pleading for years. It was the capital point of her original offence to the ultra Romish party. And yet, with innumerable instances of the evil of an exclusive creed, the King was still unable to make his kingdom free to his subjects.

Latude, who was supposed by some to be insane, was treated very gently even after his second escape. It was proposed that he should return to his own country on condition of not leaving his native province. He refused this condition, preferring to ferment mischief elsewhere.

But, after the overture for his return, he became puffed up with more self-importance than before, and became so bold and litigious, that he was re-captured, and returned to the Bastille as a prisoner of State. Here he remained, forgotten by Madame de Pompadour, (among serious after-pressing cares of the country at war,) and for

years after her death the Government kept him in
the Bastille. He would not be worth mentioning
here, only that in 1793, when the revolutionary
madness of the people turned infuriated on the
past history of monarchy, this Latude became a
hero at last, as a supposed victim to oppression
and despotism. It was then, standing in the
streets of Paris, picturesquely laden with chains,
and wearing a long beard, he denounced the late
Duchesse de Pompadour, (" Citoyenne Pompadour,") as having deprived him of his wealth,
and kept him a prisoner for life, and demanded
£60,000 from her heirs or executors as indemnity
—which was paid !

So Latude, thanks to his insane love of notoriety, had his reward at last. Never mind that
it was for a foul lie, and paid by brutal ignorance,
as unreasoning as his insanity. He had £60,000,
and became a hero at the lower theatres on the
Boulevards, where he was represented as the
Martyr of a King's Mistress.*

To return to 1753.

* "11 Juin, 1793. Tout ce qu'on a écrit sur Latude"
(above quoted) "a été pris dans les Mémoires qu'a publiés
l'avocat Thierry, sous ce titre : 'Le Despotisme dévoilé, on
Mémoires de Latude '—1792, 1793."

It has been said how Madame de Pompadour turned often from cares of State to the society of her daughter. What personal ambition she had left was involved in this daughter. Her highest aspirations were for this child, whom she jealously guarded against the evils that had beset her own earlier days. She not only often went into retreat with her, at the Convent of the Assumption, but had her, when circumstances of Court and State life permitted, under her own care at Choisy, Belle Vue, and elsewhere. The King was partial to the child, and not only tolerated her presence, but " desired that she should treat him as her father, comporting himself as though she were his own child." Both he and the Marquise had ambitious views for " Mademoiselle Alexandrine," although the mother severely rebuked her daughter when, on more than one occasion, she, in company with her play-fellows at the convent, behaved arrogantly, as though she were a King's daughter instead of the child of the financier d'Etioles.

" 1748.

" I have received a letter concerning you which afflicts me. It is said that you are haughty and imperious with your companions. Why

afflict the heart of your mother ? I had so recommended you to be gentle, modest, and affable, as
the only way to please God and your fellow-crea-
tures. Have you so soon forgotten my lessons ?
Do you wish that I should blush for you ? . . . . . .
No fine airs ; they are suitable to none ; least to
you. If you are brought up like a princess, remember you are far from being one. Adieu, my
dear daughter, you know I only breathe for you ;
and that it is for you I love life. If you promise
to amend, I pardon and embrace you." *

The Court chronicle says : " As to Mademoiselle Alexandrine, she resembled Madame de Pompadour greatly; she was very pretty, and animated,
and showed much haughtiness on account of her
mother's position. But this defect was attributable
rather to the flattery that was lavished on her *en
pension* than to her own disposition. At the convent with her were young ladies of the highest
distinction ; among the rest the daughter of the

* "Louis XV., finding every day with his favourite, Alexandrine her daughter, took a fancy to the child, and made her
call him ' Papa.'

"The Duc de Fronsac, son of Marshal, Duc de Richelieu,
was the young nobleman about the Court whom the King
much desired should marry Alexandrine."—Mems. de la Cour
de France.

Prince de Soubise, who afterwards married the
Prince de Condé. She disputed precedence with
these. Her mother, on being informed of it, said
gravely but simply, My daughter has been wanting in politeness." This is why the Marquise
wrote the above letter to her child.

The King desired that Mademoiselle Alexandrine should be betrothed to the son of the
Duc de Richelieu ; the bride-elect was too young
to have any voice in the matter (being about 12
or 13 years of age) ; her mother was willing that
the King should so arrange the destiny of her
child, having no objection to the young bridegroom selected for her by his Majesty, and the
match being such as, in a worldly point of view,
to satisfy her ambition for her daughter. But the
Duc de Richelieu, who had not forgotten the
affair of Madame de Popelinière, and not being
capable of belief in the duration of the King's
purified attachment to the Marquise, declined
the alliance. The King was more annoyed by
this conduct than the Marquise, but he, with the
traditional love of the House of Bourbon for that
of Richelieu, would not punish the Duke for his
refusal, even had Madame de Pompadour (more

quick to discern the double motive) not interceded
for him. *

Besides, she had other views for her daughter,
which were so lofty and successful, that some
French writers believe that they discredit the
assertion of the Duc de Richelieu's refusal.   It
is certain that about the time that he was reported
to have refused the alliance, the young Alexandrine was promised, and formally betrothed, to
the Duc de Pecquigny, of the family of Luynes.
It has been seen how the Duchesse de Luynes
wrote, at the Queen's desire, to the Duchesse de
Pompadour a letter of affection and re-assurance
on her instalment as Lady of the Tabouret.   It

---

* "The Duke de Richelieu," says his especial chronicler,
" replied that much honour was done him, but that he declined the alliance, because his son belonged to the Empire.
But though he might so boast of royal blood, it is difficult
to believe that he should reject this marriage which would
have given him the place in the ministry he desired, &c. &c.
He had but to regard the young Alexandrine as the daughter
of a financier of considerable wealth, and, notwithstanding,
his boast of blood, it would not have been hard for him to
remember that his family was not too ancient or exclusive.
His servile deference to the Marquise had been remarkable,
and every day the daughters of financiers married with the
oldest titles in France."

will also be recalled that the Cardinal de Luynes
was one of the Queen's directors.   This alliance
was superior in every way to that of de Richelieu's son, more agreeable to the feminine instinct
of the Marquise (who had been disgusted with
the Marshal's scandalous gallantries), and more
flattering to the position she had conquered.
The idea of it seems to have revived her.   There
was no immediate cause for anxiety.   The pres-
sure on her nerves was lightened.   She appeared
with the King at the Opera, and there saw
Rousseau's celebrated *Devin du Village*, at Car-
nival time.   Rousseau himself was present.*
Rousseau, mad, excited, his brain heated by
study and anxiety ; a very monomaniac of

---

* Witness " Les Confessions " de J. J. Rousseau.   Jean
Jacques Rousseau, born at Geneva, in 1711.   His mother
died soon after his birth.   Neglected.   Father a watchmaker.
Apprenticed to an engraver at 14.   Ran away into Savoy.
Roman Catholic Priest took him to his new convert, Madame
de Warrens, who had run away from her Protestant husband.
Mighty friendship sprang up between the run-away youth
and lady.   J. J. R. sent to a Jesuit seminary at Turin.
Afterwards fled back to Madame de Warrens.   Subsequently
got his living by music.   Went to Paris with his composition
" Le Devin du Village."   Afterwards ups and downs of all
sorts, till he died (self-poison suspected) in 1778.

genius, yet shabby, — shrinking into a corner
before the, to him, unaccustomed splendour of
the audience he—the unknown—had convoked.
Thinking the actors bad because they did not
do him justice; believing some silly women
angels because he heard them murmur applause;
exalted above humanity, yet fearing, heart-
beating, trembling, because he heard no clap-
ping of hands. The King was there, and it
was not etiquette to clap hands in the Royal
presence. And there was the Pompadour, herself the greatest artiste and actress of her time,
splendid to look upon, with smiles of approbation
that the King understood, but Rousseau, no
courtier and a rustic genius, did not see.

The curtain fell. Instinct told the author
and composer that he was a success. Gasping
for air, ashamed to look the multitude in the
face, he fled; albeit the King had sent for him
and desired to say a word of royal approbation,
and something more. The words of a Bourbon
were not bald, nor their favours empty. Rousseau
rushed back to his garret, and tried to cool
his head. But the King, under the Pompadour's
direction, was not to be evaded.

A royal messenger arrived with a hundred Louis for Rousseau (the Republican) from the King; and 50 Louis from the Marquise.

Rousseau, for once, was glad there were kings on earth, and flattered when, a few days afterwards, feeding upon royal bounty, he was told that his Majesty was for ever singing to himself snatches from the *Devin*, and that the Marquise intended herself to represent the part of *Colin* at *Belle Vue*. This she did, triumphantly, with all her old *verve* and spirit; not acting the worse for a conscience void of offence to man, though she knew the hand of Heaven's retribution was upon her. She loved those pieces, as she declared, which brought the drama down to the level of human nature, from the stilted representations in which its true intention had been lost, and by which kings alone were flattered.

Then came fresh rewards to Rousseau ; 50 Louis from the Opera, and 500 francs from Pissot, the engraver. The Marquise had made "Colin" the fashion by her inimitable representations—so that the piece which, as says Rousseau, "never cost me but five or six weeks of work, brought me more money, notwithstanding my

misfortune and loggerhead conduct, than ' *Emile* '
has since yielded me, though that cost me twenty
years of meditation, and three of work." He
had previously been angry with Madame de
Pompadour, because she could not pull his friend
Diderot out of prison directly his seditious
writings put him there. Now, Rousseau began
to grumble that in spite of the pecuniary ease
in which her favour placed him, the success of
his " Devin," that she had inaugurated, was the
cause to him of infinite annoyances, because of
the jealousy it bred. " I remarked," says he,
" neither in G—— nor in Diderot, nor in hardly
any of my literary acquaintance, that cordiality,
that frankness, that pleasure to see me, that I
had believed to have found in them, until then."

Voltaire was on the watch in Prussia, and
ever ready to spring up afresh in one shape
or another, when his self-love was piqued by
Paris doings. It was proposed to play in French
private Palace theatricals, a burlesque of his
"Semiramis." The political atmosphere was, like
the " King's " dissatisfied conscience, gradually
getting too cloudy for tragic representations in
the entertainments intended to divert Versailles.
Soldiers were being drilled and educated, ships

were building, France was on friendly relations with Austria. But Frederic was trafficking with England. Canada was unsettled. The Cabinet of France was watchful and uneasy. It was no time to play at tragedy. " Semiramis " was to be burlesqued! Voltaire never pardoned success, if not his own. Rousseau's triumph maddened him. Now he heard that his Semiramis was to be parodied at Fontainebleau! "He could not understand," says a commentator, " that the grandest chefs-d'œuvre have their parody for the reason that the sublime is akin to the ridiculous." He could not write to his former patroness, the Pompadour, whom he had so outraged, so he addressed himself to the Queen of France, concerning whom he had formerly indited sarcastic verses. " Think, Madame," wrote he, " that I am the servant of his Majesty, and consequently yours :—a word will suffice to prevent a scandal, the results of which will lose me. I hope that your Majesty's humanity will be touched, and that after having painted virtue, I shall be protected by her." *

The Queen interposed, and the parody of Semiramis was not represented. " It was a fine

---

* Correspondance générale. See Appendix 2.

thing," as he himself would say, to see Voltaire begging the Queen of France to protect virtue— his virtue—Voltairism.

Just as he was writing his *Pucelle d'Orleans* in Prussia, a mightier will than that of Voltaire interposed in the matter of Court comedy. After all, a real tragedy was manifested there, though not Voltaire's,—The Reality of Retribution, though no poetic fiction. The daughter of the Marquise de Pompadour, the newly betrothed, who bade fair to rival her mother in beauty and grace, was taken ill at her convent. The mother flew from the Court festivities, of which she was the soul, to join her child. Anxious, hopeful, prayerful, watchful. All in vain. The physicians shook their heads, though all the dower of the Pompadour would reward their skill. The Nuns moaned and prayed. The young companions wept. All in vain. The girl died. The mother who had said " you know I only wish to live for you," saw the last remnant of her ambition blasted. The one object of her pure love passed from before her eyes. What was the world now to her who had nobody left in it, belonging to her, to care for ? Would she have exchanged the glory

of having done great things for her country, for
the possession of a conscience unstained, as
became the mother of that perfect innocence
she had so guarded in this young life that was
taken to heaven ?

The Duchesse de Pompadour was away from
the world, for a time, with the coffin of her
child which contained all the human hope she
had. She went to bury her at the Convent of the
Capuchins, that simple but pious order for which,
while struggling with proud prelates, she had ever
had the deepest veneration. Laying aside the trap-
pings of her rank and dishonour, she conformed
to these models of abnegation and misery. This
order, entirely created for the people, " of a
sublime democracy," abjuring all worldly goods,
had always been fondly protected by her. In
return it offered her a refuge in her unutterable
woe. She laid her daughter down among these
true servants of heaven. She planted the cross
above her grave, and placed on it the virginal
wreath ; and knelt down—she, the mistress of a
King.

Shuddering at the past,—shrinking from the
inevitable future,—the time that must pass before
she could rest there, too. She had work to do

still. She would do it. She had pledged herself to the King not to desert him in the coming time of his need. But what was the world
and its wars to her? She, alone in the midst of
her splendour, with her body stricken by disease,
—her beauty fading,—her youth passing away.
Surrounded by enemies. Let preachers preach.
Let moralists cant. Let poets fabricate justice.
The story of a real life, fairly lived out, is God's
best teaching.

CHAPTER III.

" Here I am," cries Voltaire, who had just been pleading for virtue in France, " with the great Frederic, a silver-gilt key hung to my coat, and twenty thousand francs of pension ! " Long ago he had been a sort of improvised prime minister to the great Frederic.* " I have still," says Voltaire, " that paper where I asked him, ' Do you doubt that the House of Austria will not re-demand Silesia of you on the first occasion ! ' And here is his answer on the margin :

' Ils seront reçus, biribi,
　　A la façon de barbari, mon ami.'

This negotiation of a new sort finished by a discourse that the King held with me in one of his moments of vivacity against the King of England, his dear uncle. These two kings did not love each other. That of Prussia said : ' George is uncle of Frederic, but George is not uncle of the King of Prussia : let France declare war against England, and I march.' "—In 1753 the tables were turned.

And then the charming life at Potsdam ! A King up at five or six in the morning. Dressing almost without help. In a fine room with a silver

* 1743—1744.

balustrade ornamented with well-sculptured "little loves," which seemed to shut in a couch of which you only saw the curtains ; " but behind, instead of a bed, a bookcase : and as to the bed of the King, it was a truckle behind a screen. Marcus Aurelius and Julian, his two apostles, and the greatest men of stoicism, were not worse off for a bed."

But, somehow, this hard couch did not augment the royal philosopher's dignity, as when the great King was dressed and booted, he only teased his pages, until his nerves were soothed by coffee. Then all the great men and Secretaries of State brought their despatches.

All business was settled in half an hour. Frederic, the Anti-Machiavellian, was the happy accident of an accident. His father had plagued him in his life-time, but he died rich. There was no need of talk with plenty of pelf.

" The father," says Voltaire, " was a veritable Vandal, who only thought in his reign how to amass money, and to keep up the finest troops in Europe at the smallest expense. Never were subjects so poor, and never was a King so rich. . . . . He walked out of his palace in a miserable blue coat and copper buttons, and when he bought a new coat he made the old buttons do for it. . . . . He was armed with a big stick. . . . When his son, Frederic, had a sort of mistress, the father made that young lady perform the tour of the *Place de Potsdam*, driven by the hangman, who whipped her under the eyes of his son.   But after all, the son deceived himself and his father."

The kingdom had been ground down by an iron rule to passive obedience and military routine. There was not much to do, even when the King in boots went to review his troops in his garden, so that sometimes "the Great " amused himself by looking at his men through the window, under which his sentinels marched like machines wound up by the hour.   It must have been a relief when dinner-time came, which meal was as good as it could be in a country where there was neither game, nor passable butchers' meat, nor a chicken, and where wheat was brought from Magdebourg. After dinner, his Majesty retired, and, shut up alone, made verses.   Then a young man came and read to him.   A little concert began at seven o'clock, without women's voices.   The King played the flute.*   Then came the supper, with " the

* Playing the flute brought about the hangman's Tour de Potsdam, above named.   Frederic used to accompany the

singular ornament," that so struck Voltaire, stuck
in the midst.   So altogether it was a fine life, that
of Potsdam, only Voltaire, the erratic, got tired of
it at last.   Three or four years, summer and winter,
were enough for a foul poem, seething scandal,
and scant food.   Particularly when one of Voltaire's best friends at the Prussian court kindly told
him that his Majesty had declared that he meant to
fling him—le Roi Voltaire—aside "like a sucked
orange, when he had got all he could out of him."

It was time for offended dignity to be off.
Voltaire packed up, and started to pass a month
with Madame la Duchesse de Saxe Gotha.   (It
was Doctor la Métrie, "the frankest Atheist in all
Europe," upon whose proscribed body France had
set a price, who had warned Voltaire of his fate.)
He might have got trampled on as well as sucked,

---

lady who played (and was whipped) on an old *Clavecin* out of
tune.

While King Frederic played the flute during the *Pucelle
d'Orleans* visit of Voltaire, he (Voltaire) wrote to De Richelieu:
" Could not you have the goodness to persuade Madame de Pompadour that I have exactly the same enemies as she has ?   If
she desire that I return, cannot you tell her that you know my
attachment for her, that she alone would make me leave the
King of Prussia, and that I have only quitted France because I
have been persecuted there by those who hate her ?"

if he had stayed, for Frederic was not scrupulous in the treatment of his friends when he had exhausted them. For example: There was that poor Pöllnitz, his chamberlain, who had told him and us so many good stories about his travels. Well, when the great Prussian King got tired of his talk, and had all his best stories by heart, he would say, " Won't you change your religion for the fourth time?" (Pöllnitz was an impressionable man, and had been of all creeds in all nations.) Or: " O mon Dieu, my dear Pöllnitz, I have forgotten the name of that man that you robbed at the Hague, in changing bad money for good; help my memory a little."

But Pöllnitz had wasted his substance, and was obliged to stop and eat King's bitter bread, made with Mandebourg flour. Voltaire was rich and a philosopher. He had lined his pockets with fine pensions from Prussia and France, so he got away in time from the one, though he was ashamed to show his face in the other. " I breathed!" says he.

Then, " I gently continued my road through Frankfort. It was there my eccentric destiny overtook me. . . . . There was at Frankfort a man named ' Freitag,' banished from Dresden, after having been put into the iron collar and condemned to the wheel-barrow. Since then he had become agent of the King of Prussia, who willingly made use of such ministers, because they had no wages but what they could pick up from passers-by. This Ambassador and a merchant named ' *Smith*,' condemned to expiation for having issued false coin, signified to me on the part of his Prussian Majesty that I must not go out of Frankfort until I had restored the precious property that I had carried away from his Majesty. 'Alas,' said I, (always Voltaire,) ' I carry nothing away from Prussia, not even the least regret. What then are those jewels of the Brandebourg crown that you demand?' ' It is, Sir,' says Freitag in execrable French, ' the work of *Poëshie* of the King, my gracious master.' ' Oh,' says I, ' I will give him back his prose and his verse with all my heart, although I may have more than one right to the King's work. He has made me a present of a fine copy printed at his expense. Unfortunately this copy is at Leipsic with my other baggage.' Then Freitag proposed to me to remain at Frankfort until the treasure had arrived from Leipsic. . . . . . . On the 17th of June, 1753, arrived the grand bale of Poëshies."

Voltaire " faithfully " gave them up, but he and his niece, Madame Denis, who in his company, were arrested, and the latter treated most ungallantly, at bayonet point, with four soldiers—sentinels—for her bed-posts. The merchant *Smith* got hold of half the baggage.

Voltaire thus lost—so he says—the sum that Frederic had paid for his journey to Prussia. " It was impossible," he declares, " to pay more dearly for his Prussian Majesty's Œuvre de *Poëshie*."

Some time afterwards he went to drink the waters of *Plombières*. " I drank, above all, the waters of Lethe, being quite persuaded that misfortunes, from whatever source they come, are good only to forget."

He was received at Plombières with public acclamations, (long afterwards Frederic declared, that had Voltaire been an old Greek, he would have been worshipped as a god,) but Cardinal Tencin frowned darkly on him at Lyon. This Cardinal had made his fortune by dubbing Catholic that Law whose financial paper-system beggared France.

At last Voltaire was havened at Ferney,* although his conscience was *not* steeped in the

* Appendix 3.

waters of Lethe, as declares Marmontel, who
visited him there.

They talked of the Pompadour. "Ah," sighed
Marmontel, "she is no longer happy,—she is not
well."

Voltaire, being man enough to forgive the
benefactress he had injured, when she was smitten
by misfortune, said :

"Let her come and play tragedy with us
here. I will write her the parts fit for a Queen.
She is beautiful; she ought still to know love."

"Ah!" said Marmontel, "she also knows
profound grief and tears."

"That," said Voltaire, "is exactly what is
wanted in tragedy."*

Never having felt grief for aught but himself,
he was powerless to imagine that which had be-
fallen the woman who told him, long ago, that she
believed in her own destiny. No longer haughty,
defiant, splendid, as then. But :

"What decrepitude, what degeneration in outward form! Yet still large and fine eyes; but
what a look darts forth from those two .caverns!
It seems as though a whole being, body, soul, de-
taches itself when she looks towards you. Ex-

* Appendix 4.

tremely thin. Dressed in a sort of négligé, which fashion has adopted. Beautiful hands and teeth, but white lips, which she has a habit of biting, so as to bring colour into them," (or to keep down inward emotion, as when, a few years before, her husband was cheered at the Opera to insult her?) " with the gift of tears." *

Here is (minus some uncourtly acerbities) the picture that hatred and jealousy drew of the Duchesse de Pompadour, when she was about 36 years old, — a childless mother, — with nothing but regret behind her, and nothing but increasing suffering before her. She is again at

---

* Such is the description of an unsympathizing and jealous court lady (Madame la Maréchale D....), in whose portfolio were said to be preserved the accounts recorded of Madame de Pompadour's letter to her husband, &c.—The inference of this lady is always malignant, but now, that her superb rival is overwhelmed by trouble and sickness; the Maréchale confesses that formerly "The Pompadour was handsome and pretty at the same time, and equally remarkable for her vivacity and languor. The different characters appertaining to her were evinced by her varying countenance. She was, at will, superb, imperious, calm, playful, curious, attentive, intellectual, childish, ... of a fine and well-cut figure, middle height, and without defect, knowing well how to set all that off by toilette. Without deranging the attitude of her body, her face was a perfect Proteus."

7 *

Versailles, in 1755, "where," she says, "what augmented my pain was the necessity of appearing cheerful, when a despairing melancholy was devouring me."

The King, although of a sombre temperament himself, tried to cheer her. " It will now be my turn," says he, " to play comedy, Madame, and to sing little couplets, that I may make you laugh as you have so often made me laugh."

She told him one day that the Count de Maurepas, who was exiled from Court, wished to return to Pontchartrain, his château close to Versailles. Several of his friends had interceded for him with the Marquise, and she laid the case before the King, entreating compliance as a favour to herself. The King granted it, but he was struck by this proof of forgiveness of enemies. " Madame," said he, " Monsieur de Maurepas has grievously offended you, and yet you intercede for him ; truly, you have a noble soul. I admire it." It was not possible, however, to get the King's consent for the return to Court of de Maurepas. His disgrace outlived the Marquise.*

* A year after Madame de Pompadour's death, Horace Walpole visited the Count de Maurepas, Ex-Minister of Marine at Pontchartrain, and found him still exiled from King

About this time the Prince de Condé was married to Mademoiselle de Soubise, (she who, as a child, had disputed precedence with the daughter of the Pompadour,) and Marshal Belleisle's son was married to Mademoiselle de Nivernois. To a faithless wife who had just buried her husband's daughter, the sight of young brides was mournful. The Jesuit party was more eager than ever to secure the Dauphin now that, by his children, his future dynasty seemed secure. But the Archbishop of Paris, and the Bishop of Orleans, &c. were at one time exiled to their country houses. Sorbonne threatened to cease instruction. The King was distracted. Religion was brought into contempt by this Church quarrel. The flame of the feud spread even to Silesia, to judge from the following letter from Frederic of Prussia to Baron de Dancklemann, Minister of State for the ecclesiastical department,—

..... "I have resolved that you intimate to the respective regencies and consistories of Silesia, to admonish the Protestant clergy of that province, without exception, to abstain entirely in their ser-

and Cabinet, so that when politics were mentioned,—though de Maurepas was habitually gay,—a melancholy look overspread his face, a look of pain.

mons from all controversies which may excite
bitterness and animosity among my subjects of
different religions.   That they content themselves
by teaching and explaining in their sermons the
principles and dangers of their creed; that they
abstain from all injury and declamation against
those of a different religion.   That they give, on
the contrary, by their conduct and doctrine, the
example of moderation and tolerance."

Again: " To the Prince Schaffgotfch, Bishop
of Breslau. My paternal solicitude for my subjects of Silesia has always had for its object to
maintain among the inhabitants, of two religions,
union and a good harmony. . . . .   But having
learned that, according to ancient and pernicious
custom, sermons of controversy are preached in
the churches and Roman Catholic convents, ...
absurd and indecent arguments, which, instead
of edifying the auditors, have only for their object to excite hatred and nourish aversion between fellow-citizens of different religions,". . . it
is commanded that such be " entirely abstained
from, under penalty of chastisement. . . . . . .

Potsdam, 25th April, 1756."*

* "Lettres Diverses," &c. Published in Mems. Histo-
riques de Frédéric II, dit le Grand, Paris, 1828.

Frederic attributed Church discord in France to weak government. Absolute and unprejudiced himself, he scorned a King who, having faced the battle-field, trembled before the sword of the Church. One night at the Opera of Berlin, a French company of dancers was to appear. Frederic was seated in his box, and the Marquis de Valori, French Ambassador, in a box near him. It was some little time before the curtain drew up, and the legs of the dancers were just visible below it, while the corps was being arranged for the ballet. " Valori, Valori," shouted King Frederic to the French Ambassador, " there 's the picture of the Administration of France, all legs, and no heads." One head, he thought, would have crushed the Bull Unigenitus. A diversion from it came at last. "In 1755, the English made their *début* by attacking the French towards Canada, and by seizing, without any declaration of war, more than three hundred merchant ships, whose value was estimated at 30,000,000 livres. The English, in possessing themselves of these vessels, and of three ships of war, made at least 6000 officers, mariners, and sailors, prisoners, and a thousand five hundred soldiers, or new levy men.

" The only inconvenience that the English had
to fear was that the French might revenge on Hanover their losses in America or elsewhere." * Voltaire, who had returned his pensions and Chamberlain's gilt key to Prussia, declared, from his
haven at Ferney, that " England made a war of
pirates on France for some acres of snow,"
while at the same time the Empress of Austria
" appeared to have some desire to retake, if she
could, her dear Silesia, that the King of Prussia
had snatched from her.   With this design she
negotiated with the Empress of Russia and the
King of Poland. . . . . . . The King of Prussia preferred the alliance of England to that of
France, and united himself with the House of
Hanover, reckoning to prevent with one hand
the Russians advancing into Prussia, and with the
other the French from coming into Germany."

" The Court of London had compared its maritime forces with those of France; it had calcu-
lated what efforts the English and what the
French colonies could make." *

* " Fastes de Louis XV. Vol. ii. pp. 39, 40. Published
Chez la *Veuve Liberté*, 1782. A Ville-Franche." A book
tinged with Prussian blue, and therefore here preferred, for
impartiality, in preamble of war between France and England.
Presently, those who fought Kings and Princes, may speak
for themselves after a hundred years' silence.

" The Electorate of Hanover was placed under the safeguard of the King of Prussia.* This
Prince, who was the friend of France, allied
himself with England to prevent the entry of
foreigners into the Empire, and he ought to be
seconded by Hesse, the House of Brunswick, and
even by Russia. The English flattered themselves with having tied the hands of France, or
at least hoped to reduce her by this policy to
carry on the war far from her frontiers, in a country
of which conquest would be more difficult than that
of Flanders and of Brabant; they hoped that being
almost impossible for a French army to maintain
itself there, the restitution of Hanover would not
oblige them to restore America.

" These projects, meditated with wisdom, were
executed with imprudence. The troops that
France advanced to her coasts spread alarm, or
rather consternation, in England. The govern-

* The King of Saxony and Poland, without declaring himself openly, had promised to join himself to " a simultaneous
effort against Frederic II.," and the family alliance with
France, in the person of Madame la Dauphine, gave an impe-
tus to political rapprochement between France and Poland.
Voltaire says that the Polish King was only regarded as
Elector of Saxony in the matter; " *car on ne négocie point
avec les Polonais.*"

ment remembered the enterprise of Prince Edward
in the last war, and thought already to see a
French army upon the Thames. Strange thing!
a people which boasts of ruling the sea fears a
descent into its island; it forgets the conquest
of America, and is only occupied with its own
salvation. It calls to its succour Hessians and
Hanoverians, whilst the French cause to pass
freely their convoys in America, where the haughtiness of their enemies had already irritated and
stirred up the greater part of the *naturels du
pays*."* Versailles, through M. de Mirepoix,
indignantly demanded of St James's an explanation
of " les Actes de piraterie de la Marine Anglaise."
Henry Fox, Minister of Foreign Affairs, replied,
" The state of war does not always result between
nations from real combats, but from certain acts,
from certain measures, which announce hostile
intentions; none can dissimulate the armaments

* Maria Theresa had never considered the cession of Silesia
definitive; " I have sacrificed," she said long ago, " my dearest interests to the tranquillity of Europe in ceding Silesia;
but if ever war re-kindle between myself and the King of
Prussia, I will re-enter into all my rights, or I will perish for
them—I, and the last of my house." She, therefore, anxious-
ly watched the Transatlantic storm brewing.

of France.   Why such great squadrons, and in-
cessant transport of troops to Canada?" (Here be
remembered the loose screw in the Aix Treaty, as
shown by Pompadour to Belleisle.) "The Britannic
Government could only advise as to the dignity of
its nation."   Versailles proudly rebutted: " That
which has come to pass is but a vast system of
piracy, and unworthy of civilization."

" England suspecting France of secret negociating with Austria, told the King of Prussia of the
danger that threatened him, and engaged him,
without trouble, to prevent his enemies and dis-
concert their projects. Whatever may be the cause
of it, the entry of this Prince in Saxony lighted up
one of the most extraordinary wars that Europe had
yet seen;* and in consequence of that bold step,·
England saw herself obliged to conquer America
in Germany, and to make such costs that the
greatest success could never repay. . . . . . The
face of Europe then changed. . . . . . The old system of equilibrium was overthrown. . . . .
Actually, France, the House of Austria, Russia,
Sweden, and the Empire, made war against England and Prussia; and the Kings of Spain and

* See Treaties, transcribed.   Also, Royal Autograph Letters, in following chapters, and Appendix.

Sardinia, and the United Provinces, simple spectators of this quarrel, observed an exact neutrality." While England was making her *début* in the New World the Pompadour wrote to the Ambassador in London : *

"1755.

"I think as you do, M. l' Ambassadeur, that you cannot remain decently at the Court of London : and it is hoped soon to see you here. . . . I know not what will be the result of war, but if

---

* In 1753, just before the death of her daughter, the Marquise wrote :

"In spite of all your hopes and your promises, and the falsehoods of the Court of London, we look upon war as inevitable, but without alarming ourselves : all the hearts of the Indians in America are for us : we have ships, a good army, and good friends. My Lord Albemarle, who occupies himself more with his pleasures than politics, has nevertheless presented a grand memorial, in which he complains that it is at the instigation of the French that the savages of America attack his nation. It is sad that this wise people cannot make itself loved, and it is undignified to complain of the fact. . . . . Lord Albemarle also complains that France builds vessels. . . The English have not tact. . . . . Pray make my civilities to the Duchess of Queensbury. . . . . I have an idea that we shall soon see you again. . . I shall be very glad and very sorry, for I love not war. It never does much good, and always a great deal of harm. . . . . Adieu."

fortune take part with justice, we shall not have much to fear. . . . . . . They say that our navy is on a tolerable scale, and capable of making head against the English.   God grant it !

"Nevertheless, notwithstanding the promises and confidence of our ministers, the King is not without fear, nor the nation either.   It is a sea war we are going to have, and the sea is not the element of the French; we may even say that they dislike it. . . . Do not fail to bring with you an exact list of the English Navy, the number of their vessels, of their sailors, of their troops for sea or land. . . . . Inform yourself with ability of their designs, of their negotiations with the princes of the continent, of their resources, projects, &c.

"We flatter ourselves that we shall have superiority on land, so that for certain losses that we sustain at sea the continent will repay us. . . . . It is believed that King George finds himself compelled to take this violent step, so opposed to glory: that the merchants of London, by their credit and clamour, lead their King by the nose, and oblige him to make war, whatever inclination he may have for peace. . . . . You see, Monsieur le Duc, that there are inconveniences everywhere;

in absolute monarchies Kings can do all the harm
they wish ; in mixed monarchies they cannot do
the good they would.   For us, try to do as much
as you can, in loving and serving our King and
his friends." *

The French Ambassador, with such letters
in his pocket, might well be thus described
by Horace Walpole, — " I overtook M. le Duc
de Mirepoix t' other day, who lives at Lord
Dunkeron's house at Turnham Green.   It was
seven o'clock in the evening of one of the hottest
and most dusty days of this summer.   He was
walking slowly in the *beau milieu* of Brentford
town, without any company, but with a brown
lap-dog with long ears, two pointers, two pages,
three footmen, and a *Vis-à-Vis*, following him.   By
the best accounts I can get, he must have been to
survey the ground of the battle of Brentford . . . ."
Lord Hertford had succeeded Lord Albemarle in
Paris ; " but England, trying to pick a quarrel with
France, had among other things complained that

* Unhappily for France, indignation against Prussia was
mitigated by longing for liberty of conscience, which Prussia favoured.   Groaning under Church strife, French loyalty
languished.   The King seldom went to Paris.   His gloom
increased.

in France, England had been charged with regicide. How little France foresaw her own crime a few years afterwards!

Monsieur de Mirepoix declared from England (just before England struck the blow), that " England did not think of breaking the peace."

" From whence, then," cried Louis, " does it come that she is arming herself, as if for war ? "

" Sire," said de Mirepoix, " the Britons have a maxim, 'Profit by the tranquillity of Europe to augment forces.' "

Alas! de Mirepoix! your cogitations in Brentford town were too late, while England was striking the first blow elsewhere. The King of France did not wish war. To prevent it, if possible, he sent Bussi to Hanover to confer with the King of England who was there. Madame de Pompadour thought Bussi managed the affair badly, but it was too late for diplomacy. War was unavoidable. France therefore multiplied her flat boats (*bâteaux plats*), dreamed of supplanting ' William the Bastard,' by a new English conquest;* sent Admiral de la Galissonière (formerly

* " The English Government is very different to ours. It is the people who make war rather than their kings ; princes

governor of Canada) to the Mediterranean, and prepared sealed orders for Marshal Richelieu, with command of Forces in that direction. It was supposed that Richelieu and Galissonière were destined for the Colonies. The Marquise told old Marshal de Noailles that it was better to send out troops to Canada than advice. While France sought means to sustain the cost of an inevitable war, it was said at Versailles that England's subjects had volunteered resources for that purpose. Some distinguished individuals, it was declared, had offered money to sailors who would serve in the royal navy, and others offered to sustain their families at their expense until the peace, let it come when it would. The Marquise, on hearing this, said rather bitterly to her old friend Belleisle,—" It seems to me, Maréchal, that a nation which behaves thus, has the advantage over that which, for expenses of war, only gives its money by force." "That is true," said the Marshal, " but that same English nation, which voluntarily despoils itself of its wealth for a war that it thinks useful to the State, often loses its advan-

die, but the spirit between France and England subsists, and this spirit is always against us." Lettres Politiques, published in 1772.

tages in peace. A *Lord* who wishes to pave his way to the ministry by a system of pacification, intrigues for himself near the King, gains his confidence, and makes himself creatures. These demonstrate that sieges and battles ruin the State, and that by them commerce and industry suffer and perish. The cabal strengthens, the party of the postulant minister augments; he takes the upper hand, and peace is signed at the expense of blood, and of the nation's wealth." De Belleisle had not forgotten Horace Walpole's father, the peace-at-all-price Robert, concerning whom his pupil, the Marquise, received her first lesson in politics.

But where was France to find resources? Orders were reiterated in all the sea-ports for preparation, and also for a " land-war." But the Royal treasure, which was only just beginning to recover itself from the late war and all preceding evils (of the last reign, Regency, Fleuri Ministry, &c.), did not contain enough for the execution of such orders.* The controller-general said to the

* In France political necessity has often stimulated woman's devotion. Once when Saxe wanted war-supplies, Adrienne le Couvreur, the actress, sent him £40,000 by pawning her plate and jewels. Of her, Voltaire says : "The soul im-

King, " Sire, the Farmers-General offer money to your Majesty; you must take it. They lend sixty millions to the Crown at four per cent.; the

parted all,—voice, shape, and beauty." Her acting was full of expression and truth.

Marshal Saxe was dead, but his last letters on military tactics were carefully studied by the war council of France now that she was going to send forth her armies to battle without him to lead them. The following are extracts of the last letter Marshal Saxe wrote. . . . It was preserved in the archives of France, and brought to light by the 1st Napoléon. It is addressed to Count d'Argenson, and dated:

"Compiégne, 10th July, 1750.

" I have received, Sir, the memorial on the formation of Cavalry squadrons. . . . . I am of the opinion of our fathers that fortune declares herself for big (compact) squadrons; a squadron of ten ranks, and twenty files of front, ought always to break in one of ten ranks, and fifty files of front. It is more easily manageable; the diminution which happens in the cavalry is not so felt, it does not take up so much ground. It depends on the ground which one has to occupy or would wish to occupy. . . . . I would desire that there be but one standard to a squadron, because then you can give it the formation wished. An ensign, a standard, have been only instituted for the rallying of troops, and if there be two seen in one squadron, that is because out of two weak companies one squadron has been formed. . . . There is no good reason for this custom, which is but established by a defect. Standards are then attached to the squadron, and not to the company; there ought to be but one to serve as a rallying point to the squadron. These squadrons with small fronts and great depth

State in its present condition cannot do better than take it." The Marquise remembered the advice of Marshal Saxe. " When you want money, go to the Farmers-General," though the doing so was repugnant, involving personal and political ob- jections. The King borrowed another thirty mil- lions at three per cent. on " les Postes."*

The " piratical attack of the English on Canada," as it was indignantly called in Paris, caused a popular revulsion in favour of the King of France. Hitherto France had left the pam- phleteering system to her neighbours, being con- tented with rhythmical lampoons. Now, appeared a weekly newspaper entitled " L'Observateur *Hollandais*," which, at the expense of Versailles,

manœuvre much better, because the friction is less. . . . What is proposed as to supernumeraries has great advantages if only to establish certain uniform distances between the squad- rons, &c. There, Sir, is what I think on the formation of Cavalry squadrons.

Saxe,

à M. le Comte d'Argenson,

Ministre."

* "Les sécrétaires du roi, trnt du grand que du petit college furent taxés, et cet impôt, peut-être le moins onéreux de tous, parcequ'il tomboit sur des gens qui avoient achetés leurs charges par ostentation, produisit une ressource de quarante cinq millions."

8 *

commented freely on the bases of English Government, and exposed the Anglo-Prussian causes of French grief.

Ambassadors were recalled. King Louis sought the Marquise and said, solemnly, "Madame, war is declared. The English are my enemies."

Sad but foreseen news for one who had worked hard for the arts of peace! It came, too, just as Lowendhal, the pupil and companion of Marshal Saxe, died; a matter of grief to the King, and a great loss to the nation. The Marquise was also mourning another friend and able adviser, one to whom she had long looked for sympathy and private counsel in times of difficulty,—Montesquieu. The London Gazette paid this tribute to a Frenchman, just before the national shedding of blood:

"On the 10th of this month died at Paris, universally and sincerely regretted, Charles Secondat, Baron of Montesquieu, &c. &c. His virtues did honour to human nature; his writings, justice. A friend to mankind, he asserted undoubted and inalienable rights with freedom, even in his own country, whose prejudices in matters of religion and government (' *il faut*,' says a French contemporary critic, ' *se ressouvenir que*

c'est un Anglois qui parle') he had long lamented
and endeavoured to remove. He well knew and
justly admired the happy constitution of this
country, where fixed and known laws equally
restrain monarchy from tyranny, and liberty from
licentiousness. His works will illustrate his name
and survive him as long as right reason, moral
obligation, and the true spirit of laws, shall be
understood, respected, and maintained."

In 1752, M. Dassier, famous for the medals
he had struck in honour of celebrated men, was sent
from London to Paris to strike that of the Baron
de Montesquieu. "After having," says d'Alembert,
" decently fulfilled all his duties, full of confidence
in the Eternal Being he was about to rejoin,
Montesquieu died with the tranquillity of a good
man, who had never employed his talents but to
the advantage of virtue and humanity. France
and Europe lost him on the 10th of Feb. 1755, at
the age of 60 years."

The Duchesse d'Aiguillon was an intimate
friend of Montesquieu. Her regret at his loss
was a bond of sympathy between her and the
Marquise, which led to the fact of the Duc
d'Aiguillon receiving the command of the troops
in Brittany. Whether or not Madame de Pompa-

dour had reason to regret d'Aiguillon's appointment will presently be seen by her letters to him,
which, until now, have lain dormant in England
exactly a century.

The Duc d'Aiguillon, of the family of de
Richelieu, had inherited from the great Cardinal
that spirit of firmness which makes it difficult to
yield to parliamentary influence. It was hoped he
would be strong enough to control the assembly
of Brittany, as well as its troops, exposed to an
attack from England. The Duc d'Aiguillon
belonged to the Dauphin's party, and therefore his appointment, through the Duchesse de
Pompadour, does honour to her disinterestedness.

De Bernis had returned from Venice. He
was not yet in the " *Secrétariat* " of Versailles,
but the Marquise listened, and profited by, the
Abbé's acute perceptions in behalf of the King ; de
Kaunitz also arranged that all the overtures from
his Imperial Mistress should be made direct to
the Duchess, or, as we shall continue to call her,
the Marquise. This tribute of policy, skilfully
carried out by an eye-witness of Madame de
Pompadour's increasing power and capacity, has
been clumsily perverted to the impossible notion
that the Empress and the Marquise blew this war

into a flame, the one to rob Frederic of Silesia, and the other to revenge her mortified self-love.

Whatever Maria Theresa might have desired, France, in the person of the Pompadour, dreaded war as the worst evil at that particular time. Its only advantage was that it drew attention from the disgraceful quarrels between the different parties in the Church. "It was frightful," says our old friend, the Abbé Millot, " that for a dispute about some boundaries of American cantons, one was again to see the fire of war ready to recommence its ravages."

The Abbé Millot * must have known that the Marquise was, by taste and inclination, opposed to a war which impeded literary research,

* The Abbé Millot, formerly professor of History at Parma. Of the Society of Jesuits. Afterwards preceptor to the Duc d'Enghein. His party strongly opposed to, but his intellect in favour of, the Pompadour. Her patronage developed treasures of literature. She founded the Oriental chairs in the Royal library. Every Wednesday the manuscript keepers of that library were received by her with honour at Choisy, to inform her of any additions, &c. Illuminated editions of rare works (the Zend-Avesta, the sacred book of Persia, for example), known as "Pompadour Editions," scattered in the Revolution, have fetched in separate vols., 150 francs each.

and retarded the works of peace. The officers from the Invalides were called into service, a fact in favour of aged generals in other countries; although some said it was " to attack the living by the dead." Old Marshal Noailles sent in his resignation. . . . " I fear," wrote he to the King, "after having served the late King, your illustrious predecessor, to succumb beneath the weight of years and infirmities." To him the King replied : " My Cousin, whatever pain I feel at being deprived of counsels, and of marks of an attachment that have always been as agreeable as useful, I cannot but applaud the part that your wisdom induces you to take."

The Marshal de Noailles obtained for his son, the Duc d'Ayen, the appointment of Captain of the Guards, with the reversion to his grandson, the Count d'Ayen, although Louis the XV. was notorious in his abhorrence of hereditary preferment in his army, and of officers younger than himself.

The following letter of the King (Louis XV.) to Marshal Noailles, was preserved by the Abbé Millot as " remarkably characteristic."

" My Cousin,

" You know the repugnance I have to

grant reversions; your son, moreover, being younger than I, and in consequence likely to last a longer time. Nevertheless, the services rendered for more than a century by your family to my forefathers and myself, and also your attachment to my person, determine me to grant you the singular and last favour that you ask me. Happily the subject is in his 20th year (for you know that at my age children are not conformable), and that he bears promise. And notwithstanding your 80 years' accomplishment, I flatter myself that you will have time to teach him to serve me well and faithfully. You know that at every change I diminish the *brevets de retenue.* Thus, I shall only give 400,000 pounds to the Count d'Ayen, your grandson; it being understood that if any misfortune overtake his father, and that I do not confer his charge on other of his family, he who would succeed him pay the 500,000 pounds entire to the succession of the Duc d'Ayen. So zealous and aged a servant as you are, may always reckon on my friendship and regard : praying God that he may have you, my cousin, in his holy keeping.

"Versailles, this 30th day of December, 1758."

Before this the King had written to de
Noailles :

" I grant you leave to retire, as you ask.   I
grant also that of keeping your *appartement* here
(Versailles), and desire that you may long m?ke
use of the justice I render to your attachment
to my person since the day of my birth ; *mes
bontés et ma bienveillance en seront toujours le
prix.   Sur ce, je prie Dieu, etc.   Versailles*, 13
April, 1756."

Noailles preferred a sea-war, but that .vas not
liked best by the King and others of his council.
The Marquise wrote to Noailles.   In his answer
he says :

" Paris, Oct. 30, 1758.

" *You* ask my advice, Madame la Marquise,
and I am flattered, for it is a novelty to see an
old man so consulted."   It is observable that the
appointment he craved for his son and grandson
is dated just two months afterwards, an evidence
that though the veteran's advice was not always
welcome, the Marquise used her influence in
soothing the pang of its rejection.

De Noailles wrote to his grandson (the Count
d'Ayer), after receiving the King's letter, an " Instruction," which is a *multum in parvo* of the

whole duty of youth. . . . "You have been hitherto, my dear grandson, absorbed in an education which has screened you from the eyes of the
great world." The Marshal then warns him that
Envy is to be feared as much as Enmity ; he implores
him to make his first step in life so as to leave no
remorse ; to hold fast his faith and avoid fanaticism ;
to oppose to blasphemous talk, silence and a good
conduct ; to form no acquaintance with bad men ;
to join probity with religion, and modesty with
the exercise of talent : to seek good advice and
submit ; to apply himself strenuously to his
military duties ; not to mortify the self-love of
others ; to be free from affectation and slow to
blame, and liberal without ostentation ; to be
true to God, and faithful to the King," &c. &c.

"In a very old age," says the Abbé Millot,
" he, the Marshal de Noailles, was a pattern
of extreme piety. He is one of the men of our
century, who has the best proved by conduct the
beauty of submission in a superior intellect to the
dogma of Christianity, and the influence of its moral
teaching to direct and sustain a virtuous heart."*

---

* De Noailles died the 24th June, 1766, aged nearly 88
years, in the midst of a family more worthy than all his glory
to make him regret this life.

De Noailles still argued in favour of a sea-war, however disastrous. " It is," said he to the King, " only in the midst of a maritime war, and in the bitter experience even of disgrace, that your Majesty can hope to form a navy imbued with the soul which inspired it before the feeble policy of the Regency so fatally impaired it." It was Marshal de Noailles who, although too old to fight, advised the King to undertake the expedition of Minorca, and the Marquise de Pompadour who solicited its command for de Richelieu. The advice about a naval war was honourable to one who, on the brink of the grave, could already look into eternity for results ; but France, conscious of a military power and marine defects, could not exclusively adopt or approve counsel which, for the sake of ultimate glory, despised the necessity of the passing moment. How many victories, glorious at the moment, are abortive in the long run, France and England know.

The Marshal de Noailles flattered himself to the last that the attachment of Spain to France would result practically in favour of the latter. But the Court of London reckoned on the neutrality of that of Madrid. " *Le Mercure*," and the

" *Gazette de France,*" (Marmontel at one time edited the former,) grew full of French patriotism and chivalry, while " *l'Observateur Hollandais*" reeked with paragraphs justifying France in this war which had re-suscitated her heroes.

" The West Indian war," writes Walpole, "has thrown me into a new study. . . . Among all the Indian nations, I have contracted a particular acquaintance with *Outaouanouca.* . . They pique themselves on the purest dialect. . . . How one would delight in the grammar and dictionary of Crusca ! " *

* In 1860 they speak French to the Prince of Wales.

CHAPTER IV.

AT a time when France was straining every nerve
to find resources, the King had to lament the ob-

stinacy of his parliament in thwarting the taxes
that were essential to his cause. At the moment of a national war against England, when
chivalry and people rallied round the banner
with enthusiastic devotion, the Parliamentarians
(who were practised in opposition by continual
quarrels with the ultra Church party and the
Bull Unigenitus) were so antagonistic, that, says
a commentator, " one would have said that
these men wished to profit by the embarrassment
of Government and by the misfortunes of their
country, to imitate England (Cromwellians) in
assuming to themselves undue prerogatives and
rights." They threatened resignation. The President, M. de Meynières, was politically opposed to the Marquise de Pompadour, in spite of
her friendship for the late Baron Montesquieu,
President of Bordeaux. But de Meynières,
although leader of the most factious party
in the Assembly, desired nevertheless that his
son, who was in the regiment of the Guards,
should be advanced. This request was an infringement on one of the King's strongest prejudices. We have seen how he only accorded a
military command that had not been fairly earned
to the son of his faithful Marshal and friend, de

Noailles, because that loyal old veteran who
had served him and his predecessor faithfully,
pledged his honour it was worthily bestowed.
Louis, whatever his faults, must be respected in
his declaration that " if a Government owe equity
to all, it only accords, if just, its favours to those
who fortify it by devoted service!"   But de Meynières remembered the review at Compiègne two
or three years before, and the devotion of the Guards
to the Marquise on that occasion.   He remembered
her zeal in the foundation of the military school,
and how the brave old officers, now issuing forth
from the Invalides once more to serve their King
and country, owed their home to her.   Being
repulsed by the King, he demanded an audience
of Madame de Pompadour.

De Meynières was no friend of the lady of
whom he craved this audience, and through whom
he desired to obtain a favour for his son; and
therefore his own recital of the interview will be
more welcome to the cold charity of the world
than if it came from one who was not an enemy.*

---

* The army just now offered a wide field for political
ambition.   In 1752, Louis XV. had raised the Marquis de
Bussy Castelnau " Bussy, the Indian ") to the grade of Lieu-

The audience was given in the small apartments at Versailles. The Duchesse was standing near the fire, dignified and beautiful. The President paused — stammering words of apology. Was this the cast-off mistress — the shame of decency—the invalid woman who had designed "The Magdalene" in face of Parliament, and who he had hoped was dying from slow poison? With an extreme and most unusual modesty, he laid his case before her.

"I know, Madame," he said, "that I have had the misfortune to displease the King, but I cannot imagine the particular cause of my disgrace."

At these words, which were not sincere, the Marquise replied with hauteur and vivacity:

tenant Colonel, and afterwards to that of Brigadier-General of the royal troops, in recognition of his distinguished services in India, where he had served from an early age. The system of Dupleix in India had been a grasp at real possession,—territorial aggrandizement. Bussy substituted an idea; viz. to gain a moral and material ascendancy by assisting such native princes as were disaffected to the English, with munition and troops, so that by a double lever the English should be expulsed. Robert Clive it was who counteracted Bussy's idea. The impatient Governor "Lally" found Clive's energy indomitable.

" How, M. le President, you do not know?
Recall your recollections ; do they not tell
you how and when you have displeased the
King?"

" No, Madame, I cannot remember."

" And have you no friend to remind you,
Sir!" *

" On the contrary, Madame, were I destitute
of friends, I should not now have the honour of
paying my court to you, but nobody has explained
to me the cause of my disgrace."

" Indeed, that is strange," said the Marquise
with a bright but sarcastic smile. " Well, the
cause, Sir, of your disgrace is your own merit,
your science. You are the editor in chief of most
of the acts that emanate from the Chamber of Inquiry against royal edicts; the King knows this,
and does not lose his recollection."

The President was slightly confounded by a
reproach so courteous but cutting. He felt
abashed by its truth. Shame and self-love left
him nothing better to say than:

" In any case, Madame, if I have the misfor-

* This interview was obtained for de Meynières by the
learned Abbé Bayle. De Meynières' recital (MS.) was published by La Société Bibliophile Française, in 1856.

tune of offending the King, that is no cause to close a career against my son."

" The King is master," replied Madame de Pompadour ; " if he abstain from marking his displeasure, personally, against you, that is no reason why he should confer a personal favour on your son. But I am sorry for you, and desire nothing better than to be able to serve you. You know, for example, that at this moment the King desires proofs of submission from turbulen t subjects on certain matters. Many have written loyal and respectful letters ; if you and others agree to write such, it might be a service that you render to us under present circumstances, and I would hasten to show the King its value. Now, what would you that I say to his Majesty ?—' I have seen M. de Meynières to-day ; he has protested to me the most loyal devotion to your person and authority ? '

" The King will answer, ' What has M. de Meynières *done* to prove it ? ' Am I to say : ' Nothing ? '

The President declared " that this condition was impossible, and that Parliament honour necessitated resistance." " But," says he, " Madame de Pompadour only smiled, until with eloquent

9 *

vivacity she answered : ' I am always astonished at finding this pretended honour of Parliament thrust in the way of whatever the King desires, —what he wills,—what he orders. Is it not true honour to fulfil the duties of the State, to subdue the disorders of the reign, and to reconcile conflicting administration by combined acts of justice ! Honour, Sir, consists in confession of wrong, and repairing it, instead of a frivolous persistence in a conduct contrary to all rule and all good feeling. I believe that nobody doubts I respect the Magistracy ; there is nothing I would not give to be spared the pain of reproaching an august tribunal, albeit a Court that does not fail to be prodigal of its own praises. What ! is it that Court so wise, which aims unceasingly to reform government, which in a quarter of an hour is carried to such an extremity by want of self-control as to necessitate the resignation of its members ?* Nevertheless, if it be with these madmen you send in your resignation, M. de Meynières, your honour is bound not to desert their cause. You prefer to see the Kingdom, the State, the Finances perish ; in that consists your honour. Ah! M. de Meynières,

* Upon the question of war-subsidies.

it is not the honour of a true subject attached to
his King, nor even of a good citizen attached to
his country.'

" I (de Meynières) was dazzled by her eloquence of word and look and manner, and could
only reiterate what I had just said; when Madame
continued in a voice that was charming by its
varied intonation.

" ' So, M. le President, it must needs be that
the State perish ; ought the King to restore
to the Parliament exiled turbulent agitators !
If your resistance last, it will come to pass that
the King of France must fail in his engagements
with his allies, and that he cease to pay the
pensions, the troops, and maintenance of his
army. . . . . See the condition to which you
reduce the kingdom ; and you remain deaf and
indifferent ! Did not those who resigned abdi-
cate their charge, voluntarily ? The King may
retain some of these, according to their individual worth, and, in his mercy, do an act of grace
to others ; that is all he ought to do.'

" ' An act of grace, Madame ! The word is too
hard ; we are not criminals.'

" ' What I have said, M. le President, may

sound harsh.   I acknowledge it; but I am only a
woman, and not a chancellor; when those who
have the right to speak to you, do so, they will
weigh expressions without diminishing authority.
Above all things, it is essential that the honour
of the King be preserved ; and so it will be, though
by more scrupulous words.'

" ' Madame ! I wish I possessed your eloquence to subjugate the Parliament. . . . But
it is not the first time that the two Chambers have
ceased their service ; for example, that was the
case under Henri IV. from the 20th of March
to the 1st of June.'

" ' Were there exiles then, M. le President ? '

" ' One only, Madame, whom the King regarded
as a fool, and who was restored to his company
before the 6th of June.'

" ' Truly, that is very fine for Henri IV.,' replied the Marquise, with a strange mixture of
dignity and raillery. ' It is the too great goodness
of the King which renders you all so turbulent
and difficult.   But even such goodness wearies,
and your King will be your master.   Do not
attribute to ministers the just resentment of the
King, as King.   That is your habit, but they
have nothing to do with this case.   It is the King

who is personally wounded, and who will be obeyed. But I ask you, gentlemen of the Parliament, who are you, to resist the will of the King, as you dare to do? Do you presume to think that Louis XV. is not so great a Prince as Louis XIV.? Do you believe that the Parliament of to-day is greater in its attributes than that of former times?

"'Ah! I only wish the one resembled the other. But consider for yourself, what was the Parliament in 1673, after Louis XIV. had dealt with it until 1713, and you will see if ever Parliament were greater and more dignified. Why, to-day, gentlemen of the Parliament, do you find it extraordinary in a time of need that you are carried back to the execution of the *ordonnance* of 1667?'

"This admirable improvisation," continues de Meynières, "in the mouth of an elegant and graceful woman, an artiste, and a leader of fashion, so astonished me, that I replied by an unpremeditated admission, 'It was, then, Madame, that they dared not. . . .' 'Dared not, M. le President!' she interrupted, 'they dared not, and you—*you* to-day find courage to dare? Do you think, then, that the King is less powerful, less reso-

lute, than his ancestor? They dared not!—Ah!
mon Dieu, what a word you use!.... I know
it is the habit of gentlemen of the Parliament
and others so to think and speak; but there are
few who confess it, and I am sorry that, out of
your mouth, M. le President, should issue such
self-condemnation.'

"Afterwards," adds the disconcerted Meynières, "Madame la Marquise took leave of me by
some few words vague and polite, leaving me
filled with astonishment and admiration."* As
he left her, standing there alone, careless of his
wonder, and unconscious of his parting bows, she
was meditating—as proved afterwards—how to
turn the scale, so heavy with difficulties, in
favour of the royal cause. She was thinking
how to overcome turbulence, superstition, and
the want of funds in face of war. She was
thinking by what personal sacrifice she could
stimulate loyal emulation, breathe fresh life into
France, and quicken with new love the people

---

* "Madame de Pompadour," reiterates the President, "was
alone, near the fire. She scanned me from head to foot with
a haughtiness that will remain all my life in my memory.
She made no curtsy, but continued to regard me in the
most imposing manner."

who no longer shouted as in the last war,
" God bless the King." De Meynières confesses himself troubled beneath the eyes, which
even female envy declared to emit a light as
though a new soul sprang into life.

" Here was not only the artiste,—the woman
who inspired deeds of chivalry, and encouraged
men to fight for France, but the serious legislator, discussing the prerogatives of the Crown,
defending them with eloquence, versed, among
all her accomplishments, in dry parliamentary
precedent and lore. Moreover, carrying on the
discussion with tact, and refined politeness,
without a moment's loss of self-control. Who
can wonder at the absolute confidence of Louis
XV. in the Marquise, or at his devotion to an
intellect so great—devoted to him—at a time of
perplexity, war, and crisis ? "

At one time the Marquise wished that the King
would put himself at the head of his army as in
former days. She could no longer accompany
him, either as young musketeer in de Richelieu's
" elegant baggage," or by invitation of the chiefs,
who were her friends and correspondents ; but she
lived only for his glory, and she had much reason
to fear that he would be enervated by inaction in

France where he was surrounded by temptation. As a woman she had many griefs. However great the triumph of her intellectual ascendancy in France and Europe, she was still young enough to feel, at times, when faith and nerves relaxed, the anguish of her peculiar position. Let any woman judge for herself what this must have been.

But it was decreed by the council that Louis must stay in France.* It was remarked that the English might attack the coasts of France. English ships were lying off Normandy and Brittany. Also, the civil strife within the kingdom was not ended, only lessened for a moment by nearness of a common peril; and, for this reason, if for no other, Louis must reside within, or near, the capital. In spite of the Parliament, the preparations for war were rapidly and successfully achieved. Sustained by love for King and coun-

---

* The Marquise hoped that a descent might be made on England in favour of Prince Charles Edward, but, on being convinced that the cause would only insure defeat to her country, she withdrew the notion ;—the second time the head of the Marquise vanquished her heart in the Stuart cause, for which she had imbibed a poet's dream, and had personally suffered much.

try, the Marquise rallied for a time, and was un-wearied in inciting activity, loyalty, zeal.

The Minister of Marine,* her protégé, had not done badly, now his works were tested, as, in spite of England's threats and suspicions, he had 67 vessels of the line, 44 frigates, and 80,000 seamen ready for the emergency. An improvement on Cardinal Fleuri's time.

More than 200,000 soldiers marched up, ready, to the banner of France, without counting the provincial militia.

The financier, Paris Duverney, an old and esteemed friend of the Marquise, called by her in-fluence to assist in the Council since the war of 1745, provided for the deficient resources of this present war in concert with the Farmers-General. The Marquise, subsequently, in 1759, set an ex-ample to her country, which vindicates her from the charge of rapacity. She sent her own plate and treasures to the Mint for public use. In spite of the King's affection for her brother, and the public works nobly executed by the latter, it was her pride to know that the Marquis de Ma-rigny, whom the King called " Beau Frere," was not rich.

* De Rouillé.

By despoiling herself of costly superfluities, she incited others to self-sacrifice for the good of the State in time of peril. It was thus she initiated the Edict of October, 1759, which, though not obligatory, invited all subjects to contribute their treasures to the Mint,—objects of art excepted. A generous impulse passed electrically through France. There was war against England; and the aristocracy, even the bourgeoisie, assisted of their own free-will to sustain it. This conduct on the part of the Marquise redeems her from the charge of covetousness; as also the fact of her being the intimate associate of artists, and the sister of the Capuchin community (vowed to self-abnegation), from the other charge of excessive haughtiness. She has been accused of having exercised regal prerogatives in her household, and doubtless her political position rendered it expedient to maintain a certain reserve and state in her appointments. But when calumny goes on to assert that pride prevented her rising, even to receive princes of the blood, her own physician must step in to prove that physical infirmity prevented her so doing. Still young, and outwardly lovely, she was often carried on a couch to assist in the Council Chamber, as we shall see.

The private sacrifice of articles of silver and gold, of which the Marquise set the example, she turned with tact to the benefit of the fine arts. She then propounded and manifested the doctrine which has since been illustrated, that beauty in art does not consist in the matter but the manner of the thing ; that form is as perfect in common earth as in marble, gold, or silver. Above all, that gold and silver are nothing in a house by the side of a fine picture, a poem, tapestry, or even, as regards form and imagination, that fine Sèvres china which she had instituted as a national manufacture.

" It is from a time of national penury that date the highest *fantaisies de salon* (among superior works of art) that are still in vogue as this, that, or the other, à la Pompadour. While a higher price was set on pictures,—a Watteau, a Boucher even, than on sideboards laden with plate, —the internal decorations of palaces and houses became more rare and elegant as ostentation declined, and even the fans, held by Court ladies, became, as they are handed down to a favoured few, priceless as gems of art."*

* C'est à Madame de Pompadour que l'on doit " La petite poste de Paris" (a journal to amuse the people), " au prix de 10 centimes." Edit de Novembre, 1759.

In this sudden ascendancy of elegance over wealth, and this dawn of art for the million, is found the antetype of the Crystal Palace development of the 19th century. The *Expositions* of London and Paris of 1850-51, were foreshadowed by that of the Louvre thrown open to the public and strangers just a hundred years before. In the progress of art and its gatherings, the name of Madame de Pompadour must not be forgotten.*

Nor in Free Trade. On the 17th September, 1754, an edict was issued that the commerce of corn should be entirely free in the interior of the kingdom, that it should pass from province to province without need of passports, or permission (even in heretic Languedoc and Auch) to traffic in it. This liberty of corn-transport had been long craved for in France. To its want some authors

* A school was also constructed for science. Engineering was encouraged in this school. One of the sneering enemies of the Marquise confesses that "Whilst the brother of the Favourite, under the auspices of that French Minerva, carried fresh life into art and science, and into the royal manufactures under his supervision, she effected a revolution not less rapid and favourable in other parts of the administration." The number of beggars was reduced. Those who pleaded impotence to gain their own living were sent, at the expense of the State, to their native provinces, or to their relations.

attribute the disadvantageous points of the Aix Treaty.*

By this edict, agriculture took fresh root, and the people were more contented. If Madame la Marquise filled the ministry with her " creatures," as envy asserted, her creatures worked well. It so happened that the corn edict for which France had so long pined in vain was peculiarly due to her misfortunes. She had placed herself under Doctor Quesnay, " although," says her lady-in-waiting, " she knew from the first her complaint was incurable,—a mere question of time."

De Quesnay was a fearless philosopher, and was deep in the question of political economy.† This was a new doctrine to old France, but the Marquise, impressed by the truths she heard from de Quesnay concerning it, brought them before the Council, and used her power over the King to the unprecedented gain of the people. Medicine also made rapid advances, although it was not

---

* The way for all these things was contested step by step. At the first proposal to place the different schools of art in the Louvre, national jealousy resisted it. The universality of genius triumphed at last.

† Dr Francis Quesnay. Son of a husbandman in the Isle of France. Born in 1694. First taught by a village surgeon. Went to Paris, lived frugally and studied hard.

capable of administering to the heart diseased of the Marquise. Uneasy conscience originally, over-work, over-strung nerves, the struggle against envy, the effort to find the right way through the wrong, the anguish of resigning her undivided empire as woman over the King, for love of whom she had lost all and gained all, these were the ingredients of that slow poison by which there were some who supposed her perishing. The skill of de Quesnay was not equal to this. Father Sacy was the better physician of the two, and to him, forgetting the part to which he had been urged by her enemies, Madame de Pompadour was a true daughter in the faith. The reverend confessor is witness against the foul charge that malice, for political purposes (fostered by Prussia), fabricated against her. To say that she encouraged

Wrote books when Philosophy had forced something like free-press for free-inquiry. Patronized by the Pompadour. Assaulted old practice of constant blood-letting, and other fatal fallacies. Was made Secretary to new Institution for improvement in surgery. Although a genius, succeeded. Turned the advantage of a friend at Court to the good of the nation in particular, and human nature in general. Died, 1774. Was useful in promoting the sanitary reforms of Paris which were then began. His plans now continued and illustrated by good internal street government of Paris, below the surface. Public health indebted to de Quesnay then, and now.

the King in the intrigues of gallantry to which every chamberlain in his service and all France incited him, and troops of unprincipled creatures fostered,* is not only a gross indignity towards a dying woman, but a profane imputation on the religion of which she lived in the public exercise. Such reports were circulated in England, through pamphlets, published when French authentic books were contraband.

Political panders in France echoed the calumny, especially about the time of the Revolution, when every wild assertion that could bring discredit on the Monarchy was unscrupulously bruited and eagerly swallowed.† Had

---

* Witness Autograph Letters in Archives of France, unfit for publication. Documents valuable in vindicating the late Cardinal, and the present penitent (each in turn slandered as permitting, and pandering to, royal iniquity), from the individual reproach of sin which was the accumulated corruption of centuries. Welcome as affording something like a vindication of the King on plea of overwhelming temptation, from every part of his kingdom.

† It is remarkable that honest Englishmen condescend to avail themselves of the Authors of the 19th century when compiling a story of the 18th; that they should accept as a fact the "place for royal debauchery, called the *Parc-aux-cerfs*" and abominations that were practised there in 1750,

such a charge rested on the foundation of truth,
would the Church (politically opposed to the
Marquise) have received her as a penitent, confess, absolve, and admit her to the participation of
the Holy Sacrament? Would Montesquieu, who
died so calmly, have dedicated his best book to
her? Would the pious veteran, de Noailles, have
written to her that he " was flattered " by her note
of remembrance to him? Would the convent of
the Capuchins and that of the Assumption have received her as their inmate, and have treated her
presence as an honour?

It is tardy justice that out of the Archives of
England (the country where the vilest calumny
against this woman has been devoured) should
come to light, after one hundred years, letters
traced by her hand, as if only yesterday, which
bear intrinsic evidence of her courage, devotion,
and endurance of the Cross of suffering.

" The erudite Librarian of Versailles, who is
not sparing of censure and malevolence towards

---

from the evidence of revolutionary books published as late
as 1824.   For pure truth the historian must go to the foun_
tain-head. The stream is corrupt when it has been filtered
through the mire of a revolution moist with the blood of King,
Queen, nobles, and priests.

Louis XV., is obliged to confess that for this charge there is no foundation." *

* Everybody learned in the scandalous chronicles of the last century will know what is meant by the *Parc-aux-cerfs*, the scene laid by wicked invention for wicked practices of the King. Capefigue, the historian, now in France, declares "There never was such a place with such a purpose, destined for the King's ignoble pleasures. In the *Bibliothèque Impériale*, certain pamphlets published in England and Holland, by refugees there and in Prussia, have been condemned as unfounded libels, false as gross, and cast out. From the archives of the city of Versailles, it results that the site called the 'Parc-aux-cerfs' was detached from the general park of Versailles, and sold for building by the acts of 1725 and 1735, that is, long preceding the scandalous adventures which have been invented there. On this land were built the streets of St Antoine and three others, with that of St Louis and the New Market. I have sought to find any trace of a *Parc-aux-cerfs*: here exists none. What then becomes of the Royal scandals of a place that did not exist from 1749 to 1770? At that time the ground had been sold and partitioned for building a new quarter. I then went to other sites which might bear the name: no trace, no vestige. I have consulted in my life those noble old men who still survived with the cross of St Louis on their breast, have listened to the legends of their fathers: no sign, no memory of a *Parc-aux-cerfs*. There exist more than twenty deeds of sale and purchase made in the name of Louis XV., but none for this imaginary place. Let it not be imagined that history would be so complaisant as to conceal the vices of the King by suppression of place. I defend not the chastity of the King. According to the

10 *

The living historian of France, whose researches have not only vindicated the monarchy
of his country, but also human nature, from
charges black enough to produce atheism, mis-
anthropy, and anarchy, repeats an anecdote which,
though bad enough, shows that Louis XV. was not
at this time degraded below shame in vice. It is recorded as an exceptional case as regards the Marquise, who, childless, felt its retribution. One day
the King entered her apartments, leading a young
lady, and presenting her with painful embarrassment to Madame de Pompadour. A glance from
the latter sufficed to show her the reason why
the King, though too overwhelmed with shame to
speak, sought the favour of her protection to this,
her rival, who was about to become a mother. It

corrupt practices of the 18th century he lived; but that he
went so far beyond those, and with the sanction of a woman
he honoured, as to build an express retreat for debauchery, is
one of the most monstrous and untenable inventions. The
manners of the 18th century, generally, were chastised by the
Revolution, but no credible authority ever fixed this stigma to
them." It is curious and melancholy to observe from what
impure sources have been derived pretended biographies of
Madame de Pompadour. There was one by a nun who had
married a Prussian Officer. How false to fact and fatal to
morality this would be, its origin may suggest.

was a fearful test to one who, having for years striven to fortify the King's mind from the fanatic observances in which he still indulged, had also laboured, with death in view, to raise him above those debasing pleasures by the temptation to which she knew him to be surrounded.*

A Magdalene, even though a Marquise, dare cast no stone. Was this why the girl was received in silent pity?—After one painful moment, the Marquise became a sister of charity.—It was subsequently, through her earnest intercession for her rival, that mother and child were justly provided for by the King. (Louis XV. abjured the vice-stimulating practice of his predecessor of legitimizing children not born in wedlock, but he took care they were cared and provided for. In one instance he ordered that a daughter of his own should be brought up with every care, but that she should never know her real parentage.) The King was deeply touched by the generosity

---

* The King's daughters, those weary princesses who appeared as appanages of the royal household on State occasions, and then retired to amuse themselves as Horace Walpole found them, knitting and knotting, adopted of their own accord their little illegitimate brother, who afterwards became Abbé de Luc.

and forbearance of the Marquise. " Truly," he said, " you are good; what gratitude is due to you for burthening yourself with such a mission!" * And often he would murmur, as when she interceded for the mitigation of her enemy's (de Maurepas) sentence, — " You are good, you have a noble soul." In answer to these words, so often heard, she would lay her hand on the King's heart, and say : " It is to that I wish to speak."

" While arts, manufacture, commerce, municipal administration, lightened by the dawn of philosophy, were perfected in 1756, jurisprudence arose from the obscurity of barbarism and false prejudice." †   It was lamentable to the Marquise,

---

* The above anecdote was recorded by one living in daily intercourse with the Marquise, and not a friend at heart, her lady in waiting. It is observable that this lady in waiting, variously called " Femme-de-Chambre " and " first lady of confidence" by those who have cited her Mémoires (Mems. de Madame d'Hausset), was secretly ' leagued with the Jesuits. Hist. de Paris. Dulaure, Tome vii. pp. 395, 396. Pub. Paris, 1834.

† Testimony of an enemy of the Marquise, who talks of " her creatures." Also, of another enemy, a jealous woman, sneering : " Madame de Pompadour, who may be

who was unwearied in her labours for the arts of
peace, that war should again come to retard their
advancement. And now for this Political Treaty
between France and Austria of 1756, that
Treaty at which common history has jeered as the
work of diplomacy in petticoats, and of an
enervated Cabinet. France to-day declares that
if the work of Madame de Pompadour it re-
dounds to her eternal honour.

" 1st, It assured the concurrence of Austria,
when France saw herself unexpectedly attacked
by Great Britain. 2nd, The diplomatic preponderance of the Cabinet of Versailles over the Germanic body, especially over Saxony, Bavaria, and
Wurtemberg. 3rd, The cession made by Austria
to France, of a new frontier on the Low Countries,
which extended from the port of Ostend to the
sovereignty of Chimay. 4th, The reversibility of
Belgium entire at the death of the Infant, Duc de
Parma. 5th, The eventuality of a reunion to

afraid when she is dead of being insultingly cast aside
by the clergy (it is a Jesuit lady who writes), or by Monseigneur the Dauphin, or by the people of Paris, has worked
hard to assure herself a sepulchre; to deserve it she is very
earnest about the construction of a Church, called 'The Penitent Magdalene.' "

France of the left bank of the Rhine, promised by circles."

" It was not without a serious end, or without the stipulation of serious advantages, that the Cabinet of Versailles took to her balance of the account, the contingents of circles of Bavaria, Saxony, and Wurtemberg." (" This policy was followed by the 1st Emperor Napoleon. It was that which Talleyrand adopted to organize the confederation of the Rhine. Gentlemen who jested about this army of circles, called by the name of ' Cooper ' the French corps of the Prince de Soubise, destined to sustain them.") *

It was also agreed : " That if by the eventualities of the present war, the German powers found sufficient indemnities on the territory of Prussia, enlarged since 1715, the said powers engaged to yield to France the territories they possessed on the left bank of the Rhine, reserving the rights of bishoprics, of abbeys, and of manors mediatrix." †

---

* While Paris under peace operations was being laid out by new improvements in squares, the plan of war operations prescribed circles.

† " Les Traités de Paix," de Kock et du Comte de Garden, le tome iv. p. 19.

The first simple treaty (of neutrality) had been concluded on the 1st of May, 1756 (England having made her transatlantic *début* in 1755), in these terms:

"1st, The tranquillity of Europe being disturbed by the differences which divide France and England, the Queen-Empress declares that she will take, neither directly nor indirectly, part in the said differences, but that she will observe a perfect and exact neutrality during all the time that the war may continue.

"2nd, The same day (1st May, 1756)* was signed a secret convention in these terms: ' Nevertheless, if on occasion of the said war other powers than England attack, even under pretext of auxiliaries, any of the provinces His very Christian Majesty possesses in Europe, Her Majesty the Empress and Queen engages to guarantee and defend them; and reciprocally, if the States of Her Majesty, Empress and Queen, be attacked on the continent, His very Christian Majesty engages himself on his part to defend and protect them.' "

So France and Austria treated between them

* See Appendix 6. (Autograph. Mus. Brit.)

on the footing of perfect equality, although Madame de Pompadour, who has the credit—or blame — of all this, declared, as already shown by her letters, that there were but two really great powers in Europe, France and England. *England had now struck the first blow, as the result of protracted suspicion and uneasiness.*

But France and Austria were informed of the treaty of alliance that had been concluded between England and Prussia (15th Jan., 1756) so long projected : "His Britannic Majesty promises and engages to pay every year that the present war lasts, a million of pounds to his Prussian Majesty, that he may act efficaciously against his enemies. . . Moreover: His Britannic Majesty promises to send to the Baltic a squadron of four ships-of-the-line, and several frigates. His Britannic Majesty also engages to disquiet France on the coasts and in the Low Countries, to make a diversion in favour of his Prussian Majesty." *

By thus proving " facts by facts " it seems that far from the initiative being taken by France and Austria (as a feminine cabal, by which the

* Frederic usurped (*envahi*) the *Electorat de Saxe* on the 20th April, 1756.

Pompadour sacrificed France to her own vanity, flattered on the part of Austria, as alleged by credulous historians who get their evidence through the paid writers of the Anglo-Prussian alliance), hostilities not only began on the part of England, but that the Treaty between their Britannic and Prussian Majesties was ante-dated by four months to the preliminaries between France and Austria.*

The subsequent development of the question was rapid on all sides. To the triumph of French diplomacy be it said, that " a quadruple alliance was soon signed at St Petersburg : in the name of France by the Marquis de Châteauneuf; in the name of Austria by Count Esterhazy ; in the name of Sweden by the Baron de Posso ; and in the name of Russia by Count Voronsow." †

At the same time France and Austria signed a series of military conventions and territorial indemnities. " His very Christian Majesty was to

* In quoting the Treaty between England and Prussia, France is mistaken in the date by one day ; to witness :— Appendix, 6.

† See Appendix 7. Letters of the Arch-Duke Peter, and Arch-Duchess Catharine. Autographs.

support a corps of 4000 Bavarians, 3000 Wur-
tembergers, 7000 Saxons, and to pay moreover
to Austria an annual subsidy of 12 millions, for
the maintenance of an army of 100,000 men, always ready.   Her Majesty the Empress-Queen
agreed to yield to France the sovereignty of
Chimay,* Beaumont, the towns and ports of Ostend,
Nieuport, the towns of Ypres, Furnes, Mons, the
fort of Knope, and a league of territory round each
of the said cities; and moreover to cede the rest of
the Low Country to the Infant Don Philip of
Bourbon, Prince of Parma,† (reserving to herself
but a voice in the sitting of the Diet! the ad-
vowson of the Toison d'Or; the armorial bearings and the titles of the House of Bourgogna,)—
all this when she should be secure of Silesia.
Surely when historians on the Anglo-Prussian
side of the question have declared that Maria
Theresa of Austria stooped to flatter the " French
King's mistress, Madame de Pompadour," address-

* The Low Countries were then an Austrian possession.

† Another treaty assured the reversibility of the Low
Countries to France, after the death of Don Philip de Bourbon,
Duke of Parma, who would take the title of Grand Duke of
the Low Countries.   Pretty much the same terms of treaty as
had assured Lorraine to France.   Documents publiés par
M. de Garden.

ing her as " dear cousin," and " dearest sister,"
merely to get back Silesia, and that Madame de
Pompadour sold her country, and lit up a seven
years' war, because her head was turned by this
flattery, the State documents of England and
France could not have been so liberally placed
within their reach as now?

Progress forbids prejudice to be as blind in
the middle of the 19th century as at the time
(a hundred years ago) when France drove out
religious liberty, and Prussia, fostering licentious
thought, paid unscrupulous pens to fabricate lies.
Can an age, which boasts of free inquiry and
of impartial judgment, be so obstinate as to prefer fictions that blast the memory of a great Empress chastened by adversity, and of a penitent
woman whose wish unto death was to serve her
King and country, to honourable facts? Were
the fiction not nullified by facts, England had a
most unworthy enemy in the country she chal-
lenged to fight her.

" The King of Prussia was not only a military
genius of the first order, but he knew how to combine, to divine, and to use whatever material favourable to his cause might be found in the philosophers, the pamphleteers, writers, and refugees

whom he tempted to group themselves around him. By aid of these atheists, Frederic could disfigure facts, and impose on Europe by disseminating the writings distorted to his own views and policy. The King of Prussia, united to England, began hostilities, and carried disorder into Germany." These writers had the art of representing to Europe (to the world at large, of non-access to Cabinet councils and State Papers) that this crowned aggressor was the victim of the injustice and ambition of France and Austria. His scorn of women must have found a rich satisfaction in such representations; France and Austria then being governed by Maria Theresa and the Marquise de Pompadour.

Soon after the King of Prussia had burst like an 'illustrious brigand' into Saxony* (as we shall see), an event occurred in France that shocked public attention from news of the Camp to that of the Court.

On Jan. 4th, 1757, the King, after dinner, was going from Versailles, where he had been to visit one of his daughters who was ill, back to Trianon, where he was staying, and had ordered that the

---

* Aut. Letters between Kings of Poland and Prussia, for reasons, why. Appendix, Vol. ii.

carriages for himself and suite should await his return. At six o'clock he re-appeared, preceded by his equerries, having on his right hand the Dauphin, and behind him the Duc d'Ayen, the son of old Marshal Noailles. Just as he reached the last step leading to the court-yard, he suddenly stopped and said, " Somebody has pushed me roughly with his elbow." He thrust his hand under his vest on the left side. Then, drawing it back, covered with blood, he added, calmly : " I am wounded. Let them take care of Monseigneur le Dauphin." A moment afterwards he pointed to a man amongst the people who had assembled to see him re-mount his carriage, and declared ; " It is he." This was a man about 45 years old, dressed in brown, with a brown over-coat, and, unlike the other people, with his hat on his head. (Previously he had been observed by the Dauphin, who had said to him, " Do you not see the King ?" upon which one of the body-guard had knocked his hat off.) " Arrest him," ordered the King, " but do not kill him." The man was taken prisoner. All this happened in about five minutes. The man did not attempt to fly.

It was found that the knife had entered the

left side between the fourth and fifth rib, and that the blood flowed copiously. The King never lost his calmness for a moment.

Though the Court was not at Versailles, where the Palace was in disorder, the King was obliged to remain there. He was undressed by the gentlemen in attendance on him, and laid on a mattress, but before the surgeons could arrive he fainted as from suffocation. When M. de la Martinière, the first surgeon, came, he found that the wound was about "four inches deep," but not mortal. The knife had glanced aside (although it was a clean stroke), which favourable accident was attributed to a chance fold in the linen next the skin. (The shirt was preserved with much veneration.) In spite of His Majesty's calm in the midst of the terror surrounding him, there was subsequent fear of fever, not so much from the effect of the wound, as from the evidence it gave of a plot being in existence against his life. This idea excited the patient. The Queen was apprized of her husband's danger, and she lost no time in joining him at Versailles, where she evinced much grief at his condition.

Subsequently, the symptoms were such as to induce forebodings as to the result. The King, preparing for the worst, delegated the powers of Lieutenant-General of the Kingdom to the Dauphin. He said he believed it urgent that Monseigneur le Dauphin should be put in full ex-ercise of the royal authority; and the chancellor was summoned to recognise and sanction the au-thority of Monseigneur.

It was thought, from certain symptoms, that the knife was poisoned, and therefore that the King's case was fatal.

Immediately, the enemies of Madame la Mar-quise de Pompadour rallied round the Dauphin, and also her double-faced friends. The Duc de Richelieu informed the Marquise of the King's danger.*

Miserable and terrified, she listened;—saw at a glance her own fall and debasement under the power of the Dauphin, who was the tool of her sworn foes, the Jesuits; saw, too, how the system she had laboured to build would crumble to the ground, how liberty and progress would be stifled. She felt the sting of her shame, now that the man she had loved lay dying, and she was thrust aside as something already forgotten.

* Horace Walpole, gossiping second-hand ten years

The fact of de Richelieu seeking her and being admitted, refutes a charge, that at that time he was suffering from her ingratitude for his brave services to the King.

She dared not approach the King, lest the consequent strife and excitement might be fatal to him. She heard of his having asked for the sacred oils. While the priests had gone forth to administer extreme unction, Paris, as thirteen years before, was offering up prayers for him. The Church of St Geneviève, which Madame de Pompadour afterwards caused to be rebuilt, (says one of her adversaries, as an " *affaire de dévotion*,") was so thronged with people praying for the King, that the municipal authorities were unable to make their way through the crowd. The Marquise, now that the star of her destiny was supposed to have set, would not have dared to uncover her face before that multitude.

afterwards, says: " When the King was stabbed . . . the Mistress took a panic, and consulted d'Argenson whether she had not best make off in time. He hated her, and said ' by all means.' Madame de Mirepoix advised her to stay. . . . . The King recovered his spirits, d'Argenson was banished, and la Maréchale inherited part of the mistress's credit." *See Appendix. " Ministerial Enchainement and Intrigue."*

But inside her sumptuous Paris hotel, which was placarded outside with insulting lampoons, she could find consolation in the belief of a destiny less illusive than that she had sought, and of a kingdom not of this world. Her old friend, the Abbé de Bernis, (who could preach fine sermons, as well as sing love sonnets, or write diplomatic despatches,) hastened to her, and found her sick and depressed, gloomily conscious that in spite of all she had urged the King to do for his people's welfare, their prayers for him no longer sprang from such enthusiasm as at that time when her predecessor, de Chateauroux, was the object of their execration. French heroes were away at the war; the Pompadour was deserted and dying.

To know that, when the King was thought to be dying, his Counsellors were already lowering the standard of the policy which, at her dictation, had been royally established, that trusted servants of the King were turning their backs on their master, and were tottering on their principles with eagerness to worship the rising sun—if anything could rob death, to her, of its last sting, it was this. Where could she find a finer homily on the ambition which had once been hers? By what means be drawn nearer to Heaven than by

11 *

the sense of her own insufficiency, and this experience of the base ingratitude of man ?

The city of Paris, the municipal bodies, and
the Parliament sent deputies to Versailles to con-
dole, and at length, when the King was out of
danger, to congratulate. — Yes, the King lives.
The old King, not the new. "Long live King
Louis XV. !" "Down with the Jesuits !" The
King rose from his bed and received the Parliament men. Listened to long preambles. Then
said, drily: "I am quite well. Tell my Parliament to give me proofs of its obedience."

He sent word to his "good city of Paris,"
"I am well pleased with your zeal and affection,
and I assure you of my protection and friendship."

What the King said to the Marquise, nobody
knows ; but from the time of his restoration to
his Council and Cabinet, she was held more
in honour by him than ever. Those of the Ministry were dismissed who had showed signs of de-
falcation from the principles of Government. The
Abbé de Bernis was made Minister of Foreign
Affairs, having inspired confidence at Versailles
and at Vienna. The Count de St Florentin had
the department of Paris, and the disposition of
the Lettres de Cachet. The first that were signed

of these by St Florentin were for M. M. Machault and d'Argenson.* The King's faith was so shaken in his subjects, that he refused to deliver up the great seal, but kept it in his own hands, fearing a conspiracy. The Marine direction was accorded to Moras, but Rouillé was retained as adviser.

The war department was given to M. Pauliny d'Argenson, nephew to the deposed Minister. Marshal de Belleisle had full authority to direct the campaign.

Marshal Belleisle, fired by patriotic indignation, conceived the project of a descent on England. " From the origin of hostilities, the Marshal Belleisle had, from time to time, given an impulse to the national spirit, which enthusiastically responded to his idea of an expedition upon British ground." This idea had been carried into effect so far that France declares: " A profound disquietude existed in London, and the war suddenly engaged in on the Continent was instigated by England to provide a diversion for the Expeditionary Army assembled on the coasts of France." France was aware of English discontent, and London Cabinet feuds.

King George II. was furious. . . " He feared

* See Appendix ‡.

more than anything else to lose Hanover. Hanover was as the apple of his eye and the cords of his heart." . . . The Duke of Cumberland was hastily dispatched with a military force to Hanover, as soon as Pitt had quitted the Council. . . . Never was any sovereign in so pitiable a plight.* Not even the King of France.

On the 15th of January, Letters Patent had been issued in Paris, that the minute notes against the assassin should be sent to the Great Chamber. This had been deferred by the ramified examination that had been going on, and the complicated evidence which the other Law Courts had been sifting. The Grand Provost must judge the criminal. The evidence of this case of attempted Regicide fills a heavy volume. Not that there was any doubt that Damiens was the culprit, but the point to be brought to light was, whose tool he was. The man himself was not worth the trouble he gave to grave and reverend Signors, but he was invaluable, in a time

* For three months England was without a Ministry, until Newcastle and Pitt, both of whom had displeased King George, kissed hands on the 29th June (1757) and became the Government. Annals of War, 18th century, Sir E. Cust, p. 204.

of civil strife between Jesuits, Jansenists, and Parliament, as to the nest in which mischief and murder were hatched.

On Damiens was found a book of devotion, with the knife, and money — gold and silver. Regicides are generally fanatics. But they have — in almost every case in France — been the tools and victims of party-spirit. Damiens was born in the city of Arras, where the Jesuits exercised an absolute power. Some days before his attempt on the King's life, he declared that he should die, but the greatest on earth would die too. In speaking afterwards of his crime, he always said " We," but no torture could extract from him who were his accomplices. At one time —as if to throw suspicion in the wrong direction —he denounced some députés of Parliament. His accusation of the Parliament was utterly untenable, and incredible.

It was remarkable that the first words he uttered when captured, were: " Let them take care of Monseigneur le Dauphin," the echo of the King's words, which it was not likely, in the confusion, that he heard. It was also known that a girl, who was a pensionnaire of St Joseph (the same convent from which the Nun wrote the letter to Madame la Marquise complaining of forced religious vows), had declared :

" The King's life is in danger ; he is assassinated, or will be." This was treated at the time as the nonsense of a child, but the words were remembered when fulfilled, especially as they were uttered on the day of fulfilment, about four o'clock in the afternoon. Damiens struck the blow at six that evening. These words the girl, who was between thirteen and fourteen years old, had uttered in a low voice to one of her companions, after having visited some of her relations. Of course one examination led to another. Nothing came of them, although the child narrowly escaped imprisonment.

The Sœur St Joseph, who, some few years before, had written to the Marquise, complaining of finding herself *nolens volens* a nun, and imploring the King to remedy such cases, was not the only person in that conventual community who longed, in seclusion, for a Revolution which alone could set them free ; and thus the child had probably overheard some seditious talk. That clue snapped short. Others were unravelled, but none led to the true source of the crime. The

soldiers, in guard over the prisoner, were so indignant when they captured him, that, in spite of
the King's command that he should be cared for,
they pinched the flesh off his legs with red-hot
tongs, as he sat brooding over the fire in the
guard-room. Afterwards, he was placed in the
strong tower of Montgomeri, with chains of iron
round his wrists. His legs being still too sore
to support irons, he was sewed up in strong
sheets.

The knife was a clumsy weapon with two
blades. Damiens had originally been a servant
(cuistre) in a Jesuit college. Afterwards he had
gone into the service of a lady at whose house
the Marquis de Marigny (brother of Madame
de Pompadour) was in the habit of visiting.
Marigny did not like the countenance of Damiens,
and advised the lady to dismiss him as a dangerous
and ill-looking fellow. The lady did so. Afterwards, when 'M. de Marigny visited her, Damiens smashed the windows, in revenge for the
advice that had been given and taken. On one
occasion the police had been obliged to inter-
fere. Then Damiens had disappeared, and
only re-appeared as a Regicide. When asked the
reason of his crime, he said: " I did not desire to

kill the King, but to give him a sharp warning
to make the opposition of his Council cease to
the edicts of Parliament on the Bull Unigenitus."*
Here was fresh fuel to a fire which, though it had
looked pale in face of the blaze of war, had never
become extinct.

A letter was sent by Damiens to the King,
but his own prevarications had so discredited all
he said and wrote, that the letter could not save
him.   Here it is :

" Sire,—I am sorry to have had the misfortune to approach you ; but if you do not take
the part of your people, before many years hence
you, M. le Dauphin, and some others will perish.
It is grievous that so good a Prince cannot
be sure of his life, because of the too great
goodness he has accorded to ecclesiastics in whom
he places all his confidence. . . If you do not
remedy it great troubles will befall; your kingdom
is not in safety. . . . The Archbishop of Paris
is the cause of all trouble, because of the Sacra-
ments which he has caused to be refused.   After
the cruel crime that I have committed against

* From the curious collection entitled " Original Documents on the evidence of the Procédure du Procés against
Robert François Damiens."   Published, Paris 1757, in 4to.

your sacred person, the sincere confession which I
take the liberty to make, gives me hope of the
clemency of your Majesty's goodness.

Damiens."

Jesuits accused Jansenists, and *vice versa.*
Damiens was executed on Monday, the 28th of
March.   When he was on the scaffold, the Registrar asked him if he had any declaration to
make : " No," replied Damiens, in a hollow
voice, "if not that I should not be here, had I
not served the Parliamentarians."   The Registrar
retired, making a wry face.   One confessor said
to the other (Jansenist and Molinist), " Did you
hear that? "   To which the only answer was . . . .
" Ah ! "

Damiens was pulled to pieces by horses.—A
frightful end to him ; but wild horses were nothing in their momentary work to the fury the
culprit left as his only heritage.   The Jesuits
accused the Jansenists of complicity with the deed,
and the Jansenists flung back the accusation, in
these words : " *We* attempted to kill the King,
you Jesuits say !   But that would be to give us a
reign less favourable to us than that of the King ;
since, in case of his demise, the Dauphin inherits
the throne.   The Dauphin !   He who is devoted

to the Jesuits, and who, under their advice,
awaits but his reign to annihilate us altogether."

The King lived, but he never completely recovered the attack made on his life. Haunted by
the notion of some secret conspiracy in the heart
of his Capital, the natural gloom of his mind increased. The Marquise had now to exert herself
over her own sufferings of mind and body to
amuse a man ' frozen with terror.'   It was sometimes difficult for her to rouse his attention even
to the most urgent cares of State.

In proportion as the kingdom was working
out the retribution of centuries, the King's
conscience became his torment.   Louis insisted
on employing a secret correspondence, within and without his kingdom, to ascertain all
that was going on, as he feared, in reference to him, personally.   In vain Madame
de Pompadour tried to dissuade him from a
system unworthy of him as King of France, and
too much resembling that she abhorred.   She
knew that it would be to the interest of many to
foster this morbid curiosity, and to increase the
hypochondriacal fear that incited it.   The Abbé
and Count de Broglie were deputed to appoint

secret agents abroad and at home. The Duc de Choiseul — " that resolute, abrupt, proud, man"—implored his Majesty to cease this system of self-torment. In vain. The King's fears were greater than his love or his friendship. Thus the King's hand became too unnerved to wield his sceptre. It relaxed the firmness of its hold on the helm of affairs, just as a vigorous government was needed abroad and at home.

Feeling his deficiency, Louis would hold no Council without Madame de Pompadour at his side. He distrusted everybody but her. When her health (impaired still more by the shock she had endured in the attempted assassination of the King) would not permit her to stand or walk, she was wheeled on a low couch from her apartments to the King's Council Chamber. In fact, while she was gradually growing weaker unto death, the whole weight of Government devolved upon her. As, week by week, and month by month, she sank lower into the grave, her political importance rose higher and higher.

The Duchesse de Pompadour fully achieved her " destiny " when it was no longer capable of adding to her happiness in this world. All she had to do now was to work steadily on, and hold fast the faith to the end.*

She was glad to welcome her old friend, the Abbé de Bernis, to assist in the King's Council and " the Pompadour Ministry." De Bernis had a vision of the Roman Purple before him, for he had charmed the accomplished Pope Benedict; so the Pope and the Pompadour, who pitied the constrained attitude of the Holy Father, had a common bond of earthly sympathy in the Abbé who had charmed all other diplomatists out of their sober senses, had got his own way in spite of dull routine, and had blown dry husks of diplomacy to the winds. He found his beloved friend and patroness much changed. Scarcely recognizable in outward form. Hardly to be known in depth and earnestness of thought, for the brilliant creature who, a few years before, had flung back repartee, and who used to improvise a merry *rond* dancing and singing at the same moment. A shock in the right direction for the reverend Abbé—teaching him to

* A new impulse was everywhere felt. Eight new Marshals were made, among them the Count d'Estrées and the Duc de Mirepoix.

look upon the cross as something more than an
ornament.

In 1752 a painter had induced the Marquise
to sit to him for her portrait. His name was
Liotard. He had excited Parisian attention by a
long beard, and the flowing robes of a Mussulman, having just come from Constantinople, where,
according to his own account, he had painted all
the beauties of the Sultan's harem. It has already
been said that no canvas could do justice to the
mobile charms of the Marquise in her earlier
days. Many had been disappointed by the impotence of their art to " catch the life." But
Liotard entreated. The Marquise doubted his
skill and her own charms (about this time she
wrote to a friend, that her mirror reflected no
pleasure), but, always obliging to artists, she
consented.

The " copy of her countenance " was finished ;
like the sign of an inn. There she was—eyes,
nose, and mouth, without a trace of her inward
self,—her soul. Conscious of illness, painfully
alive to ugliness, unable to see herself, she
shuddered. As the vanity of woman was re-
vengeful and demonstrative in those days, it

speaks well for the Marquise that she kept her
temper and engagements with Liotard. She
recovered her self-control. She gave Liotard 100
louis, which was his price, and said, " Ah!
Monsieur, I begin to suspect your strength is
in your beard." But the charlatan was
crushed by her few laughing words. He never
rallied. Delilah herself, in cutting off the hair
of Samson, was not more terrible than the Pompadour who lightly touched an artist's beard.

When de Bernis was admitted into the Versailles " *Secretariat*," the Sanctuary of State and
Cabinet, the sight of the Marquise lying on
her couch at the head of the Council table excited his poetical fancy. " Mere beauty," he
says, " one admires and passes by, but expression
irresistibly enslaves attention." The Council felt
the electricity that darted—as confessed by female
rivalry—from the sunken eyes of the Marquise.
—The Duc de Choiseul was, as Minister, devoted
to her plans. She relied implicitly on his fidelity
to the King.

Voltaire, from his new retreat at Ferney,
jealously watched these new Cabinet Combinations. " It was then," he says, " the privelege of
poetry to govern kingdoms. De Bernis, since

Cardinal, had *débuté* by making verses against me, and then became my friend, which served him nothing; the friendship of Madame de Pompadour was more useful to him. . . . The King of Prussia in that fine book of ' *Poeshies* ' he demanded of me, slipped in a verse against the Abbé de Bernis,—

' Evitez de Bernis la stérile abondance.'

I do not think that book and that verse got to the Abbé, but as God is just, God used him to avenge France on the King of Prussia.   Madame de Pompadour presided at the negotiation." *

* This treaty with Austria was signed by the Count de Stahremberg, de Rouillé, and the Abbé Count de Bernis (on the 22nd of September, 1755, at a small château called " Babiole," near Belle-Vue), in consequence of "English piratical proceedings in America," and sinister intentions on the part of Prussia.

CHAPTER V.

BACK to the war! Court anxiety has too long
superseded Camp glory. Minorca is taken! For
a fair glimpse of French triumph, it may be as
well to get a bird's-eye view from Prussia. If we
could always see ourselves from our enemies'
point of view !

On the 21st day of July, 1756, the Marquis
de Valory (that French envoy who had been
taunted by Frederic about the French government
being like the Opera Ballet-Corps, all legs, no
head) wrote the following letter to the King at
Potsdam.*

" Sire,

I apprize your Majesty of nothing new
in announcing to you the surrender of the Fort
St Philippe ; but I obey the orders of the King,

* Autograph. "Royal Letters." Mus. Brit. Bibl.

12 *

my master, who, persuaded of your friendship and
of the concern (*part*) that you will well take in.
his success in the unjust war that the English
make against him, orders me to communicate
('*de lui faire Part*') the surrender of the famous
Fort, which by the ground where it is placed, and
the immensity of its works, was beyond harm from
the efforts of every other nation than of the
French. May your Majesty permit to me this
boasting, which is particular to me.

" Monsieur, the Duc de Fronsac, son of the
Marshal de Richelieu, arrived on the 10th in the
morning at Compiègne with the news of the
reduction of Fort St Philippe . . . . I believe that
your Majesty is better instructed of it than I am ;
may he permit me to congratulate myself upon
the occasion of so brilliant an event of placing
myself at his feet.

" I am,

with a very profound respect

of your Majesty,

The very humble and very obedient servant,

Valory.

" At Berlin this 21 July, 1756."*

* The French were first in the field. From the commencement of the differences with Britain in the preceding

To this diplomatic sarcasm, Frederic replied :

" Monsieur le Marquis de Valory,

" I am much obliged to you for the news that you have communicated to me by the letter you have done to me, of the 21st of this month. I confess that I should have been more glad to learn that of peace, or of the dispositions to draw together the two *Partis* to a good accommodation, which would be equally interesting to all Europe. And upon that I pray God, that he may have you, Monsieur le Marquis de Valory, in his holy and worthy keeping.

" At Potsdam, this 23rd July, 1756." *

Richelieu, as usual, had played with toil and opposition, and won the day. His appointment to the command of the Minorca expedition

---

year, the design was formed of taking the island of Minorca, and preparations on a large scale had been making at Toulon with wonderful secrecy and diligence. Minorca was prized by the English next to Gibraltar : they valued both as trophies of the War of the Succession, and awaking from their lethargy, Pitt and the people assailed the Government for their supineness in not showing more activity for its protection.—Sir Edward Cust's Annals of the Wars of the 18th Century, p. 174.

It is scarcely necessary to recall to the reader that Port Mahon and Fort St Philippe were in Minorca.

* Aut. Mus. Brit. Bibl.

was at Madame de Pompadour's instigation. She preferred him to be in the camp rather than at court; he, the King's arch-tempter, being an honour to the former and a disgrace to the latter. But, though the Duc de Richelieu's bad morals excited abhorrence in a corrupt Court, his good temper inspired love even among austere Puritans. On one occasion the gallant Duke pawned his most brilliant Order, that of the *Saint Esprit*, to provide him funds for unholy pleasures. Richelieu was the good and evil genius of France. He carried glory and left disgrace wherever he went.* How he pleaded for Languedoc Protestants has already been told. In 1754, was confirmed the grant of the " Rehabilitation of Protestant marriages " (the Curés attesting such marriages as civil contracts) and the Protestant assemblies were no longer interfered with. Languedoc was so grateful to the King for the clemency which the Duc de Richelieu had incited, and the

---

* Some few years after de Richelieu was worshipped as Minorca hero, Horace Walpole met him at Versailles, and profanely describes that great conqueror as " only a bit of tawdry old worn-out ; " but adds, " he is as like to myself as two peas on a dish, — two grey old parched peas."

Pompadour had confirmed, that it voted, of its own accord, a ship of war, and a second provincial regiment which took the name of Septimanie. But there were two parties in Languedoc. Always in war time, the Protestants were ready to take up arms for their faith (as they supposed), when the enemy professed their own tenets. England and Prussia were the two Protestant powers.*

Again, one good turn begot another. In recognition of Languedoc loyalty, and of Richelieu its instigator, the King appointed the Duc de Fronsac, Richelieu's son (who the King had once wished should wed Madame de Pompadour's daughter), Colonel of honour to this fine Languedoc regiment.

Colonel, Duc de Fronsac, in July 1756, was posted off to Compiègne with the good news of his father's Minorca victory over the English, as reported by the Ambassador Valory in his letter to the King of Prussia. King Louis instantly wrote to the Duc de Richelieu, to congratulate him upon " a success so prompt, and

* Autograph from King Frederic to King George, the two defenders of the faith. Appendix.

so complete." France was overflowing with joy. English ships were the bugbears of France, and she chuckled the more because her brave Admiral Marquis de Galissonière had defeated Admiral Byng in sight of the Minorca besiegers. The proverb was: "The soldiers of Richelieu have seen the English sailors fly."

Admiral Byng, as England knows, was shot blindfolded on the deck of his own ship, in retribution of Galissonière's triumph. France groaned with horror at this instance of England's *Sevérité implacable*. Meanwhile, the hero Richelieu hastened to Versailles. His road through France was a triumphal march. Arches overhead; whole populations turning out to hail him; his army at Toulon *fêtée* and caressed. Even the garments of women (the *caprices des femmes*) and the equipages in which they rode to meet the conquering hero, were dubbed by the local names of his victory. "Minorca" was inscribed in flowers on the triumphal arches over his head. One of the new streets in Paris, jutting out on the freshly planted Boulevards, was called "Port Mahon." All this was dear to the heart of a Frenchman, hero or not. All this had emanated from the heart of a Frenchwoman who loved the hero, though she was not fond of the man.   Amid the cheers of the people, de Richelieu hurried on to Versailles; and there, in presence of the King and assembled Court, he, in the language of the time, "laid down his laurels at the feet of the Duchesse de Pompadour." Well pleased, she replied to the hero's gallant homage with sportive lightness, which was the vogue of Versailles, and worth about as much as the homage itself.   The King, looking on in his sombre way, said, with a dryness that showed his inmost satisfaction (already sincerely and seriously expressed by letter), "Well, Marshal, and how did you like the figs of Minorca?"

Now about these figs there was a *double entendre*, though the King seldom indulged in a joke.

His joke now did not sting like an asp in a basket of figs. "The jokes of stupid men are cruel." Louis XV. was not stupid, and Richelieu accepted the joke as a compliment rather than a cruelty.   But an English historian* is pleased

---

* Sir Edward Cust.   Annals of the Wars of the 18th Century, p. 172.   This English historian also attributes de Richelieu's Minorca appointment to Madame de Pompadour's ill will against him; from which we may infer that a brooding Court hatred hatches a fine camp success.

to infer from it, exactly 100 years afterwards, that the King of France was so weak in character, as to be incapable of appreciating the services of his brave subject.

Not to waste time in guessing what royal sarcasm might imply under a symbol old as Adam, it was known for a fact that the hot climate of Minorca and the thirst for conquest had excited de Richelieu's troops to drunkenness.

A sort of fever broke out among them, and the more figs they greedily devoured, the worse they became. Then de Richelieu grew fearful of other *figues* (also the French for ' sneers'), as Minorca was a modern Capua for enervation.

The fear of failure spurred him on to brave deeds which were thought rash by the Cabinet. To check demoralization, which would cause defeat, Richelieu became severe in the discipline of his troops. This discipline was appreciated at Court, as the following letter may show, from Madame de Pompadour to the Countess de Brienne (whose husband, of the House of Lorraine, was grand Equerry of France).

" We are all in joy; you must partake in it. The enterprise of Minorca was at first thought rash ; now that it has succeeded, it is looked upon as a presage of new glory, and regarded as a matter of course. The Marquis de la Galissonière has dispersed the English fleet, and the Duc de Richelieu has taken the Fort of St Philippe by assault: these are happy events to which we are not accustomed in our naval wars with the English, and which are therefore but the more important and agreeable.

"Our soldiers have shown an intrepidity and a passion for glory which astonish. The Maréchal de Richelieu, seeing how debauchery and drunkenness killed so many men and made havoc in the army, issued an order that whosoever in future might get drunk, should be deprived of the honour of mounting the trenches, i. e. of the honour of getting his head broken. This threat has made such an impression on these brave men, that since that time there has not been seen one intoxicated. . . . '*Où le point d'honneur va-t-il se nicher ?*' would have asked Molière. . . . The city of Paris is going to make grand rejoicings; and for myself I will do my best. . . . ."

Marshal Richelieu was made Generalissimo of all the forces by sea and land. Admiral de la Galissonière (formerly Governor of Canada), was idolized by the nation, which gave him thank-offerings.

Before Richelieu's arrival in France he had written of his success to Voltaire, having been for more than twenty years the correspondent of that philosopher, and the confidant of the late Madame de Châtelet in those days when Voltaire was concocting Newtonianism with her at Cirey.

In answer to Richelieu, Voltaire wrote:

"Aux Delices, 16th of July, 1756.

" My hero and that of France,

" In virtue of the little note with which you deigned to honour me after your fine assault, I had the honour to tell you all that I think of it, and to write to you at Compiègne.   You are going to be assassinated with Odes and Poems ;— A Jesuit of Mâcon, an Abbé of Dijon, and a Bel Esprit of Toulouse have already sent me some.   I am the Bureau d'Addresse of your triumphs. I am addressed as the aged Secretary of your glory."*

* Voltaire versifies :

> "Des deux Richelieu sur la terre
> Les exploits seront admirés ;
> Déjà tous deux sont comparés,
> Et l'on ne sait qui l'on préfère.

> "Le Cardinal affermissait,
> Et partageait le rang suprême
> D'un Maitre qui le haïssait ;
> Vous vengez un roi qui vous aime."

While all this was going on in France, the King of Poland (father of the Dauphiness), who had wanted nothing to do with the European struggle for ascendancy, became uneasy at finding his kingdom full of Prussian troops.

Frederic (who pretended Peace, and had prayed God to have Mons. de Valory in his holy keeping, and to send him and his royal Master pacific dispositions) had demanded a passage for these troops into Bohemia *(pour aller en Bohème)*, but Augustus grew suspicious at their tarrying by the way. * So wrote to " Fredericus, Monsieur mon Frère,' le bon Frère, Auguste Rex,"† on the 29th of August, 1756, just the very day before the conqueror Richelieu re-entered France.

* The report of the intention of France to invade Great Britain increased every day, and it was deemed absolutely necessary to meet the threatened evil. Seven millions were voted by Parliament for the increase of the Army and Navy. . . . . Speaker Onslow, in presenting the money bills to the Sovereign, ventured to say :

" There were two circumstances existing which most seriously alarmed the people of England—subsidies to foreign princes, and an army of foreign stipendiaries,—and he trusted that his Majesty would never trust the sword out of his own hand to any people whatever."—Sir E. Cust's Annals of the Wars of the 18th Century.

† Aut. Letters of King of Poland. Appendix.

Then Frederic of Prussia wrote the following letter to Augustus of Poland,* forgetting that in diplomacy ' qui s'excuse s'accuse ' :—

" Monsieur mon Frère,

" The inclinations which I had for Peace are so notorious that all I could say to your Majesty would not prove it more than the convention of Neutrality which I have signed with the King of England. Since that time, by different tacking-abouts of system, the Court of Vienna has thought to find the moment favourable to put in execution some designs which since a long time it has incubated against me. I have employed the highway of negociation, believing it the most suitable to dissipate reciprocal suspicions to which divers proceedings of the Court of Vienna had given place. The first answer which I had from the Court of Vienna is so obscure and enigmatical that no Prince who wishes to provide for his safety can content himself with. The second was conceived with so much haughtiness and contempt that it ought to offend the independence of every Prince who has his honour at heart ; and although I had but insisted upon assurances that I required of the Empress

* "Royal Letters." MSS. Mus. Brit. "La Réponse du Roy au Roy de Pologne."

Queen, to be safe against all the bad enterprises
which she would be able to make against me, this
year and the coming year, she has not deigned to
answer to a demand so important. This refusal
has obliged me, in spite of myself, to take the part
which I have seen the most proper, to prevent
these designs of my enemies. . . . . Nevertheless as much for love of Peace as by the spirit
of humanity, I have again ordered to my envoy at
Vienna to make some new representations. . . . . .
I did put myself in motion on one side, but . . . if
yet the Empress wished to give me security. . . she
might reckon that I would willingly sacrifice all
the expenses of a commencement of war, to public
tranquillity. . . . . . It is neither cupidity nor ambition which directs my proceedings, but the protection that I owe my peoples, and the necessity
of preventing some plots which would become
more dangerous from day to day, if the sword did
not cut this Gordian knot while there is yet time.
There is nearly all the explanation that I am in
a condition to give to your Majesty. I will keep
fair with (menagerai) his States as much as my
present situation will permit. I shall have for his
Majesty all consideration, and for his family all
the attention and all the consideration that I ought

to have for a great Prince, whom I esteem, and of whom I have to complain, but inasmuch as he delivers himself up too much to the counsels of a man of whom the bad intentions are too much known to me, and of whom I could be able to prove the black conspiracies, paper upon table.

" I have made all my life profession of probity and of honour, and upon this character, which is more to me than the title of King which I hold but by the chance of birth, ... I assure his Majesty .... that his interests will be sacred to me, and that he will find in my proceedings more care for his interests, and for those of his family, than persons wish to insinuate, who are too much beneath me to deign to make mention of them."*

Again :

" To the King of Poland, Sept. 1756.

" Monsieur Mon Frère, ... Whatever desire and whatever inclination I have to oblige your Majesty, I see myself in the impossibility of evacuating your States, from a hundred reasons of war. .. I would that the road to Bohemia passed by *Thuringe*, forasmuch as I might not have cause to molest the States of your Majesty, but as the reasons of war oblige me to avail myself of the River

* For original Prussian vows entire, see Appendix.

Elbe. . . I cannot by a miracle turn its course. . . . and it is impossible for troops to fly."

Unto the King of Prussia writes the King of Poland . . . . . . " I appeal to the sentiments of justice and of probity of which your Majesty makes profession, and I am persuaded that you will not find that I and my States ought to suffer from the differences of your Majesty with the Empress Queen. I would desire, as to the rest, that your Majesty would give me to know the black plots of which you make mention in your letter. . . . . . I pray then your Majesty to evacuate my States, in causing your troops to go out of them, as soon as possible. I am ready, as I have already caused to be explained, to give to your Majesty all the sureties that you can exact from me, suitable to equity and to my dignity. . . . I take the part of repairing to my army to receive there at the soonest the ulterior explanations of your Majesty, protesting to you yet once more, that my intention is by no means to alienate myself from a covention of Neutrality with your Majesty, *mais que plutôt j'y donnerai les mains avec une satisfaction parfaite.*

" Dated, at Dresden this 3rd September, 1756. Au Roy de Prusse." *

* Aut. Mus. Brit. Bibl.

King Frederic then dropped the mask, and sealed his solemn promises to Poland with blood.

One evening, just as the King of Prussia was soothing his 'bon frère,' Augustus of Poland, by his epistolary promises and protestations, he whispered at supper to Sir Andrew Mitchell, the plenipotentiary of his Britannic Majesty, that he wanted to see him in camp next morning. When Sir Andrew arrived there, Frederic pointed out to him the Prussian soldiers like a swarm of hornets, and said : " Behold 100,000 men ! They are setting out they know not whither ; write to your Master that I am going to defend his dominions and my own."

" Sire," said Sir Andrew, alarmed, not being instructed in a way to keep pace with such Prussian policy ; " Sire, let us hope that by the help of God we shall soon force our enemies to a desirable peace."

" By the help of God ! " cried Frederic ; " I did not know that He was one of your allies."

" Yes, Sire," said Sir Andrew, " and the only one who costs us no subsidies." *

" The Alliance of France with Austria was

---

* Appendix : Convention between England and Prussia on Subsidies. Aut. State Doc.

characterized 'a monstrous union' after 300 years of an always sanguinary discord. The 'monstrous union' proved only just in time. Frederic's impatient sword rent asunder the veil of suspected Prussian 'sinister intentions.'"

King Frederic marches his troops into Saxony, reckoning to make of that province a rampart against the Austrian Power.* He invades Leipsic, presents himself before Dresden, enters as Master into that capital under the name of Protector. . . . . This invasion of the King of Prussia was the début of a new scene which put under arms more than 500,000 men. . . . Meanwhile the Saxon Monarch had been obliged to flee from his capital. He had proposed neutrality, and had received this overwhelming answer. " All that you propose to me does not suit me : I have no convention to make ". . Augustus repaired to Pirna on the road to Bohemia, where 17,000 Saxons were encamped, and where he believed himself in safety. Frederic commanded as conqueror in Saxony.

The queen of Poland, wife of Augustus, had not wished to fly. The key of the Archives was demanded of her, and upon her refusal to deliver it up, they tried to force open the gates ; the

* Fastes de Louis XV.

13 *

Queen placed herself before them, flattering herself that her person and firmness would be respected; neither one nor the other was respected;
she saw the State Dépôt opened and the papers
carried off which were of consequence to the conqueror to have in his possession. . . . . . .* The
Saxons saw themselves blocked up by the Prussian
Army even in the camp of Pirna; and . . . . were
reduced to the hard extremity of rendering themselves prisoners of war to the number of about 13
to 14,000 men, seven days after the battle.   The
Capitulation was singular.   The King of Prussia
declares to the Polish Monarch, that if he will give
to him that army, he does not want to make it prisoner.   Upon the demand of subsistence he replies
' Granted, and rather to-day than to-morrow. Upon
the only prayer of Augustus, that his Body-Guard
might not be made prisoners, Frederic adds ; " that

---

* The King of Prussia seems, by his Dresden cruelty in
1756, to have revenged himself for his demoralization in Dresden (1728), under "that unique Polish Majesty, the Saxon
man of Sin," the old King Augustus of those days.   After
which, as Thomas Carlyle tells us, "his life for the next four
or five years was ' extremely dissolute '. . . . . consorts chiefly
with debauched young fellows, as Lieutenants Katte, Keith,
and others of their stamp, ... wallowing like a young Rhi-
noceros in the mud-bath :—Some say it is wholesome for a
human soul; not we ! "

he cannot listen to him; that a man is a fool to let go troops of which he is master, to find them in head a second time, and to be obliged to make them prisoners a second time."

" Augustus, having lost his Electorate and his army, demands as a favour, passports from his enemy to get back into Poland. These were accorded to him without trouble, with the insolent politeness of furnishing him with post-horses. All Saxony was laid under contribution. The magistrates of Leipsic remonstrated upon the taxes that their conqueror imposed upon them. . . . they were put into prison, and they paid.

"The Queen of Poland desired not to follow her husband. She remained in Dresden. Grief soon ended her life. Europe commiserated that unfortunate family."

Such is the sequel to the state documents which, discoloured by a century, are, without it, as dry as the dust of their royal writers without the soul. But humanity was much involved in the sequel; the feelings of a daughter, and that daughter the Dauphiness of France.

When mourning for her mother, the daughter of Augustus, the ornament to virtue in any country, and the brightest domestic example to France, must have rejoiced (meek-hearted woman though she was) to hear King Frederic spoken of as " illustrious brigand." Such deeds as these made him greater than ever in war, in which, as with the Jesuits, the end justifies the means. But even philosophy, which had so looked up to him, flinched.

As before said, France had inclined towards Prussia with a yearning for liberty of conscience, there exemplified. The Duc de Choiseul had brought philosophy into the Cabinet of Versailles. Madame de Pompadour was, by antagonism to the Bull Unigenitus, impelled towards it. In Paris, flowing in through the press from hidden sources, it was deepening, ramifying.

But this sudden exemplification of philosophy on the part of the Prussian King re-kindled ancient loyalty and indignation against practical atheism. France sang:

> " L'Anti-Machiavel, mon Cousin,
>   Est un Roi débonnaire
>   Mais qui s'affiche tel, mon Cousin,
>   Et fait tout le contraire, mon Cousin,
>   Voila d'un Mandrin l'allure, mon Cousin,
>   Voila d'un Mandrin l'allure."

and

> " De tes amis trompés, tu deviens le tyran.
>   Prince ingrat! Tu n'est depuis cette victoire
>   Qui fera pour jamais détester ta mémoire
>   Qu'un faux sage, et qu'un vrai brigand!"

"But," as observes the impartial authority quoted, " on the other hand his aggression was regarded as a *chef d'œuvre* of policy, wisdom, foresight, activity, and audacity."

Frederic converted everything he could lay his hands on in Saxony into money, except the Palace and Art Galleries.

As to Dresden porcelain, it was scattered all over Europe, reminding one of the British proverb of a bull in a china shop.

To the people and soldiers Frederic said: " I am monarch of your country, and therefore your master; obey me." Success with the people is virtue. King Augustus protested against the fidelity of his own subjects—his soldiers especially—" being turned against him." His heroic Queen never recovered the insults of the illustrious brigand (while she defended the State documents which, with political perversions, were ruthlessly published to the whole world); and with bitterness against the time-serving nature of man, the King of Poland turned for sympathy to Austria.

" The Emperor of Germany addressed a remonstrance to his Majesty, Frederic, requiring him to desist from his unexampled, highly crimi-

nal, and most culpable rebellion; and at the same
time called upon the generals and officers of
the Prussian army to abandon their impious lord,
that they might not be participators in his guilt."*

Maria Theresa, indignant and alarmed — as
after this Saxon invasion there could be no longer
any guarantee in public faith, political treaties, or
the boundaries of nations—prepared her armies
(in 1757), and Elizabeth Petrowna, Czarina of
Russia, sent into Lithuania 100,000 troops, under
General Apraxin, thus threatening Ducal Prussia.
A strong fleet lay in the Baltic. Maria Theresa
of Austria did not suspect that, instead of defending Saxony against her, the illustrious brigand
was about to burst into Bohemia (from which en-
sued the famous battle of Prague), nor did Elizabeth Petrowna of Russia suspect that, at the
very time she had sent her troops to sustain right
against might, the Prussian Mandarin and King
George were coquetting with the Grand Archduke
Peter and Archduchess Catherine, her well-beloved niece and nephew, the heirs to her throne,

---

* " The Saxons of all ranks, from similarity of dialect, manners, and ideas, were more inclined towards the Prussian than
the Austrian service." Annals of the Wars of the 18th Century. Sir Edward Cust, p. 176.

under the shadow of her palace roof, and in the very heart of her court.*

The Archduchess Catherine, who afterwards was declared by Frederic to be greater than Semiramis, and worthy to take her place between Solon and Lycurgus,† was the only royal woman he tolerated. He killed the Queen of Poland. He played treachery with Elizabeth Petrowna of Russia. He dodged Maria Theresa, and threw the whole odium of the fiercest war that ever deluged Europe with blood upon her and Madame de Pompadour.

The faithless conduct of the Philosopher King, shocked back the soul of Europe to the Pope of Rome. The Austrian Marshal Daun had his sword blessed by the Holy Father to fight with it against " Frederic the Atheist." (Marshal Daun was stationed in Moravia, and Prince Charles of Lorraine near Prague ; under the latter acted our old friend, the Irish-Austrian Marshal Brown.)

* See Appendix, 7. " Original letters from the Grand Duke Peter, and the Grand Duchess Catherine (afterwards Empress of Russia), with letter of King Frederic to the Archduchess Catherine, &c. (MSS.) labelled, " Very important." Literally translated.

† Original letter of King Frederic to the Empress of Russia. Aut. Appendix.

The Dauphin of France, excited by his ex-clusive creed against the two Protestant powers, (Prussia and England), and urged to revenge his wife's wrongs as perpetrated by Frederic on her father and family, rose from his usual apathy, and wanted to buckle on his sword, which was also blessed. As in former days, his zeal was restrained by Cabinet policy ; and his advisers, the Jesuits, by no means wanted to lose their hopes of future power in him.

The Abbé, Count de Clermont, who, as told in the last war, had a special dispensation for fight-ing, was made General. King Frederic, when he heard of this elevation, said, "I swear that he will soon be raised again by the Archbishop of Paris."

France, spasmodic with hope and fear as to the fate of her colonies,* infested by "uncivilized

---

* 1757. 1761. "After the first blush of success, 'Tout va tomber en décadence.' Will the idea of Bussy be frus-trated, and Chandinagor and Pondichery tremble in the balance ? Will these establishments fall into the power of the English ? Canada, too, which had been moved by *une impulsion si Grande,* is it only to be conquered by the Eng-lish ? And will the Sugar Isles lower their *Pavillon* before the Britannic Squadrons ? If so, let England thank the im-pulse of Guillaume Pitt. One knows not what may be

pirates," determined to avenge herself on piracy and " the illustrious brigand," by seizing hold of Hanover, that apple of the King of England's eye.

" Sixty thousand men," as the English chroni-dler tells us, " under the Marshal d'Estrées, received orders to march upon the Electorate, and to commence by seizing the estates of the King of Prussia on the Rhine." The Duc de Richelieu was jealous that the command of this army was not given to him. Then, among French generals, began that system of recrimination that France had so clearly seen, when existing in the last war among English generals, to be the cause of England's failures. The system of military tactics was also in a state of transition. Some generals inclined to the old, as exemplified by Saxe, and some to the new, as practically illustrated by Frederic of Prussia. The King of France, though the king over heroes, bewailed more than ever the loss of his old servants and staunch soldiers, Marshals Saxe and Lowendhal. Again he mourned, " I have only captains left." And Madame de Pompadour dreaded lest thousands of men should be lost for the sake of one man.

achieved by a firm hand and a powerful head for the policy of a State." Plaintes de Versailles.

The tables were turned.

But soon France had reason to flatter herself that a new halo of glory was dawning over her camp. News arrived at Versailles that the French army, commanded by Maréchal d'Estrées, had passed the Weser, taken Embden, laid Hanover under contribution, had fought the Duke of Cumberland, and had so closed in his army that no other resource was left him but capitulation.* Hanover and Brunswick were in the power of the French. The second army of the Rhine roused itself to march into Westphalia, and to make its junction with the army of Hanover under the Marshal Duc de Richelieu.†

Six thousand Prussians had assisted in the defence of Hanover. King Frederic would spare

---

* This capitulation was signed at Closter Seven,' on the 8th of September, with the guarantee of the King of Denmark. The principal article was that all the troops should disperse. Prussian pamphlets declared that it was with the money of Closter Seven that the Duc de Richelieu built the " Pavillon de Hanovre," upon the Paris Boulevards. Certain it is that the Streets d'Hanovre and de Richelieu owe their names to this period.

† De Richelieu and the Count de Lynar shared the credit of the Closter Seven Convention. De Lynar believed himself inspired by Heaven to stop the shedding of " precious Lutheran blood."

no more troops just then from his other operations.
While pretending to be putting Dresden into a state
of defence, he had concentrated his forces on
Bohemia. The Prussians suddenly advanced
against Prague; one body of troops under the
King, and the other under veteran Field-Marshal
Schwerin.

Prince Charles, of Lorraine, resolved to remain on the defensive, until (out of Moravia)
Marshal Daun should join him, with his sword
blest by the Pope. Marshal Schwerin soon made
Prince Charles change his position ; but the
Austrians poured down such a volley on the
Prussians that the latter were flying in all directions just as King Frederic rode up with fierce
reproaches. Stung by these, Schwerin got off
his horse, snatched a colour from an ensign's
hand; cried, " Let the brave follow me ; forward, my children ! " and rushed to the front !
when, shot dead, he fell with the flag he had
held, like a pall over his body.* — (Just in
the same way had fallen the Chevalier Belleisle,

---

* Schwerin had served under Marlborough and Eugene.
All who have been to Berlin, must remember the monument
to Schwerin's memory. Frederic called Schwerin his tutor in
war, but worried him in time of peace.

Marshal Belleisle's brother, ten years before at Exilles.)

On the other hand, Marshal Brown was carried off the field, mortally wounded. Prince Charles, hesitating whether to capitulate, sent to ask the dying general's advice. Frederic had summoned Prince Charles to capitulate. The dying Marshal Brown (who formerly had so bravely fought the French), roused himself. "Est-ce que sa Majesté croit que nous sommes tous de C—ll—us ?" he gasped: "Tell my Prince that I advise him immediately to attack the enemy. Does the King of Prussia take us all for poltroons?" (Brown died on the 26th of June.)

At this juncture, up came Marshal Daun out of Moravia with an army of 40,000 men, but he thought it better to lie in ambush beyond Kölin. Frederic, however, sent off 25,000 men to watch Daun. Then the Prussians fired red-hot shot into Prague. The garrison there were living on horse-flesh. Maria Theresa dispatched a Captain of Grenadiers (who—disguised—slipped through the besieging army into the city) with an address, which even at that hour of horror and extremity incited fresh Austrian courage, loyalty, and devotion, "for our King, Maria Theresa."

Marshal Belleisle who, years ago, had defended
Prague with 15,000 men declared : " Si j'y étais
avec la moitié des troupes que le Prince Charles
y a, je détruirais l'armée Prussienne."

Meanwhile, Daun's troops were impatient at
his delay. But, holding his own counsel to the
last, Daun, on St Barnabas' Day, the 11th of June,
with the sword of the Church in his hand, and reinforced by 200,000 more men, advanced to attack
the "Atheist King" before Prague. Frederic ex-
pectedthis.   He left the greater part of his army
to the Prague blockade.   He dodged Daun.
On the 18th of June Frederic prepared to fight the
battle of Kölin against Marshal Daun and General
Nadasti.   Prince Ferdinand of Brunswick (pit-
ted against the Abbé Count de Clermont in
Hanover) came up with a powerful artillery.
The conflict was desperate.   Then came the " illustrious brigand's " retribution.   Saxon revenge,
roused by the sight of blood, played its part.   The
Saxon dragoons cut at the Prussians, crying,—
"Take that for Striegan ! "*   The Prussians were
mowed down.   Over and over again Frederic
rallied his troops.   " Would you live for ever ? "
shouted the philosopher King.

* Striegan—A Saxon defeat 12 years before.

Daun had two horses killed under him, and was wounded, but he seemed to bear a charmed life, everywhere in the midst of the fight, sword in hand, inspiring his men. The Prussians were compelled to fly.

"My hussars," cried Frederic, "my brave hussars, will you suffer all to be lost?"

At last King Frederic stood alone, in front of a battery, tracing figures on the sand with his stick. Respect for him kept his few followers at a distance. Somebody at length ventured to address him. Frederic seemed unconscious. "Sire," asked this somebody, "do you mean to take that battery single-handed?" Then, for the first time in his life, King Frederic wept. Afterwards he rallied, and, with assumed cheerfulness, cried, "Let us retreat."

The loss on both sides was terrible.

Daun allowed Frederic to retire to Nimburgh, and to cross the Elbe. The Blockade of Prague was raised. Rejoicings at Vienna for Prague and afterwards at Versailles for Hanover were unbounded. Medals were struck in Austria and France, and the order of Maria Theresa was instituted. (Scandal proclaimed that if that hero Marshal de Richelieu had not tarried on his way at Strasbourg to say gallant things to the Duchesse de Lauraguais, sister of the late Duchesse de Chateauroux, Marshal d'Estrées would have never reaped half his laurels.)

But to go back to Kölin.—

Sir Andrew Mitchell (who had so devoutly prayed God soon to inspire the enemies of England and Prussia to a desirable peace, and who had been so profanely replied to by his Prussian Majesty) sends over "in my most Secret" a sad account to the English Ministry of King Frederic,—fortune-forsaken, in July, 1757. *

"The King of Prussia, after the battle of Kölin, retired to Leibnitz, lodged in the Bishop's Pallace, where I also was lodged. He was for some days low-spirited and saw nobody, but as he recovered he admitted me in the afternoon to pass some hours with Him, and in consequence of some conversation we had, he sent me this Paper enclosed in a cover in the beginning of July, 1757. Prefixed to this statement is a huge envelope, addressed,

"A Son Excellence,

"Monsieur de Mitchel,

"Ministre Plenipotentiaire de S. M. Britannique."

* MSS. Auts. Mus. Brit.   "Mitchell Papers."

Sealed with crown of Prussia, and containing,
  " Substance of the Arguments
    Of which may serve himself,
      An Austrian Minister
        At London, to draw
      Subsidies from England.
  In the year, 1763."*

Which " Substance of Arguments " shows how
King Frederic beguiled the weary time in the
" Bishop's Pallace" and recovered his spirits by
devices of political chicanery, and the dream
of irresistible English gold. But " low-spirited"
though Frederic was, he took care to conceal
his weakness from King George, on whom he
depended for future subsidies.   He knew that
gold is only given freely to those who know how
to turn it to the profit of the donor. " To be
beaten and to seem beaten is the devil itself."
The philosopher recognised the wisdom of that
old proverb when he wrote this

  " Lettre de S. M. Le Roy de Prusse

    A S. M. Le Roy de la Grande Bretagne.

  * Translation from the original, (MS. in the " King's
own hand "), labelled " Of Singular Importance." Appendix. U. 4.

Ce 20ᵉ Juin 1757.

" Monsieur Mon Frère,

" To conform myself to the desires of
your Majesty I have sought the means which might
put me in a condition to send a detachment
to the Duke of Cumberland, and to the Landgrave of Hesse Cassel; I have found none more
suitable than that of attacking the army of Daun,
camped in the environs of Kölin. I marched
there the 18th, after having attacked it at 2 o'clock
in the afternoon, and after having taken two Bat-
teries and two Villages furnished with Infantry.
We have been repulsed at our left, and obliged to
retire to Nimbourg. The consequences of this
battle have been that I have seen myself obliged
to raise the blockade of Prague; and as for the
beginning that puts me out of condition to make
detachments, to work incessantly to repair my
losses and to put myself into a condition to repair
this check, I write to your Majesty things in the
greatest truth, without augmenting my advantages
or diminishing my losses. I hope in some time
to be able to send (*pouvoir lui Mander*) some more
agreeable news, there is nothing to despair of
(*rien de desespére*) after eight battles that we
have gained consecutively; this is the first lost,

14*

and that because the enemy had three posts
furnished the one behind the others, after having
taken from them the Battalions of the attack, and
those that they had sent to sustain them had so
strongly suffered that they found themselves
reduced to nothing, and that the combat finished
for want of combatants. We have repulsed the
enemy twice to our right, and it has not had the
heart to disquiet us in any manner.

"*Je ne desespère de rien.* I despair of nothing,
and I can assure your Majesty that you will see of
it the consequences; some time only is necessary to
recover (remettre) the troops, after which I hope
to find means to repair our check. I am with the
most high consideration,

"Monsieur Mon Frère,

"Of your Majesty

"Le bon frère." *

The defeat of Frederic was the death-blow of
his mother, whom he loved. Her fate was retri-
butive of that he had inflicted on the Queen of
Poland. Meanwhile, the Prince de Soubise
marches towards Leipsic, declaring, "France
shall free Saxony of the Prussians."

Armed Russians are advancing. Closter Seven

* Autograph, Coll. Mitchell Mus. Brit. Bibl.

convention is signed on Sept. 8th.   The French, elated, direct their steps towards Magdebourg (the place where Voltaire declared Prussian flour came from for Potsdam *petits soupers*, and also the place of residence of "Monsieur de Mitchel").   The army of the circles is round about Prussia with the auxiliary Corps of the Prince de Soubise, the Swedes have invaded Pomerania, and the Austrians and French surprise Berlin.

Despair again prostrates Frederic.

Meanwhile, the Maréchal d'Estrées (who in his youth had been in garrison at Weissembourg, and was the first love of Marie Leczinska, now Queen of France) thus addressed the University of Gottingen which had solicited his protection :

" Gentlemen,

" The University of Gottingen is too celebrated by the great men it has produced, and which have put the seal on its glory, for me to pass by this particular occasion of testifying towards it my particular esteem.   The University may tranquillize itself concerning the *désagrémens* which war carries in its trail. . . . . I am not ignorant how such are prejudicial to the sciences, and I shall be careful that the march of troops does not trouble an University so famed and excellent. It is in these sincere sentiments that I am truly, &c."

Just as Marshal d'Estrées had issued this address the Duc de Richelieu threw his troops into Brunswick, and devastated the Provinces of Prussia.

Frederic the Great believed himself lost.

For the first time in his life the "illustrious brigand" longed for peace. He therefore wrote this letter to Marshal Richelieu.

"September 6th, 1757.

"I feel, M. le Duc, that you have not been placed in the post you occupy to negociate; I am, nevertheless, persuaded, that the nephew of the great Cardinal de Richelieu is made to sign treaties as also to win battles. . . . It concerns only a trifle, Monsieur (Il s'agit d'une bagatelle), to make peace if one wish it. . . . He who has deserved statues at Genoa, he who has conquered the Isle of Minorca, notwithstanding immense obstacles, he who is on the point of subjugating *la basse Saxe,* can do nothing more glorious than to work at the restoration of Peace to Europe. Work at it, Monsieur, with that activity, which enables you to make such rapid progress, and be persuaded that nobody will have more gratitude, than your faithful friend,

"Frédéric."

Richelieu answered:

" Sire,

"Such superiority as your Majesty may have in every way, there would be, perhaps, more to gain for me in negociating, than in fighting face to face, such a hero as your Majesty. I believe that I should serve the King my master in a manner that he would prefer to victories, if I could contribute to a general peace. But I assure your Majesty that I have neither instructions, nor notions on the means to arrive at such a result."

The letter ends with a promise of sending a courier to Versailles with the overture of Prussia, and with general, and rather fulsome, assurances of esteem and respect.

Voltaire declares that it was he who, as the friend of both parties, had induced King Frederic to write to the Duc de Richelieu. Voltaire protests also: " In these extremities, it came into his head (the King of Prussia's head) to kill himself !

" He wrote," says Voltaire, " to his sister, Madame la Margrave de Bareith, that he was going to
put an end to his life. He could not finish off
without making some verses. The passion of the
poet was still stronger in him than his hatred
of life. He wrote then to the Marquis d'Argens
a long epistle in verse, in which he confided to
him his resolution, and said adieu to him. . . .
However singular the subject of this epistle may
be, there are certain bits in it pretty well turned
for a King of the North. . . . He sent to me this
epistle written by his hand. . . . There are many
passages in it stolen from the Abbé de Chaulieu
and me. . . The ideas are incoherent and the verses
are generally badly made, but there are some
which are good; and it is much for a king to
make two hundred bad verses in the state that
he was. He wished it to be said that he had
preserved all his presence of mind, and liberty
of spirit, at a moment when other men have
none.

" The letter that he wrote to me testified the
same sentiments : but in it were fewer roses and
myrtles, *Ixions*, and less profound grief. I
combated in prose the resolution he had taken
to die, and I had not much trouble in deter-

mining him to live. I advised him to try a negociation with the Duc de Richelieu, to imitate the Duke of Cumberland. I took, in short, all the liberties that could be taken with a despairing poet who was ready to give up his kingship. He wrote in effect to the Marshal de Richelieu ; but *receiving no answer* he resolved to fight us. He sent me word that he was going to combat the Prince de Soubise, and finished off his letter by verses more worthy of his situation, of his courage, and of his mind,

> ' Quand on est voisin du naufrage,
> Il faut en affrontant l'orage
> Penser, vivre, et mourir en roi.' "

This is the letter Voltaire (who we see was not without a flaw) wrote to King Frederic :

"October, 1757.

" Sire,

" You wish to die. I speak not to you here of the painful horror with which this design inspires me. I conjure you to suspect at least, that, from your high rank, you can scarcely see what is the opinion of mankind, or what is the spirit of the times. . . As King, they tell it not to you ; as philosopher and great man, you see but the examples of the great men of An-

tiquity. You love glory ; you place it to-day in
dying in a way that other men might rarely
choose, and that none of the sovereigns of Europe
have ever imagined since the fall of the Roman
Empire.

"I add—for this is the time to say all—that
nobody will regard you as a martyr of liberty.
You know in how many Courts they persist in
regarding your entry into Saxe as an infraction
of the rights of men. What will they say in
those Courts ? That you have revenged on
yourself that invasion. . . . He whom I have
called the Solomon of the North, can say much
more in the depth of his heart. A man who is
but King may believe himself very unfortunate
when he loses his states, but a philosopher may
forego his states. Again, without mixing myself
in any way with politics, I cannot believe but
that there will remain to you enough to be always
a considerable sovereign. What would be the
use of being a philosopher if you knew not how
to live as a private man ? Or, if in remaining a
sovereign, you knew not how to support adversity ? "

Frederic faced his fate. " Fortune is a
woman," wrote he, " and I do not pay my court

to the sex;" "but," he added, "if I lose my kingdom, any prince will be glad to hire me as his general."

There is always great valour in the man of genius who reunites all his forces to attempt a last effort. Frederic felt that he must perform a prodigy, or yield.

Again he traced figures on the sand, but this time they were circles.

Now it so happened that the army of circles, profanely called by the French, "Cooperage," was composed of bad troops, the offscouring of all the fractions of Germany, Wurtemburg, Bavaria, Badenites, &c., with their own petty jealousies among themselves, and rather inclined by language and custom towards the Prussians than towards the French.

The Prince de Soubise was a brave officer, but the instructions of Versailles placed him under the orders of the Prince Hildeburghausen who commanded in chief.

Thought Frederic to himself: "I have but 38,000 men, and this army is 60,000, but my troops are trained, *les troupes d'élite*, and those are nothing but raw militia men, ready to desert, and certain of disorganization in full battle."

On the 5th of November, Frederic spied
the French Army on the march, to the sound
of clarions and kettle-drums, from a hole in the
roof of the Castle of Rossbach. He descended,
dined, conjured his men to trust in God, promised
them double-pay, stepped forth, and gained
a battle. The treason of the German circles helped him to victory. Eight thousand
men under the Count de St Germain took no
part in the battle. The Count de St Germain
was a fervent admirer of King Frederic, his
correspondent and his friend. (Even old Marshal
Belleisle was smitten with the perfection of Prussian tactics.) St Germain was a philosopher; he
believed that King Frederic was fighting for
liberty and the Encyclopédie, and that he, St
Germain, was ranged on the side of superstition
and barbarism,—France, and Austria. Whether or
not St Germain was too great a philosopher to
care for the loss or gain of a battle, the Prince de
Soubise did care. On him, a philosopher too, but
devoted to the King of France, and the most intimate friend of Madame de Pompadour, the whole
odium fell of the loss of this battle of Rosbach.

The French declared it was a victory unworthy of King Frederic; as a great general, he

would not have crowed so loud over it had it
not been due to his effort over his late depression. France was harassed in India and elsewhere. * But the King of France showed no unjust nor ungenerous irritability towards the Prince
de Soubise for the loss of the Battle of Rosbach.
" *C'est un des beaux côtés de cette âme royale ; elle
ne restait pas seulement fidèle aux heureux.*"

The people of France of course pasquinaded
the Prince de Soubise, and even stuck their squibs
upon the gates of his hotel in Paris.

> " Soubise dit, la lanterne à la main :
>   J'ai beau chercher où diable est mon armée,
>   Elle était là pourtant hier matin,
>   Me l'a-t'on prise, ou l'aurais'je égarée ? †

In the mean while, Madame de Pompadour
wrote to de Soubise :

" You have no cause to justify yourself to me,
but to the King, and to the people, who are surprised and irritated at this unfortunate affair of
Rosbach.

" A general beaten, is always a bad general in

---

* See Appendix. " India.—Colonies," &c.

† These lampoons were attributed to de Maurepas, who,
exiled from court, retained his fatal love for rhyme at Pont-
chartreaux.

the opinion of the public : the Parisians above
all are furious ; they have committed a thousand
indignities at the gate of your house.   See what
are the consolations of my position, and what I gain
by serving my friends ! . . Nevertheless, the King
esteems you always. . . . . It is said that the King
of Prussia spread a snare for you and that you fell
clumsily into it.   It does not behove me to judge
of these matters ; but 'it seems to me without
error I may say, that a battle is a game where the
losers pass for fools ; and often, unjustly.

"I hope, Sir, that on another occasion you will
show what you can do, and thus force your enemies to admire you, and those of your King to
fear you. . . . .   It is very sad for you and the nation, that Fortune began through you to turn her
back on us, and that you are the first to make us
shed tears.   But, nevertheless, lose not courage.
Your friends will be faithful and useful to you.
Reckon upon that.

" . . . . Come and prove before all France that
you have done the duty of a good general at Rosbach, and that your defeat is the fault of Fortune,
and not yours. . . . This will be the first pleasure
to me since the news of that unfortunate battle. . .

I shall welcome you with all my heart. Console yourself, and keep well."

King Frederic roamed over the field of Rosbach consoling the wounded vanquished French and German circle men. At last he came upon a French Grenadier defending himself furiously against three Prussian Cavaliers. The King asked the Grenadier if he believed himself invincible?

"Yes," said the Frenchman—whose national politeness came to his aid at his last gasp— "Yes—Sire—under you." *

A number of hares, startled by the fight, tried to run away. The French soldiers shot at them. Said the Prussians to each other, "We shall win; the French are killing their brethren instead of us."

Frederic was soon diverted by sterner work. The progress of the Austrians hurried him off to Silesia. King George (in hope from the glimmer of Fortune's favour at Rossbach) declared, as a pretext for regaining "the apple of his eye," that far from Hanover enjoying the repose promised by the Closter

* Appendix, to p. 223.

Convention, she had been treated as a conquered Province, and was represented as such in the Edicts of the King of France. The Duc de Richelieu threatened to strew all Hanover with rubbish, even to the palace of the King, if its army committed the least hostility. Ferdinand of Brunswick, who was in command, replied: "At the head of the army, I will give ulterior explanations." *

Immediately upon this, two corps of French troops were attacked and put to flight. Richelieu, in revenge, ordered the pillage of Zell, and to set fire to its faubourgs. It was burnt to cinders, even to the Orphans' Home.

Ferdinand, Duke of Brunswick, marched rapidly at the head of Hessians and Hanoverians. Under Marshal Richelieu served the Princes Conti, Condé, and Clermont. The French were routed. Hanoverian peasants fell furiously on the scattered French troops.

The Duc de Broglie, advancing to sustain the retrograde march of the French, valiantly attacked the Hanoverians under Prince Issembourg and put them to flight. The Count de Clermont had shown uncertainty, and he was replaced by

* See Appendix. "Melée."

the Marquis de Contades, created Marshal of France.

The Prince de Soubise, by Versailles' mercy, afterwards redeemed the affair of Rosbach (from that time he got out of the circles, and took a simple command in the army of Westphalia). He revenged himself by gaining the battle of Lutzelberg, in Cassel. De Soubise there took 20 pieces of cannon and 2500 Hanoverians. The bâton of Maréchal was then conferred upon him. The hereditary Prince of Brunswick was the most determined adversary of France ; " at the head of 40,000 men subsidized by England." It was his audacity which stimulated de Broglie to take the offensive. The people of Silesia had opened their arms to welcome their old rulers, the Austrians. But in December the victory of Leuthen caused a Prussian Te Deum to be sang by the men on the battle-field ; Frederic regained possession of Breslau, the capital of Silesia, and wintered in Saxony.*

* A Frenchman declares : "The Campaign of Bohemia, Silesia, and of Prussia considerably resembles the marvellous strategy of Napoleon in 1813, against all the forces of Prussia, Austria, and Russia, ' depuis Dresde jusqu'a Leipzic.' That which saved Frederic was the division of the ' Coalisés,' the un-

Versailles professed to be outraged by the English " odious violation of the convention of Closter-Seven." The Duc de Richelieu was recalled by the Cabinet. He had been nicknamed by his troops " Le petit père le Maraud." Versailles was vexed by German complaints of the lawless manner in which he had permitted his troops to live on the conquered soil.* De Richelieu excused himself by the fact of England unscrupulously sowing a lucrative crop of disaffection among her enemies' troops. But Richelieu's German game of " diamond cut diamond" was bad for French Camp and Cabinet ; the Parliaments

certainty of their simultaneous movements ; the art which he had above all, to give birth to incidental questions before Peace. That which lost Napoleon, was that Europe then felt all the perils of a division of forces ; it had need of grouping itself, re-uniting itself to vanquish a common danger ; Napoleon could divide nothing, separate nothing ; the armies held themselves like one man, and that is why he yielded in that struggle of all against one only."

* Richelieu's carelessness on this point roused the courage because it piqued the indignation of the Hanoverians. They showed fortitude and even gaiety under hardships which were endured in the hope of routing the enemy. Rapacious French officers were so severely condemned at home that Marshal Belleisle gave them a taste of the Bastille.

being more inclined to cast odium than to yield gold, or to give glory.

From the Secret Cabinet correspondence of Versailles, Madame de Pompadour had reason to know that English gold was being sown by large crops in Germany.

The diplomatic correspondence was transacted direct with the *Secrétariat* of Versailles. The intimate relations of De Bernis in Italy, and of the Duc de Choiseul at Vienna, perfected the system.

Some of the French Cabinet correspondents were little suspected as such in the countries where they resided for information ; but a study of the plan shows, in all its simplicity and scorn for diplomatic technicalities, a subtle and profound system of initiation which other countries would do well to emulate until such time as the reign of Peace shall begin. Amongst the names of "those admitted to the secret correspondence by order of Louis XV." (a list too long here to transcribe) there is evidence of France's faith in feminine tact, as the following extracts show: "Le général Mounet, in starting for Poland. On his return, trusted with direction of Secret Correspondence."

15 *

" Madame la Générale Mounet, initiated by her first husband, M. de la Fayardie, resident in War- saw." " The widow of the Sieur Tercier." &c.

––––––––––

Madame de Pompadour, therefore, held in her own hands proofs that English gold was tampering with the loyalty and honour of French allies, and (as it is only fair to fight enemies with their own weapons) she seems, from forthcoming evidence, to have determined to get English gold for the advancement of French glory in this war which had been forced upon France by ' English Pirates.'

It will be remembered that she had appoint- ed Richelieu's relative, the Duc d'Aiguillon, to the command of the troops in Brittany. Brittany, celebrated for a turbulent parliament, did not love d'Aiguillon (who was of the Dauphin's party), but still less did Brittany love the English. Between the races there was hatred, " fierce and ancient as the Moyen age ! "

The English thought to make a diversion on the coasts of France to favour the two armies of Hanover and Prussia, and to give time for English gold to bring forth fruit in Germany. *

* The English historian who complains after the Minorca victory of the Pompadour's ingratitude to Richelieu, accuses

After Anson's and Howe's successes at St Malo and Cherbourg, the English fleet transferred itself to St Brieux in Brittany; disembarked without obstacles, the English advanced to St Cast; there the Duc d'Aiguillon met them at the head of the single militia of Brittany]; the attack was so impetuous that General Bligh left 700 prisoners and more than 4000 dead on the shore.*

her afterwards of sharing his Hanoverian plunder. France says :

"William Pitt conduisait fièrement le Ministère Britannique ; dans sa haine contre la France, il avait compris que la question des subsides ne devait jamais arrêter un gouvernement fort, une grande Nation, et il avait largement ouvert à Frederic 2nd un crédit sur la banque de Londres."

"On the 5th of June, 1758, Lord Anson with 22 vessels of the line anchors in the Bay of Cancale near St Malo, disembarks there with 15 battalions of light troops and artillery ; the English encamp before the town, burn three frigates of the King, 24 privateers, 70 merchant ships, 40 little ships (bâtiments), also magazines of hemp, of pitch and tar, and retire at the end of 8 days. (Admiralty Report.)

"A second fleet displayed itself under Commodore Howe in the Bay of Cherbourg ; it disembarked its troops under General Bligh and the famous Duke of York. The end in view was to attack the Works of Cherbourg. On the 6th of August, the English attacked the place ; the garrison of about 100 men, surprised, retired. The English penetrated into the Town." Mémoires Contemporains.

* Lord Howe, perceiving the sailors in the boats to be a lit-

This triple explanation (of Versailles *Secré-tariat* information—English gold in Germany,—and the position of the Duc d'Aiguillon in

tle disordered by the enemy's fire, ordered himself to be rowed in his own boat and brought away as many men as it would carry, and was the last to leave the shore; but finding it impossible to lend any further aid, he silenced by signal the fire from the frigates upon the enemy, who showed their sense of his moderation and humanity by giving immediate quarter and protection to the conquered. About 700 men were killed, drowned, or taken prisoners; but the French had suffered severely in the contest. M. de Redmond, the quartermaster-general, the Marquis de la Chastre, M. de la Tour d'Auvergne, the Chevalier de Polignac, and about fifty officers of rank, were either killed or wounded, and of course a proportionate number of men. The ministry of the day could hardly pretend that they were going to take Paris with 6000 men: nevertheless the Duke d'Aiguillon was regarded as its saviour, and gained great glory, though the Bretons, who regarded him as a tyrant, disparaged his victory, and declared that he was never to be seen during the fight.—Sir Edward Cust, Annals of Wars, 18th Century.

Paris was content to rhyme on the occasion, thus:

" Anglois, ne partez pas si vite,
    Pressez vous moins!
Vous avez fait courte visite
    Chez nos Malouins.
Que diront vos compatriotes
    Dans leurs chansons!
Vous n'aviez pas quitté nos côtes
    Sans Aiguillon."

Brittany) may throw light upon the following letters from the Duchesse de Pompadour, the originals of which are now in the British Museum.

Here is the first to the present purpose.*

                      " 25th, Evening.

" You will judge, Sir, by the answer of M. Boulogne, which I enclose, that the letter I wrote to him yesterday has determined him to send to you the *Sr. du Mesnil*. I do not know him, but much good is said of him, and he has been brought up by M. de St Florentin, who will instruct you more what he is worth. The letter of M. Berryer will make you see that he desires as much as we do the success of our affair. I fear much it may fail for want of money. The Controller has not answered to that part of my letter. . . . I cannot believe that M——— cannot find a million in so many commercial cities. You are right, Sir ; it is very true

---

* The French newspapers of the day report : " Le Général Bligh ayant fait, le 4 Septembre, une tentative à St. Brieux, en Bretagne, fut répoussé très vivement par le Duc d'Aiguillon, qui le joignit le 11 à St Cast, et le força de se rembarquer précipitamment. Il fit 700 prisonniers et causa une perte aux Anglais de plus de 4000 hommes, tant tués que noyés. De 13,000 qu'ils étaient, 8000 à peine se rembarquèrent."—Mercure de France.

that my spirit and my heart are continually occupied with the affairs of the King ; but without
inexpressible attachment for his glory and his
person, I should often be beaten back by the continual obstacles which oppose doing good. I
should have preferred the great 'roguish trick,' *
and I am sorry to be obliged to content myself
with the little one. It does not at all suit my
Lucifer humour. Send to me the grade that you
desire for M. de——, I engage myself to solicit it.
Your projects have appeared to me excellent, and
it seemed to me that the Ministry thought as I
did. You wish then absolutely that I reckon on
your heart ; but truly I shall do myself no great
violence in desiring that you may be capable of a
friendship worthy of that I am very disposed to
have for you.

Good night, M. Cavendish.

"I have had fever again last week, and I rally
very slowly."

Then, under cover to the Duc d'Aiguillon,
sealed with Pompadour Arms.

" France, 1759.

"You are in truth very amiable to find re-

* "*Niche.*" " Nich, or roguish trick " (financial).

sources for our affair.   I flatter myself of success, notwithstanding all difficulties, because I reckon on the fortune of *Cavendish.*   I would that it extend unto 40 millions, which to us are very necessary.   I confide to you that ——— has sent to the Controller-General that those correspondents in Paris warned him that gold would not be put to this loan, *l'or ne mettroit pas à cet emprunt.*   It is necessary that you be informed of this fact, but do not appear to be so.

" . . . . My health is always miserable. I have again had this night a rigour of fever. I see, with pleasure, the interest you take. If friendship follow that interest I shall be much tempted to accord you mine, for I have a very good opinion of *M. Cavendish.*"

Afterwards comes a third autograph on this gold scheme between the Marquise and her English friend, addressed under cover to

" M. le duc d'Aiguillon,
Bretagne.*

" Rejoice, M. de Cavendish! 1st, I am not dead, and . . . . I flatter myself you are not sorry.

* This letter to "M. Cavendish" comes after others to

"2nd, The letter that M. le Controller-General will write to you to-day will prove to you that notwithstanding my misfortunes I have not forgotten our conquest.   Give your orders quickly ; there is not a moment to lose.

"There is nothing so false as he who told you that the Ministers did not approve this project.

"Good-night, M. de Cavendish.   This is too much for a poor head, feeble and convalescent.

"Sunday evening."*

the Duc d'Aiguillon, which are placed according to narrative.   The paper is discoloured by a century.   The handwriting is faltering and uncertain, as though penned in the moments of exhaustion and suffering.   Being on a matter of State secresy, the Marquise could employ no secretary, as usual, to write it.

* Egerton Collection.   Mus. Brit. Bibl.

CHAPTER VI.

THE MARQUISE designed a medal in honour of
the Victory of Lutzelberg, to achieve which victory

she had incited her friend, the Prince de Soubise. This medal was struck, and may now, among many others designed by her after more brilliant victories (especially that of Fontenoy) in former years, be seen in the Bibliothèque Impériale of France.

On one side of this medal is a globe, adorned with three Fleur-de-lis (a ' France' as it is called), resting on a circular column, round which are bound the Laurels of Victory. On the other side is the globe ' France,' resting on prostrate banners, and leaning over it a child (the Genius of France). Upon the child's head descends a flame of fire; his left arm rests upon the globe, adorned with Fleur-de-lis ; in his right hand is a budding Palm-branch, with the stem of which he traces the circle of the globe.

To the last, the Marquise thus stimulated the patriotism of her country, and the waning love of the people for the King who, wrapt in increasing gloom, required her to rally all her failing energies for his counsel and support. France was gradually overwhelmed by repeated losses. The first idea of the Cabinet of France had been to concentrate all her forces so as to save her Colonies, and to punish England on the spot for having violated the Aix Treaty. But this was impossible, as we know. The sea war, by the movements of the King of Prussia, was converted into a land war ; so that the hand of France was crippled in the endeavour to retain her beloved Canada. Volumes would not suffice to tell battle by battle in both hemispheres between France and England. Moreover, these battles are the chronicles of England, as they form a list of her boasted conquests.

Nevertheless there were bright gleams of glory for France, gleams that shone through clouds at home and hardships abroad. One of her difficulties was the new system of military tactics employed by Prussia, which made warfare still more arduous to a nation just mourning for her greatest leaders, and some of whose chiefs, incited by Voltaire, were disaffected in favour of Prussian philosophy.

In October, 1757, Voltaire (flattered by Frederic's late appeal to him concerning suicide), wrote to the King of Prussia, servilely :

" My old age has left me all my vivacity for that which regards your Majesty, though diminishing it for all else. I see only that with the valour of Charles XII., and with a soul very superior to his, . . . you will have greater reputa-

tion than he in posterity, because you have won
battles against more warlike enemies than he,
and because . . . you have re-animated arts, founded colonies, and embellished cities."

Yet, from Voltaire's record of Frederic's sui-
cidal intentions after defeat, that great hero
would not have been able to have withstood misfortune so nobly as did France; nor have been
merciful, as was France, to d'Estrées; who—
having mastered Westphalia, Hanover, Brunswick, and the Duke of Cumberland—did not
hold fast his grip of the Electorate. D'Estrées,
guilty of infirmity of purpose in not prosecuting
to the utmost a victory gained, was recalled.

Richelieu had been appointed to succeed him
by the King, with whom de Richelieu too often
prevailed at home and abroad. But, when de
Richelieu was disgraced for rapacity, Voltaire
asserted it was a Court intrigue that had recalled
the brave d'Estrées from the Camp, although a
hundred military letters declare that the day of
the Battle of Hastembeck ought to have been the
last day of the Hanoverian army. Then come
accusation and counter-accusation. Some of them
fall on the head of the Marquise de Pompa-

dour, but the following letter acquits her of a vindictive share in the recall of Marshal d'Estrées. It is addressed to his wife :

" I sincerely congratulate you, Madame la Maréchale, on our friend's glory; my friendship for you, and my esteem for him, redouble the joy I feel at his victory. The Duke of Cumberland was always unfortunate against Marshal Saxe, and he has not better succeeded against his best pupil. But in the midst of my joy, I feel a true grief to behold the command of his army taken from him at the moment of victory. A man whom I do not love, full of ambition and vanity, has persuaded that he is the hero destined by Heaven to finish off this war that goes too slowly. It is he who is to succeed the brave d'Estrées. Our dear Marshal must therefore return, but covered with laurels, and honoured by the esteem of the Public. Your own virtue and courage put you beyond the power of fortune to injure. Trust to me as your best friend."

Marshal Richelieu exceeded the authority confided to him, in signing the convention of Closter-Seven. England's violation of that convention cost France in Hanover and Brunswick

what she had gained. Many were the plans
which, for want of funds in war-time, the Marquise was obliged to leave for an after-genera-
tion to execute, although she is accused of
having shared Richelieu's plunder. Suffering
in body herself, she yearned to enlarge and
humanize the public hospitals. She fain would
soothe pain, but the world was full of fire
and blood. In vain she cast her worldly
goods to the Treasury; in vain she strove to
increase national resources by works of internal manufacture and art. In vain she wrote
through the hours of the night, her head
fluttering with pain, weariness, and sickness, to
do good to the King and to redeem the past while
she had time. In vain, her bright fancy struggling through the lowering clouds, caught at the
rays of victory and devised how to vindicate the
Genius and Glory of France to posterity. The
tide was too strong against her.

The cross was laid most heavily upon her when
she had reached the very summit of power, and had
attained the goal of human ambition. It pierced her
in every direction. Envy;—Hatred;—Detraction;
—the King's waning energy and wavering humour in Council, the knowledge of his fanatical

weakness and private vices, the continued strife against him of the Parliament, and the unceasing quarrels that disgraced the name of religion between the Jesuits and their opponents; the increasing want of funds at home and abroad, the ever-dreaded news of fresh losses of war on land and on the sea.

All this the Marquise had to bear. And more. Her friend, de Bernis, was opposed to her at this moment in Council. He wished to effect a peace which must inevitably have offended Austria, and have driven that power into an alliance against France, for whose honour there was now no possible retreat in the disastrous war which had been forced upon her. De Bernis was beloved both by the King and the Marquise, but his policy flinched in this time of crisis and of danger. De Choiseul (in confidence with the Empress of Austria) could not co-operate with de Bernis. The Marquise therefore solicited the Cardinal's hat for de Bernis from Rome. He received it by the King's hand in November, 1758; when he, the new cardinal, delivered up to the Duc de Choiseul his portfolio of foreign affairs. Always popular in Rome, de Bernis afterwards received there the title of " Protector of the French Church."

The people for whom the Marquise had done so much, and in whose behalf she had effected free trade in corn, murmured for bread. The glory which they loved they had no longer, and Famine began to dog their footsteps.

They were rendered impatient and even impious by the restrictions which party-spirit had imposed upon them in the name of Religion. They began to doubt truth altogether. Traditionally believing the King all powerful, they blamed their once Well-Beloved for the hard things that party-priests, Parliament, and unsuccessful War brought upon them. Louis XV. had retrenched his own household, and by personal sacrifices had shown his practical sympathy with the people under increased taxation, but none now cried " God bless the King."

The Generals of the army, damped by defeat and by bad news from across the Atlantic, were restless, dissatisfied, and fearful of the growing murmurs of the nation. Some wanted to send in their resignation. The Duc d'Aiguillon, for example, desired to throw up the command of Brittany. He was detained there with the greatest difficulty by the Marquise. Her letters to him are sad to look upon, not only as the discoloured memorials of a hundred years whose human generations they have outlived, but as bearing evidence of the writer's struggle to be gay under intense depression,—of painful energy in sickness,—of the loyal pulses of a heart which had loved, and ached, and was soon to cease throbbing.

At the time these letters were written, the Marquise was not only compelled to recline on her couch at the head of the council table, but, conscious of her fading beauty, she was glad when her illness prevented her rising from her bed so as to face the light of day. Perhaps none but a woman, so situated, can understand the anguish of such consciousness. She was anxious to preserve every element of her power over the King to the last, yet warned of her fading beauty by the cruel glances of triumph among Court rivals.

The saint-like Queen was blest by an easy conscience, and in the affection of her children. The penitent mistress of the King, enduring the increasing anguish of a mortal malady, was unloved, uncheered, unsoothed, and alone.

In the lonely watches of the night, the life of the Marquise was its own homily for her consideration. At night, thinking of duty and de-

16 *

falcation, she wrote the following letters to the
Duc d'Aiguillon,* whose appointment as Governor
of Brittany she had generously advised; generously, because his party was opposed to her.

Nevertheless, the Duc d'Aiguillon had been
restless—wanting to flinch and shirk his duty
when it became onerous in sight of British ships,
although an English historian apostrophizes him :
" Look to it, d'Aiguillon; sharply as thou didst,
from the mill of St Cast, on Quiberon and the
invading English ! "

The incitements of the Marquise to d'Aiguillon
for his own honour, and that of France, were
generous, because he was fiercely opposed to
herself and de Choiseul.   His party in 1757
had been accused of the King's attempted assassination, and was even supposed by some to have a
hand in the mysterious illness of the Marquise
herself.   When victory came, she wrote :†

* Of the Duchesse d'Aiguillon, Horace Walpole declares :
" She is delightful, and has much the most of a woman of
quality of any I have seen, and more cheerfulness too."
Horace equally admired the wife of the rival chief, the charming Duchesse de Choiseul.

† The writing as of one in a recumbent posture. On a scrap
of paper, as though the letter were the effect of impulse, and
showing how far the writer was from thinking that exactly one

"A M. le Duc d'Aiguillon, Tuesday, 19th.

" It is with regret, Monsieur, that I have not told you all that I thought the day before yesterday, on the glory wherewith you have clothed yourself. But my head was in such pain that I had not strength to say one word to you. We have sang your *Te Deum* to-day, and I assure you it was with the greatest satisfaction.

" I had predicted your success, and indeed how was it possible with so much zeal, intelligence, a head so cool, and troops so hot, who emulated their chief, to fail in avenging the cause of the King, and to gain a victory ? It could not be otherwise. The little note I wrote to you before your brilliant day, must have apprized you of my mode of thinking of you ; and, by the justice of which I make profession, I beg you to tell me truly if you are very angry with me for not having yielded to your representations, and to those fine reasons which you recounted to me. They were worth nothing at the time, and I find them still more detestable to-day.

" Another would not have done as well as you.

hundred years afterwards it would be brought to light in the archives of the enemy over whom she was inciting d'Aiguillon to achieve victory.

I should have been in grief instead of joy. You would have lost yourself for no real reason why. So I defy you to say that my head is not better than yours. . . . . Messieurs Lebroc and d'Aubigny can certify the interest I take in the General and his troops."

But, though the Marquise thus playfully boasts of her head, she says nothing of her heart, which, when news of Duc d'Aiguillon's success arrived, induced her instantly to write the following note to his wife, who was in Paris, and who had shared with herself the friendship of Montesquieu.

"A Madame la Duchesse d'Aiguillon,* à Paris,
Saturday.

"Accept, Madame, all my congratulations upon the brilliant success of M. d'Aiguillon. Nobody can have a more lively or sincere sympathy in that success. You have, I hope, forgiven me for not having yielded to his solicitations (to leave his post) a month ago. So far I congratulate myself. For the good of the thing and for its glory, I have the honour to be, Madame,

"Your humble and obedient servant,
" — Pompadour."

* Aut. Mus. Brit. Bibl., sealed with the Pompadour's arms, in red wax. Written upon curiously illuminated paper.

Nevertheless, d'Aiguillon grew restless again in 1760. Whenever he was harassed by the turbulent Parliament of Brittany, or English ships looked threatening, he seems to have wanted to leave the helm of the Government he had formerly so eagerly solicited. Yet, such are human justice and historical truth, that this restless hero has got all the glory of his command, and the Marquise, who lashed him to it, has incurred the odium of whatever went wrong in Camp, Court, or Council. She writes again in 1760,* at different times.

"A M. le Duc d'Aiguillon.

"You will instantly agree, Monsieur, that I am quite insupportable, to be always in the right. How, then, dare I tell you that with the best and the greatest qualities you have a little head which gets hot too quickly! You now experience, at this moment, how odious I really am. I know not how you will find goodness enough to pardon me after such an affront.

". . . . You wish to leave Brittany. *Belle Folie* which plagues your head! I will not spare you more than upon the first occasion. . . . . .

"I blush to see that you have less cour-

---

* Auts. Egerton Collection.

age than I have. You know the inconveniences
of your little command, and I, of all administrations, since there is not a minister who does not
come to tell me his troubles. Let there be no
longer question of yours, I entreat. I desire to
give my unlimited friendship to M. Cavendish, if
his soul be worthy of it."

Again, the Marquise wrote, when a short
time afterwards good news came for the King
from turbulent Brittany.

"1760.

" I congratulate you, M. le Duc, on the zeal
which Brittany has just evinced. . . . . I predict
that the states will consummate marvellously, that
you, according to your custom, will have served
the King well, and that when all will be concluded . . . I shall have to ask your pardon for having been always in the right. It is a great fault, but
since it is founded upon the good opinion I have of
your zeal for the service of the King . . . . . I hope,
Monsieur, you will pardon me. . . . . You are quite
right, not to speak of the cold blood of the Parliamentarians. I am absolutely of your opinion, and
M. Choiseul's project of arrangement, adopted by
the Council, gives me the greatest pleasure, because
it offers to us the means of requiting those unwor-

thy citizens who abuse the wants of the State, to induce their master to commit acts of weakness. You cannot yet sing ' *Nunc Dimittis.*'

" You must not, during the war, think of leaving those mad Brittany men. Nevertheless, seek who may replace you, for I have nobody in view. I do not wish M. de —— for this purpose. He is too much of an attorney, too avaricious. He has not a soul noble enough. . . . I restrict myself, Sir, to wishing you good-night, perfect health, a happy end of the year, with many other good things."

In June, 1760, the Marquise had spurred up d'Aiguillon to make the English " repent of their audacity" if they presented themselves before Brest (the French King's capital station for his ships). " You have not forgotten that I was a good prophetess two years ago," she writes (the date of Lord Howe's Brittany defeat), " therefore I pray you to have confidence in me if they present themselves.". . . . . The conclusion of this letter implies a wish for retirement, equal to her desire for revenge upon the English who had, in 1759, made havoc among the French ships and sailors of Brest. " May God will that upon this point my castles soon be not airy ones (*Châteaux en Espagne*), and although I do not propose to live with my neighbourhood, you will be excepted from the general law. You see that I yield to you in nothing for the horror of this world.". . . . In another place, referring to the Parliamentarians, she says, " I have to think for bacchanals, as you have for Brest. . . All that you tell me of the souls of *Bretons* is nothing in comparison to those of this monstrous country here." *

As the writer's "horror of this world" increased, so did her regret for the loss of her only child. In 1762, the Countess de Baschi wrote to the " Duchesse de Pompadour " concerning the design for the tomb of that child, in which design the mother (King's mistress) had fondly symbolized her dead daughter as " Innocence."

" Of all the griefs you have experienced," writes Madame de Baschi, " the sharpest is that caused by the loss of your child. . . . You have not been able to forget her. Why renew your affliction by the sight of her tomb ? "

Madame de Pompadour always wrote at night.

Seeing that the long night of the grave was before her, there is something pathetic in the playful " *Bon Soir* " which concludes her loyal

* Autographs.

appeals to Frenchmen, less in need of heroism than herself.

Sometimes she journeyed during the day to her daughter's grave. She found peace at the Capuchin sepulchre. At Court she saw the littleness of human greatness, and felt there the deadliness of human passions.

Politics only did not retain the Marquise in the Cabinet and at Court. Louis XV. was too unhappy for her to leave him while she had life. Dark clouds had descended upon his domestic life, as others uprose in the political horizon. In 1759 the young Duchess of Parma, being on a visit at Versailles, died of the small-pox. She was the King's favourite daughter. Afterwards, having lost the flower of his nobility in war, Louis stood by the coffin of his eldest grandson, the little Duke de Bourgogne, whose cradle had been rocked by the riots of Paris, as recorded.

The Duc de Bourgogne, just ten years old, was hurt when playing with one of his comrades. Afraid to complain lest his companion might be blamed, the accident was not known until too late, when its results were incurable. Three other sons remained to the Dauphin, (whose health was

always precarious,) but fear for them harassed
the King when mourning for his favourite daughter and grandchild.   The Queen had long looked
for, and found, comfort from heaven alone.   But
there was terror in the King's grief.   He reverenced the Queen, but her presence was a reproach
to him.   Superstitious, he might well believe that
his sorrows were signs of Heaven's vengeance.
To drown conscience, he sought anew those pleasures which were customary to his century, and
to which Richelieu and other courtiers invited
him.

Regard for the Abbé de Bernis had been a bond
between the Duchess of Parma and Madame de
Pompadour.   When the Abbé was removed from
the council and the Duchess was dead, life became more dreary for the Pompadour.

Under the same roof with her at Versailles,
were many who daily watched, with malicious
joy, her painful consummation of the destiny
which had been turned from a sceptre to a cross.
How long would it be before Death would achieve
its work upon her, and before the King would
e exposed as a target to their own personal ambition?   But although the Marquise was
surrounded by examples of human littleness,

her well-practised patience was at last nearly
exhausted by the Duc d'Aiguillon, who got
all the worldly glory of his day, is handed down
to posterity as a hero, and was already mightily
rewarded by his King for doing the duties to
which he was compelled by her. In 1760 she had
occasion to write this Chief another letter, which
is ominously sealed with black, and bears the suitable device of a dove holding an olive branch and
the motto :

"Soar, and hold firm your duty."

" The great zeal and ability with which you
served the King in Brittany, Monsieur, made me
take the most sincere interest in you, of which I
have given you proofs with pleasure whenever I
have had an opportunity to do so. This same interest demands of me to scold you severely concerning the letter that you write to me. What
has become of the zeal of which you gave such
proofs ? How is it possible that a moment of disgust makes you forget it ?

" To vulgar souls alone it appertains to send
in a resignation because of an inconvenience ; but
that of M. d'Aiguillon ought to be above such,
and to have no other object but the use he may be

to his master.   You give your bad cause the worst possible construction to yourself.   Do not, I beg, believe me dupe enough to adopt it.

" Sound your conscience.   You will find there all I tell you.

" M. de St Florentin, who brought me your letter yesterday evening, has been witness of the manner in which I spoke to his Majesty of the matter this morning. He has assured me that you shall be satisfied; but I am angry, very angry, with you. . . . . . . That little head of yours, of which I warned you the day of your departure, has played too great a part.

" I know not when I shall forgive you; you well deserve that I interest myself no longer about you.

" Good night, Sir,—rancour holding and very strong.—August 20."

Then—" Assuredly, Sir, your lieutenants are worthy of their chief, and that they be so always he must remain with them until the Peace. . . . I am infatuated for the service of the King, and nothing will deter me from it.   Let us talk no longer on the subject. . . . . . It is said that those gentlemen, 'Milords,' wish to fight again.   I desire

with all my soul that it may be with the same result."*

The same result! This is what Horace Walpole wrote of that result in 1758, to his friend
Harry Conway, who, ever since Fontenoy, Horace thought was born to fight the French.

"1758.

" Well, my dear Harry, you are not the only
man in England who has not conquered France;
Even Dukes of Marlborough† have been there
without doing the business. I don't doubt but
your good heart has been hoping, in spite of your
understanding, that our heroes have not only taken
St Maloes, but taken a trip across the country to
Rochefort, only to show how easy it was. We
have waited with astonishment at not hearing that
the French Court was removed in a panic to Lyons,
and that the ladies had gone off in their shifts, with
only a provision of rouge for a week.

" Nay, for my part, I expected to be deafened

* Autographs.

† The Duke of Marlborough (successor to *the* great Duke)
commanded the troops against St Malo. In the expedition
against Rochefort, the year before, Harry Conway was second in command.

with encomiums on Lord Anson . . . . who after
being allotted Madame de Pompadour as his share
of the spoils. . . had imitated Scipio.

" Alack ! we have restored nothing but a mile
of coast to its rightful owners. . . . . Commodore
Howe, with the expedition of Harlequin, re-em-
barked. . . Well! in half a dozen wars we shall
know more of France.   Last war we discovered a
fine bay near Port l'Orient ; we have now found
out that we know nothing of St Maloes."

The year 1759 was fatal to France in the East
Indies and in Canada.   In October of that year
Quebec was taken by the English.   " It is most
remarkable," observes Sir Edward Cust, " that in
the two armies the two first commanders in each
(Wolfe and de Montcalm) should have been killed,
and the two second wounded."

When Wolfe, dying, heard that the French
were in retreat, he said, " Now God be praised,
I die happy."   When the Marquis de Montcalm
heard that his wound was fatal, " So much the
better," said he, " I shall not live to see Quebec
surrender."   De Montcalm then received the last
offices of his religion, and died,—a brave soldier of
God and the King.   The loss of Canada and its
heroic defender, de Montcalm, profoundly afflict-

ed Louis XV.   He believed that the hand of
Heaven was against him at home and abroad.

Marshal Belleisle, to whom Madame de Pompadour had originally pointed out the Canadian
weak point of the Aix Treaty, never recovered
the taking of Quebec by the English.   Belleisle
was eager to the last for an invasion of England.   Cannon were tried at Choisy as to the
distance they would carry; flat boats were built;
—but money was wanting, and the flat boats
were unrigged.*

On the 26th of April, 1761, the Marquise wept
at the loss of her old friend and political tutor.
Marshal Belleisle was 77 years old when he died.
Another grief to the King, who could not replace
this, his faithful subject.

In 1759 Horace Walpole writes to Harry Conway, the would-be French conqueror :

"Their situation is desperate; the new account
of our taking Quebec leaves them (the French) in
the most deplorable condition; . . . they will be
less able than ever to raise money; we have
got ours for next year. . . . . . They must
try for a peace; they have got nothing to go

* See Autograph Letter from English Spy in France.
Appendix to p. 257.

to market with but Minorca. In short, if they can't strike some desperate blow in this island or Ireland, they are undone : the loss of 20,000 men to do us mischief would be cheap. I should even think Madame de Pompadour in danger of being torn to pieces if they did not make some attempt. . . . . . .

"My dear Sir, think of this! Wolfe, as I am convinced, has fallen a sacrifice to his rash blame of you. If I understand anything in this world the letter that came on Sunday said this : ' Quebec is impregnable ; it is flinging away the lives of brave men to attempt it. I am in the situation of Conway at Rochefort; but having blamed him, I must do what I now see he was in the right to see was wrong, and yet what he would have done ; and as I am commander, which he was not, I have the melancholy power of doing what he was prevented doing.'

"Poor man! His life has paid the price of his injustice, and as his death has purchased such benefit to his country, I lament him, as I am sure you, who have twenty times more courage and good nature than I have, do too."

The bells of London were " worn threadbare with ringing for victories!" The bells of Paris were muffled.   To the last, Marshal Belleisle said, in the metaphor peculiar to his day and to his antique studies: " An enemy can only be conquered on its own soil.   Carthage would not have fallen but before the legions of Rome."*

In danger, as Horace Walpole guessed, of being torn to pieces by the hungry mob, the Marquise saw the possessions of France passing from her country as life was ebbing away from herself.   She knew that the hearts of the Canadians were French, like the language of their tongue ; and the Council remembered that in Ireland, subject to England, was the faith of France.   M. Thurot, of Irish origin, once prisoner in England with Belleisle, had declared that Irish Catholicism was always ready for ignition against the Anglicans and the Presbyterians, and that " 10,000 Frenchmen would suffice to set Ireland on fire." " But," observes M. Capefigue a hundred years afterwards, " two things were essential, a navy and money, although hatred was so strong in France against England, the despoiler of Canada, that private pecuniary aid was offered for the Irish invasion."

* See Appendix, Vol. I. (" Paris Gossip "). Letter of English Spy. Autograph.

17 *

In the London Newspaper-Gazette was put, under the article of Bankrupts :—

"Louis le Petit, of the City of Paris, peace-breaker, Dealer and Chapman." "It would have been better," says our English Gossip commenting upon this, "if they had said ' Louis Bourbon of petty France.' "

A certain old gentleman, 'Vyner' by name, rose in that enlightened Senate, the English House of Commons, and in a fit of maundering bathos about unprotected females, urged that "*peace ought to be made, if only for the sake of that poor woman, Maria Theresa of Austria,*" just as King Frederic was fighting, "like a second St Michael to prevail over that dread dragoness, and hold fast Silesia."

The Marquise had constant need to use her seal to fighting Frenchmen, with the motto,—"Hold fast your duty,"—a duty of despair and desperation. Although de Richelieu had pillaged Hanover, — although de Soubise lost Rosbach, — although de Broglio was so unmanageable and quarrelsome that he had to be with-drawn, — although d'Aiguillon was restless at the northern helm,—although all this, and much more, the young chivalry of France, perishing for want of a Saxe or Lowendhal, fought bravely,

with honour untarnished, with valour unques-
tioned, with patriotism unsubdued. They fought
to the death for what they deemed a good cause,
in face of despair.

To Harry Conway, who fretted because he lost
a chance of fighting, again wrote Horace: " How
can you be such a child? You cannot, like a
German, love fighting for its own sake! .... The
mob of London would forget you" (a hero)...."for
the first Lord Mayor's Day or hyena that came to
Town..... In my passion I could almost wish you
were as worthless and as great as the King of Prussia. If conscience be a punishment, is it not a
reward too?"

The woman at the French Court, the head of
the French Cabinet, cherished every ray of glory
which illumined despair, although she knew that
she would be forgotten for the first rare show or
hyena that came to Paris. From daily experience
she learned, as did afterwards Goethe from Homer,
" that in our life here above ground we have, properly speaking, to enact hell."

Horace Walpole profanely asserted that heroes
of England were just then as " scarce as gold
pheasants." Heroism is estimated by success.
England could afford for her gay son to have

his joke, for all the people were bowed down to adore what John Bull loves next to money,—Success.

English heroes dead and alive were in America. Rejoicings in London. Plaudits for King George. Caps on bayonets for King George's kinsman, Frederic the Protestant hero. In Paris, silence. Muffled bells, stifled execration. Tears. The fine new buildings then in progress were in danger of being stopped. Industry was paralyzed. Art and Science languished. The new Boulevards and the Champs Elysées were watered with tears. France was almost starving. It was then the time when, as before said, the Pompadour sent all her plate, gold and silver, to the Mint.

The gentlemen of France strove to hold fast their duty according to the Pompadour motto. Many a little Rataplan inspiring song, sung at this day among Frenchmen, owes its origin to an attempt then, a hundred years ago, to make the men sing in face of death and defeat, and with empty stomachs.

And in the midst of all this it was necessary to rally internal industry, or discontent would have burst into a Revolution.

On the 9th of November, 1759, an edict (not

obligatory) was published, inviting the wealthier classes of France to yield up their household treasures (*Vaisselle plate*) in return for "*billets de monnaie sur les fermes.*" The Marquise had set the example. The King had retrenched his palace expenditure. A generous impulse electrified the kingdom. The new buildings and adornments of Paris were continued. The King held Reviews. The people began to hope against hope when they saw a busy hive of workmen, and their King, still looking every inch a King, in presence of his troops, as if preparing for fresh conquests.

But it was not only France that suffered. England had sedition in her provinces. Prussia saw her Silesia and Rhine States ravaged. Austria was making efforts beyond her means, to sustain two hundred and eighty thousand men on war footing. Philosophy announced conquering Kings as the scourges of humanity. In 1760, on the 25th Oct., George II. died of apoplexy.

France hoped that now would begin a new reign of peace. A new King of England might be more English than Hanoverian, and less inclined to subsidize the King of Prussia. The

Cabinet of Versailles hoped to make a reasonable peace. A special mission was given to M. de Bussy (no relation to Bussy " the Indian "), to travel to London and to confer with Pitt, and M. de Stanley was sent to Versailles under pretext of a " Cartel " for prisoners.

Versailles was rejoiced to make this effort, for the sake of singing men with hungry stomachs and scarcely staunched wounds, to effect a peace that should not compromise the national honour for which these men had fought, famished, and bled.

Bussy, formerly the Duc de Richelieu's secretary, and who once had been sent to confer with the late English King in Hanover (but who then failed because the Anglo-Prussian Treaty was secretly agreed upon), came to London.

War experience had confirmed the Duc de Choiseul's opinion (as Ambassador at Vienna) on the necessity of the Austrian alliance. Having resisted Cardinal de Bernis' timid policy, the Council at Fontainebleau now decided that war must continue rather than comply with " Pitt's hard conditions." This was the more disastrous, because of the fact that her most vigorous adversaries of peace were the Protestant

and Jansenist refugees then in London, at
Berlin, and even in Paris.* Their intrigues,
fostered by their cupidity, seconded the wearisome oppositions of the Parliament. . . . . †
The King of France was profoundly grieved, and
sharply irritated. In council he could not contain himself. The Marquise de Pompadour,
though equally grieved, strove to calm the " Very
Christian King." " Ah ! " cried the King, " I
am no longer young. This war misery has lasted
too long already ! "

The " Secret Notices " in the Holdernesse
Despatches forwarded through Prussia (See Appendix), may give some idea of the snares which
involved the French Cabinet. Those notes of
Secret Intrigue seem to confirm France's suspicion that the mystic Count St Germain played
into Prussia's hand at Rosbach. They also hint
that mystic " Mediums " to-day are as likely to be
employed by Cabinets as by spirits. Madame
Pompadour wrote to Bussy : " So we must
keep on to the end, and put the English to shame

* See Appendix to p. 264, Autograph. Secret notice of
General Yorke to Lord Holdernesse.

† See 2nd " Secret Notice from French Court," Autograph.
Appendix.

in the face of all Europe in exposing their ambition and disinclination for peace. Nevertheless, it is believed here that in the funds they are almost as badly off as ourselves. Their national debt is immense and increases every day; soldiers and sailors begin to fail them . . . Properly speaking, our wars with that nation are but wars with shopkeepers, but are the more difficult to terminate because the spirit of commerce desires no rival. There are a thousand distinguished individuals in London who make great fortunes by the ruin and even by the massacre of their countrymen. They wish that this cruel game should last for ever. They may easily buy the Ministry and Parliament in a country where everything is to sell. In fact, it seems that when war is declared on the Stock Exchange of London, St James's follows suit six months afterwards. If the King of England had but honest ministers who loved the public and despised clamour and money! You complain of your disagreeable situation in London. I doubt it not; but here we give example of patience. Suffer generously for your King and country."

War was to continue. France must still face the foe abroad with—as says an English Spy (see Appendix)—"fear of rebellion in her provinces, of descent upon her coasts ; and with money still scarcer than horses." Reinforcements were nevertheless ordered by Council.* Voltaire cried from Ferney, "Vive le Ministère de M. le Duc de Choiseul!" In August, 1760, Voltaire wrote to an Encyclopédiste: " This ministry will make a merit of serving you." The Marquise secretly consulted the Duc de Choiseul on the expulsion of the Jesuits from France.   She strove to fortify the mind of the King, and to brace it up to an act which would strike the fetters from his own soul, and from liberty within his kingdom,—an act which would enable all the sons of France to rally round her banner, let their creed be what it might.

By expelling the Jesuits their perpetual strife with the Parliament must cease, and all

* The financier Etienne de Silhouette, superintendent of Farms General, had been inducted into the Ministry by the Marquise, although, formerly, he had respectfully declined the King's overtures. Silhouette's system had given fresh means to Cabinet and to Camp, but it was offensive to the Court, inasmuch as it decided in one clause that all exemptions from taxes, formerly allowed to people of the Court, should be suspended for ten years. This clause, by which the Marquise suffered equally with others, increased her unpopularity. French and English historians take opposed views of Silhouette.

who were expatriated for not submitting to their authority might return. She reminded the King of a conversation held some years before between the King of Prussia and Voltaire, which plainly showed one source from whence Prussian supremacy, under which France was languishing, was derived. Also it involved the principle of England's greatness under the rule of Hanover. This conversation shall be related in Voltaire's own words:

"I spoke to His Prussian Majesty (in 1743) of a publication which has had a great run in Holland for the last six weeks, in which it is proposed to pacificate the Empire in secularizing the ecclesiastical principalities in favour of the Emperor and of the Queen of Hungary. I told him I wished with all my heart the success of such a project, which was to render under Cæsar the things that were Cæsar's. . . . That the Church ought only to pray to God . . . that monks had not been instituted to be sovereigns."*

This project, although exceeding in some respects that which was meditated by the Marquise (who clung to a religion which became

---

* King Frederic called this "*Taking a round in the street of the Priests.*"

daily more necessary to her as life receded), was
regarded by the King of Prussia at the time
when Voltaire called his attention to it as one
of the "great engines" of the times. England and Prussia had both illustrated the working of this great engine. England and Prussia
were the types of progress and common
sense, while France, although higher in the
scale of social civilization, and fine arts, was the
type of old customs that had degenerated into
corruption. Reform was needed. As the Marquise had written to Montesquieu years before :
" Let us cut off the decayed branches, but spare
the tree." Would time and opportunity be given
her for this work? Her days were numbered.*
But, needing all her elements of power, she shone
at Versailles, to the last, with an outward magnificence which was burthensome to a suffering body
and to a weary spirit. " A chevalier of St Louis is
her train-bearer. A lady of quality is in attendance
upon her behind her chair. She alone is seated in
presence of royalty. The King stands near her,
amused by her words, and in the background is
the Marquis de Marigny, her brother, decorated
with the order of the Saint Esprit, whom his Ma-

* See Appendix. Note to p. 269.

jesty salutes as 'beau-frère.' Princes and heroes
emulate with each other in doing her the slightest
service."

Photography has rendered such a picture
of the Duchesse de Pompadour familiar to England in the 19th Century. Nobles and ladies
stand round about her, and the King is at her
right hand, while bowing at her footstool is her
protégé, Gluck, the musician, offering to her the
work of his genius, "Orfeo!" Beautiful the
Pompadour still looks, with lofty coiffure, fan in
hand, and flowing robes, as she gracefully bends
towards the musician. She smiles, but it is in
face of death.

Here is the reverse of the medal, a pen-
and-ink portrait, by one of her female enemies at
the same date. " Her malady is long and dangerous. If it be poison, it is slow. The King has
become alarmed. He sends to inquire daily about
her health. She dreads to rise from her couch
and to face the daylight. She imagines that a couch
of rose hue will give bloom to her livid face. At
the Court she dare not show herself with so much
audacity. Long ago, her emaciation warned
her of the decomposition of her body. Each day

her toilette, her dress, become more and more difficult. She saw her malady afar off, and she found nothing either in her reason nor her spirit which helped her to resignation."

One of her female revilers accuses her of painting her face, and another attacks her for having laughed at others who adopted this custom of her century and country. A coarse pamphlet, published in 1802, declares that she saw in every Jesuit her poisoner. If so, she must have been singularly forbearing to have suffered so many years, without once uttering such an accusation. Although propped up outwardly for occasions, how now would this miserable wreck of a woman find strength and courage for a conflict with a power which had been too mighty for Kings or for Popes to grapple with?—strength for a conflict which might end in her being deprived of a place of Christian burial,—she who had planned the Magdalen Church, it was said, for her own sepulchre!

In the mean while, the star of Frederic the Philosopher was in the ascendant. In January, 1762, one woman was removed out of his way in the person of Elizabeth-Petrowna, Empress of

Russia. Upon her death he writes, with his own hand, to his friend Count Funkenstein (from Breslaw, the capital of Maria Theresa's beloved Silesia) : " Here is the first ray of light which appears, Heaven be blest for it. Let us hope that fine days will follow the storms, — may God grant it ! "

And 'M. Mitchell' encloses in his 'most secret' that " His Majesty said to the Marquis, in a Letter dated the 1st of February : The Emperor of Russia is as well affected for my interest as the best Bourgeois of Berlin could be. We make peace, and perhaps we shall also make an Alliance. The Swedes are no longer our enemies, they are changed by a rebound, and your domicile of Berlin will be tranquil, and my provinces sheltered from devastations. . . If assurances fulfil themselves I shall be able to make an honourable peace with the Court of Vienna, before the end of this year. I flatter myself that this diversion will come to pass ; you will see that I have the lightness of the stag, and the strength of the lion, ... Death, in brushing off this woman, has deranged all the fine projects of my enemies ! . ." " The Solomon of the North " even grew poetic

and pathetic to " Mon cher Monsieur Mitchel "
upon " The Origin of Evil." *

* Mitchell Papers, manuscript writings of the King of
Prussia—Museum Britannicum, Folio 6845.   See Appendix
for original document, announcing the Death of the Empress
of Russia, and for "Original Letters of the Grand Duke and
Grand Duchess Catherine."

CHAPTER VII.

THERE is no philosophy greater than that of listening calmly to the words of one's own enemy. To turn them to one's own advantage is the practical part of philosophy.   In 1763 Frederic of Prussia wrote: —" I have remarked, that there, where are most monasteries and convents, the people are most blindly attached to superstition. . . . There is no doubt that by destroying these asylums for fanaticism the people are enlightened. The question is, whether to destroy the cloisters, or to diminish their numbers. The moment for this question is arrived because the Governments of France and Austria are overwhelmed by debts, which have exhausted the resources of industry without being able to be liquidated. The attrac-

18 *

tion of rich monasteries and convents is tempting.
. . . . . As soon as the people are cooled, the
Bishops will become like little boys, of whom
Sovereigns will dispose according as they will,
and to the circumstances of the times that follow." The Protestant hero saw nothing in
Monks and Monasteries but tools and encum-
brances, to be used or rejected according to
temporal expediency; but the woman in France
(by whose protection the correspondence of the
Encyclopédistes was sent under cover to the department of foreign affairs) considered Frederic's acts
as types of the times, although she regarded some
religious orders as the most glorious symbols of
a sublime Democracy. The Capuchins, for example.

" Mingling with the people," says M. Capefigue, " Capuchins, above all, formed the beloved
militia of the Church militant on earth ; the men-
dicant orders of Saint Antoine, of Saint François,
were at the head of all consolation."

Voltaire accepted, or conferred upon himself,
the title of " Temporal Father of the Capuchins
of Gex."

There were many among the " philosophers,"
who, although rebelling against fanaticism and

superstition, submitted to the truth of revealed religion, which, in France, was overgrown by these. Practices inimical to the liberty of the subject, and to the soul's freedom, were fostered by the Jesuits, as was illustrated not only in the Bull Unigenitus, that fruit of an Ecclesiastical Upas-tree, but also by other superstitious encouragements of which reason loudly complained in Paris. Then, as now, in other parts of Europe, were impostures which, if not regarded as impostures, were looked upon at least as appertaining to witchcraft.

The history of Magic in the 18th century in France, abounds in tales far more astounding than the Spirit Rapping and Table Turning of the present day, or even of Clairvoyance, Mesmeric-Trances, &c. &c. The 'Convulsionists' were an acknowledged sect.* There were different orders of superstition, each manifesting its own set of painful practices. Not that the Jesuits were to be held responsible for all of these, but, as they were the chief educators of the people, and the people were driven into the fold by means of terror, as in the case of compelled con-

* Cerémonies Religieuses de Bernard Picard, &c.

fession, and all the horrors of death in face of
the Bull Unigenitus, it was time that the public faith should be purged of practices that
were maddening and unholy. In vain those who
indulged in " Magic" were arrested by Government. Terror of one sort had produced superstition, and terror of another sort only increased
it, and provoked secret assemblies which were
nests of epidemic madness. The best correction,
as said Voltaire, to such a madness would have
been ridicule and indifference. A free circula-
tion, of opinion would have ventilated the corrupt
atmosphere which encouraged the noxious growth
of the evil. But the press, as we know, was
gagged. Philosophy, the daughter of oppression,
was stifled and forced to run for the free air of
life into other lands, where she gave birth to
sedition against the mother-country. Reason
degenerated into atheism abroad, and fear into
madness at home. France, warring against England and Prussia, types of Progress and Reform,
rose in self-defence to protest against error and
to shake off the dust of centuries. The canker-
worm was at her heart. It must be cast out.
France's children at home were divided among
themselves. Superstition was stronger than

Religion. Reason was enthralled. A new banner must be raised. Liberty, — liberty of thought, of speech, of press, of life, of death. Liberty for Frenchmen to fight for France, and to serve her faithfully, whether they believed in the Bull Unigenitus or not.

This amnesty, it will be remembered, was what the Marquise first proposed, long before the Bull Unigenitus had become such a bugbear. She had proposed it when France was glorious in victory over the English, and had still an Exchequer. The Marquise then, with new life dawning for her, happy and beloved, had proposed it to recruit the army of France, exhausted by war. It was her first offence to the Jesuits, who sought to grasp and to keep temporal power in France. Had the King granted full liberty of conscience to his subjects in 1746, when his campaigns were glorious, France would not now have been humbled in face of England in 1761, nor possibly have lost her colonies for want of men and money. It was too late, now, to avert these evils, but not less urgent to lay the first stone for a better state of things at home and abroad, especially as the Parliament was again mutinous.

In 1761, the Marquise wrote one more letter

to the Duc d'Aiguillon. Her knowledge that he was a partisan of the Jesuits may have helped at this time to impart a coldness to her style, although his conduct had been enough to exhaust her patience. The letter is sealed with her arms, and addressed to Nantes :

"M. de Fitz James* had thanked the Commander of Languedoc, when I received your letter, but, whatever may be the interest that M. de Choiseul, M.˚de St Florentin, and myself may take in you, we should never have thought of

---

* The Duc de Fitz James, a Stuart, beloved in the Court of France, heir of the Duke of Berwick (who was killed by a cannon in service of the King of France), was a descendant of James II. In 1761, the same date as the above letter, the Duc de Fitz James, "a man of energy and will, with the spirit of a soldier," was appointed to the Government of Languedoc, which, like Brittany, possessed a turbulent Parliament. Afterwards M. de Fitz James had to arrest the members. A universal cry rose against this exercise of military authority. The Parliament of Toulouse decreed that the body of the Duc de Fitz James should be taken, but this could not be as he was a Peer of France. D'Aiguillon, as a Richelieu, no doubt regarded Languedoc as his right. The Bishop de Soissons (who, in 1744, refused to absolve the King until he put away Madame de Chateauroux) was also named Fitz James, and grandson of James II.

Languedoc. Your condition was assured in a very solid way, and suitable to the re-establishment of your health (*delabrie*). It will be very necessary to disencumber yourself of your Bretagne, if it trouble you too much, for assuredly we wish you no evil. Bonsoir, M. le Duc."

The Jesuits, who had opposed liberty, must be cast out. But the Archbishop of Paris declared, " Let a scaffold be erected in the midst of my own court and I will mount it to sustain my rights, to fulfil my duties, and to obey the laws of my conscience." It was then that the Duc de Richelieu, being sent to confer with the Archbishop, answered in the words of Voltaire : " Your conscience, Monseigneur, is a dreary lanthorn that lights nobody but yourself."

But, though dreary, it was a steady light. This fine old bigot, the Archbishop, swore that sooner than compromise his conscience he would see Madame de Pompadour burned alive. Such outspoken intolerance was respectable. More so than the policy of others, which had planted one of the enemy's company in the household of the Marquise, to insinuate herself into her confidence. This fact known, the extreme fanatics on the

other side of the question assume that the malady
from which the Marquise was dying, was a slow
Jesuit poison.

The Duc de Choiseul,* who was in the daily
habit of conference with the Marquise, says that
her lady in waiting was commissioned to make her
mistress understand that if she (the Marquise)
would use her influence in favour of the Jesuits,
they would do all in their power to maintain her
in the lofty position which she had attained in
spite of them.   These were the words used :

" The Jesuits have in view but the salvation
of their penitents.   But they are men ; hatred,
without their knowledge, may influence their
heart, and inspire a rigour greater than circumstances may absolutely demand.   A favourable
disposition may, on the contrary, insure from the
King's confessor great compromises... "

These words were scornfully remembered,
and repeated by the Marquise (who was not subject to a religion of terror, nor of self-interest)
to de Choiseul.

When, after the attempted assassination of the
King, the political power of the Marquise was
greater in the kingdom and over the sovereign

* Dulaure, Hist. de Paris.   Pubd. 1834.

than before, and when the Parliament threw back
the imputation of regicide on the Jesuits, who
alone might profit by it,—they malignly, but
unskilfully, cast the calumny on the Marquise.
This charge was so illogical, that it was scouted
even by her other enemies. There could be
no doubt that the stability of her power
was alone to be maintained by the King's life ;
that death to him would be instant downfal to
her. There was bitter proof of this in the short
interregnum of the Dauphin's power during the
King's illness. Neither would the " Philosophers " have derived benefit by the King's death.
As the succession must inevitably fall to the
Dauphin, they would have been entirely crushed
in France. There was no need to tell the King
that the Jesuits only would have profited by his
assassination, and that if the attempt were not
the unaided deed of a madman, they alone,
within his kingdom, were likely to have instigated
Damiens to it.

It is probable that the hypochondriacal mind
of the King had brooded over this suspicion
until it had become a morbid nightmare.
Not so to the Marquise, whose tone of thought
was more vigorous, who spoke of Damiens as " a

madman," and who was amused by his assertion
that " if the doctors had only let him be bled, he
should never have struck the King."

But the Marquise took means to strengthen
the King's mind, to disperse the clouds of
fanaticism from his soul, which operated more
strongly against the Jesuits than any extreme
assertion that was not proved. She amused
him with the writings of the Encyclopédie,
some of which were dedicated to herself. Many
of the authors were among her earliest and
best friends. Louis XV. became interested in
their arguments. His friend and counsellor,
the Duc de Choiseul, had helped the Marquise to import such writings under cover of
' Foreign Affairs.' Many of the articles that kept
appearing in Paris, in spite of all obstacles, were
like light thrown upon darkness in the middle of
the 18th century, making darkness visible. The
King saw the chaos that surrounded him. He
knew, too, that his triumphant enemy of Prussia
had encouraged philosophy, while he had been
compelled, by the power greater than himself
within his walls, to cast it out. The Bourbon
began at last to open his eyes in admiration at

the utilitarianism of the Brandenbourg monarch, and to protest in favour of a new principle.

There were other events in the Papacy which stimulated the belief of Louis XV. that the root of evil was at home. Pope Benedict was dead. In 1758, Clement XIII. had ascended the Pontifical throne. This new Pope had been a blind and passionate partisan of the Jesuits, and yet—such is the force of expediency—one of his first acts of Papal power was to condemn their celebrated work, " The History of the People of God, " both in Italian and Spanish. He also renewed the condemnations pronounced against some of their acts by his predecessor, Benedict. The Pope could do no wrong: *ergo*—the Jesuits could not always be infallibly right.

The Pope wished to save himself and his throne by wise concessions of temporal power to temporal sovereigns. It was a great blow to the Bull Unigenitus.*

---

* Pope Clement XIII. (he who burnt the Jesuits' book as a matter of expediency, although he was previously devoted to that Society) was implored to suppress the Order altogether by the five Courts of Paris, Madrid, Lisbon, Naples, and Parma, but the Pope turned round,

The order for this Suppression was still balancing at Rome, when the King sent the Duc de Richelieu to the Archbishop of Paris to entreat him to moderate his zeal. The Archbishop's scaffold answer has already been recorded. As neither the Marquise could be frightened into concessions by the Jesuits, nor the Archbishop by the King, there could be no compromise in the matter.

Three years after the Jesuits were suspected of having instigated Damiens to assassinate the King, an opportunity of open attack upon them occurred. Great events from little causes spring. So in this case of importance to France.

The Company had had a law-suit against some merchants at Marseilles, which, going adverse to

and among other things excommunicated the Duke of Parma for having increased his power by a supposed infringement of the temporal wealth of Rome. Then did the five Courts declaim against Pope Clement XIII., who found himself hemmed in so tightly by them, that he consented to give in to their wishes. The very eve of the day upon which he was to have signed in favour of the five Courts, Pope Clement XIII. died. Heresy, run mad, declares that the Jesuits poisoned him to prevent his act of common sense which would eventuate in suppression of their Company.

it, the Jesuit fathers were on the 8th of May,
1761, condemned to pay to these merchants the
sum of £60,000 sterling in reference to Bills of
Exchange, drawn by Father Lavalette, Jesuit ;
and £2000 sterling of interest money into the
bargain. This law-suit did not do honour to the
good-citizenship of the Jesuit Fathers, any more
than did the memorials which, now published,
insisted on the attention of the Parliament to
their aggressions on the civil rights of their
neighbours. President Meynières — he whose
interview with the Marquise has been recorded
—relates also how Parliament had been compelled to decree the arrest of a certain St
Nicholas who had refused to administer the
Sacrament to a sick Ex-Oratorian, &c.

Parliament, therefore, now enjoined the Jesuits to place with the Registrar a printed copy
of the constitutions of their Society, especially of
the edition published, in 1757, at Prague, and
ordered that these constitutions should be examined, and that an accurate report should be
made of them. This report was not favourable to
the Jesuits.

On the 6th of August, 1761, Parliament

decreed that the books approved by the ' Society of Jesus,' " containing immoral maxims and subversive of established order," should be torn and burnt in the Court of the Palace, at the foot of the great staircase by the executioner of high Justice, as seditious, destructive of all principle of Christian morality, and teaching a murderous doctrine, not only against the safety and the life of citizens, but even endangering the sacred persons of sovereigns."* It was forbidden to Jesuits to teach in the colleges, and to the subjects of the King to follow their lessons.

After this strong step, the King staggered. In spite of the remonstrance of the Parliament, it was decided that the Act should not be put in force for one year. The 28th of November following, it was ordered that the Bishops or Archbishops who were in Paris should be charged to pronounce upon these four points :

" 1st. Upon the utility of the Jesuits in France, and upon the inconveniences which may result from the different functions confided to them.

---

* "Procédures contre l'Institut et les Constitutions des Jésuites." Quoted by Dulaure (in the 19th century), Hist. Paris, p. 400.

" 2nd. Upon their conduct, upon their opinions contrary to the safety of the persons of sovereigns, upon the doctrine of the clergy of France, contained in the declaration of 1682.

" 3rd. Upon the subordination that the Jesuits may owe to Bishops, and their encroachments upon the functions of Pastors.

" 4th. Upon the Constitution that they would be able to bring into France on the authority of the General of the Jesuits."

But such, as says Dulaure, was the terror still inspired into France by this expiring power, that this Assembly of Prelates decided in its favour by 45 against 6, out of 51.*

The Parliament then demanded of the Universities and seneschals under its ward, memorials on the Establishments of the Jesuits in their circuits, and received a great number condemnatory of the practices of the Company, and of the means it employed to gain the end of power.

On the 5th of March, 1762, an Act was passed that certain extracted passages of condemned Jesuit writings should be submitted to Bishops and Archbishops, and that translations of the same be laid before the King. . . . From the

* Procédures contre les Constitutions des Jesuites.

Secreta Monita, or Secret Instructions, was sifted
the real danger to which the Company exposed
public and political morality and also the safety of
the State. In it were found the artifices recommended to the members of this Society to possess
themselves of the minds of Sovereigns, and in-
fluential government individuals, &c. &c.

Ultra Protestant and 19th century historians
dwell as unctuously on the " *Secreta Monita* "
as on the secret sins of Louis XV. Extracts
of assertions sustained and taught by so-called
Jesuits, exposed the root of manifold evil in
the state, and by what manœuvres their power
was sustained.*

In the month of November, 1764, an Edict of
Louis XV., King of France, decided the gene-
ral and definitive expulsion of the Jesuits from
France.†

* "Summum Pretium a viduis semper extorquendum, in-
culcata illis Summa Nostra necessitate." (Secreta Monita,
Cap. 1, Art. 7.)

† By this Edict France took the initiative in her own concerns which POPE CLEMENT XIV. subsequently adopted in
behalf of other nations. Pope Clement XIV. (Ganganelli)
in signing the Anti-Jesuit *Bref* said : "I do this with pleasure
because I have long reflected on the for and against of the
question, but I foresee that my signing this will cost me my

France breathed. France awoke as from a long trance. The quarrels between the Parlia-

life." (Afterwards, on the pontifical palace-wall were inscribed the initials "I.S.S.S.V." "In Settembre Sara Sede Vacante," "In September the seat will be vacant," — which prediction was fulfilled.)

"In perpetuam memoriam.

". . . . Being inspired by ardent desire to proceed with confidence and safety in the deliberation of which we are about to speak, we have spared neither c are nor research in discovering all that belongs to the origin, progress, and actual state of the Regular Order, commonly called, 'The Society of Jesus,' and we have found, and do recognise, that it was instituted for the salvation of souls, by its holy Founder, for the conversion of Heretics, and particularly for that of Infidels, and for the greater increase of piety and of true Religion : and that for the more easy and Happy attainment of that desired End, it was consecrated to God by the most strict vow of Evangelical Poverty . . . with the Exception only of Colleges of learning and of Sciences, to which it permits the receipt of Revenues, on condition that the Society employ none of these, nor convert them to its profits nor to its wants nor uses. . . . .

"It appears, notwithstanding, incontestable, that almost from the origin of this Society it has sown seeds of discords and jealousies, not only among its own members, but with the other Regular Orders, the Secular Clergy, the Academies, the Universities, the Public schools of fine Arts, and even with the Princes and among the States by whom and in which it has been received; and moreover that these Contests and Dissensions have had for their object, sometimes the quality and Nature of Vows, the power of expulsion from their Order, the

19 *

ment and the Bull Unigenitus were over. Men were
not afraid to die without permission of that bug-

reception of Sacred Orders without Sacerdotal Sanction and
without Solemn Vows, against the Decrees of the Council of
Trent, and those of Pius V. our predecessor of holy memory.
Sometimes the Absolute Power that the Superior General attributed to himself; and also other points concerning the
Government of Society; sometimes divers articles of Doctrine,
of schools of Exemptions, and the Privileges that the Ordi-
naries of places, and other persons constituted in Ecclesiastical or Secular Dignity, pretended to prejudice their jurisdic-
tion and their Rights.   Moreover, there have been laid to
the charge of members of the Society very grave Accusations,
which have not a little troubled the Peace and Tranquillity of
the Christian Republic. . . . .

   "Many complaints, sustained by the Authority of divers
Princes, have been brought against the said Society. . . .   We
have certainly observed with the greatest grief, that the remedies" (employed) "have not had either the virtue or force to
uproot and disseminate so many troubles, accusations, and complaints brought against the said Society. . . . . . .   Our very
dear sons in Jesus Christ, being persuaded that no remedy
could be durable and effectual to conciliate the Christian
Universe, unless the whole Society be extinct and suppressed.

   "WE EXTINGUISH AND SUPPRESS the said Society, we take
from it and abridge all and every of its Offices, Ministrations,
and Administrations, its Houses, Schools, Colleges, Hospitals,
Farms, and Places whatever, in whatever Province and Kingdom be they situated, and by whatever they appertain unto
it; its Statutes, Customs, Usages, Decrees, Constitutions,
however they may be confirmed by Oath, by Apostolic Approbation, or otherwise. . . .   To this effect we declare broken in

bear.   There was liberty in France for Conscience.   But, the 'Contradiction' removed, hideous self-assertion soon showed itself.   The people at last blessed and praised the Pompadour, but she had cause to doubt the deed she had done.

Liberty eventually owed much to this woman,

Perpetuity, and wholly extinct all authority whatever, whether of the Superior General, of the Provincials, Visitors, and all other Superiors of the said Society as much spiritually as temporally. . . . . . As to those who are in sacred Orders, we give unto them power and permission to quit the Houses and Colleges of the Society, to enter some one of the Regular orders approved by the apostolic see. . . . . . Finally, we exhort all Christians, and we conjure them by the bowels of Jesus Christ, to remember that they have all the same Master who is in the Skies, and the same Redeemer who hath dearly bought them ; that all have been made regenerate in the same bath of Water, by the Word of life, and made Children of God, and co-Heirs of Eternal life. . . . . that they make all but the Body of Jesus Christ and are members one of the other ; and that by consequence it is Absolutely Necessary that they be united altogether by the common link of Charity and be at peace with all men. . . . that they hold in horror offences, rancour, quarrels, and all that the old Enemy of the human race hath devised ; to trouble the Church of God, and put an obstacle in the way of the Eternal Felicity of the Faithful, under title and very false pretext, of the opinions of the Schools, or even of Christian perfection.

"Given at Rome at Santa-Maria (Mr) under the Ring of the Fisherman, the 21 of July 1773, and the 5 of our Pontificate.
" Signed, A. CARD. NIGRONUS."

who, in defiance of danger and death, struck off
the shackles of France; but none knew better
than she did that education in all parts of the
world had been deeply indebted to the Jesuits.
In their expulsion, she was signally impartial between priests and Parliament. But soon she feared
that, instead of Reform, she had favoured Revolution. "Philosophism," let loose, began to show
that no belief was possible.

Tear down old custom, and what will remain?
"The whole *dæmoniac* nature of man will remain,
hurled forth to rage without rule or rein,—savage
itself, yet with all the tools and weapons of civilization." *

The Marquise recoiled from the chief Parliament men (who had helped her to cast out Jesuits), such as the Jansenist hunchback, Chauvelin, who madly vented his spleen by attacking
the points which she revered in the Jesuit system,
viz. Obedience, Order, and Self-abnegation.

In strange contrast to this hump-backed monomaniac is the fine pastel portrait of the Marquise de Pompadour (by Latour), standing calmly
by a table on which is placed a large volume of
the ' Encyclopédie.' This picture finds an ap-

* Carlyle's ' French Revolution,' p. 18.   Pub. 1848.

propriate place in the Louvre, which, in 1758, she caused first to be thrown open to the public of all nations.

It is this Chauvelin who is indicated in the popular doggrel on the expulsion of the Jesuits :

> " Que fragile est ton sort, société perverse !
> Un boiteux * t'à fondée, un bossu † te renverse."

Chauvelin worked to revenge himself, and the Marquise worked to redeem France. But, though triumphant, she had cause for anguish, just as it was written of her :

> " Au Livre des destins, chapitre des grands Rois
> On lit ces Paroles écrites :
> De France Agnés chassera les Anglois,
> Et Pompadour chassera les Jesuites."

The Pompadour was dying, and time was wanted to test the result of her work.

Although a new revenue was opening to France by the reversion of Jesuit benefices, she who foresaw this could not leave her country a prey to those same English that Agnés Sorel—at whose name her heart had beat in youth—had cast out.

In 1762, just as intolerance was about to be expelled from within the walls of France, the Mar-

* St Ignatius.   † Chauvelin.

quise had written the following letter to her coadjutor, de Choiseul, who was then at Vienna.

"To the Duc de Choiseul.   1762.

"I am ill; nevertheless, I will try to answer
you. . . It is a question of better policy and of reparation of faults. You begin at a difficult time,
but your glory will be the greater if you triumph
over your difficulties, as I hope. What has come to
pass among the Russians is unprecedented. What
masters ! What subjects ! The Empress Elizabeth
dies, her nephew succeeds to her, and his wife sup-
plants him, all in six months. Poor Peter was
very wrong to quarrel with his wife. . . . I do not
think it will do to trust to this new Empress. . . . *
Neither must we hope great things from the
Spaniards. I think them sincere, but they are
irresolute and inactive. . . . As to Germany—Germany has always been a tomb of France — in
this war, the tomb of her glory. . . . As to
this *Pacte de famille*, ... the English have
dreaded it ; just now they laugh with reason at
their fears and our hopes. The safest thing is
to make peace, but the work will be difficult

* See Appendix, Autograph Letters of 'Poor Peter' and
of his wife. Also King Frederic's Autograph notice of the late
Czarina's death at the end of preceding chapter.

with a people puffed up by victory, the natural enemy of the human species, and especially of the French. M. le Duc, if you bring this affair to a conclusion you will have the glory of saving your country. It is not a question of durable peace: that is impossible. The English and French cannot remain long friends. The reciprocal hatred of the two nations, the rivalry of commerce, the opposition of interests and of alliances, will soon replace the sword in their hands. That is why I think it so necessary to try to conserve some establishment in Africa and in the Indies. It is the only way of saving our commerce, of repairing and augmenting our marine, of fortifying ourselves everywhere, and of attacking the English whenever the opportunity to do so present itself.

" The capture of our merchant vessels before the declaration of war, was an infamous action that the French will never forget until they have avenged it. How humble we are ! We give to our enemies ribbons and fashions, and they give to us laws ! I hope that will not last. Try, M. le Duc, to make peace on the best conditions we can. Afterwards, prepare yourself for war." *

* See Appendix, Original peace-letter, &c., of the Duc de Choiseul to the King of England. When preliminaries of

But in her last days the Pompadour found no
peace for herself.   In every great popular movement the mud is sure to turn uppermost.   The
penitent Marquise had thought to give liberty to
France, and soon she found that in driving out the
Jesuits she had forced open the way for atheism
to step in.   The faith of the people was shaken.
Their liberty became, for the moment, licentiousness.   The colleges for public instruction,
hitherto under Jesuit control, were closed.   Meanwhile, the Jesuits bore their misfortune with dignity.   Some who, though deprived of their habit
and vocation, remained in France, found a refuge
in powerful families who became deadly enemies
of the Marquise.   She was accused of every social evil by these partisans of the Jesuits, just as
they were accused of every crime by parliament
monomaniacs, like the hunchback Chauvelin.

The once gay de Bernis, now robed in Roman
purple, was faithful to the patroness of his earlier
years.   He had dedicated a poem to the King, in

peace were submitted by the Under Secretary of State to
Lord Granville, he was just dying. "It cannot prolong my
life to neglect my duty," said Lord Granville, and proceeded
to his task in the same spirit as did the woman in France,
but with more satisfaction at the national result.

the preface to which he declares that " people are only submissive to kings in proportion as they are submissive to God, and that kings are only just to their people in proportion as they recognise a supreme power." *

To the Marquise de Pompadour, in spite of her late political difference with him, de Bernis wrote :

" Madame, suffer also that I see you, whose esteem and friendship are to me more precious than all human grandeur. . . . . And it is possible that my counsels may not always be useless to you." †

What pain and weariness all this conflict of private feeling and public duty caused to the Marquise may be seen by the following letter to her friend the Abbesse de Chelles.

" A Madame L'Abbesse de Chelles. 1762.

" I recommend to your prayers the King, France, and myself, with all others. Heaven is never deaf to the prayers of the holy. We are going to work at Peace, but God only can give it unto us. It is a grace, Madame, that you are worthy to ask and to obtain. How happy you are, to have left this base and wicked world !

* " La Religion Vengée." Published in Paris, 1812.
† Published, 1772.

" There are beautiful women who envy me, and
I envy their freedom. Reason, years, the misfortunes of the times, contempt for the petty vani-
ties of courts, which are pitiable when known,
have thrown me into a black melancholy which
disgusts me with everything. I once desired grandeur, and here I am satiated with it. . . . I am
obliged to wear joy on my face, when death is in
my heart. . . . . ' Sire,' I say to the King, ' I
am content ; ' and at the same time I scarce can
refrain from weeping at seeing myself compelled
to dissimulate. . . . . In my spirit there is but
weariness ; ˙sadness overwhelms me. These are
an invitation from Heaven, but I continue to wear
my chains. I salute you, Madame, with the respect and the affection which your virtue deserves.
Love me. Pity me. Pray for me."

The writer of this letter had given free access
to " philosophy ; " but now, jaded in spirit, she
found no refuge in it. Her intercourse with her
faithful friend, Cardinal de Bernis, although
sneered at by coarse contemporaries, was a solace
to her soul ; for even in past days, when he first
was transplanted to the Court by her influence,
and when she tried to fortify her uneasy conscience by " philosophy," de Bernis, in his writings,

had attempted successively to refute the "systems" by which she strove to justify herself, and he had warned her that " Christianity, vainly attacked by Impiety, would finally triumph over Pride."* Her late resistance to the Cabinet peace policy of de Bernis was afflicting to the Pompadour in face of such letters as this from the Marshal Duc de Broglio.

 " Du Village de Berghen, 14th April, 1759.

 " Madame,

 " . . . . . A little accident has happened to one of your protégés.† I sent him about 11 o'clock at night to reconnoitre whether M. le Prince Ferdinand would retire. He came back at the end of half an hour, and made his report to me in a very satisfactory manner, but with an air of emotion. I saw him getting very pale; which was a little matter of scandal among the officers present.

 " ' Are you afraid, Sir,' I asked, harshly, ' in the midst of us ? '

 " ' Pardon, my General,' he gasped;—and fainted. The others present ran forward to his assist-

* " La Corruption de l'Esprit et des Mœurs." 1747.

† The young chivalry of France placed itself under the special patronage of the Marquise.

ance, and found themselves in a stream of blood. His arm was broken by a ball in acquitting himself of my commission, but this accident did not hinder him in coming to render an account of his duty. . . Madame, in my little army I have a thousand young fellows of that sort; and in a day of action there are numberless such deeds of heroism of which no one speaks nor hardly thinks."

Now, when, three years after the receipt of that letter from the Duc de Broglio, the Pompadour was going to work at peace with the Duc de Choiseul on more dignified terms than those formerly prescibed by de Bernis, she was not only depressed at heart, as she expressed herself to the Abbesse de Chelles in the foregoing letter, but she was borne down by the prescience of the short duration of peace, as may be seen in her letter to the Duc de Choiseul.

It was then, while also looking forth on the tide of social corruption which she, individually, could not stem, she cried, bitterly, " After us the Deluge ! "

These words have been perverted against her by those who, not having access to the private records of the speaker's life, have seen in them nothing but a selfish and time-serving

policy. They were the words of one on the brink
of the grave, looking back upon the comparative
unprofitableness of human counsel in face of a
nation's destiny; the words of a sense of human
nothingness in face of death; the words of a prophetess before a mighty revolution. She who
uttered them worked on still, although with the
desperation of something like despair, of which
the motto was, " After us the Deluge."

Those who have perverted this saying have beheld in this woman only a King's mistress. They
know her not as one who had walked to the brink
of the grave over thorns.

Her picture hangs upon English palace walls.
Need Morality so fear real life refutes her maxims,
that, while keeping the copy, she should turn
away from the original of that picture?

Some among Englishmen, more merciful than
others, have only regarded the Pompadour as
Artiste. It is true that she excelled in Art, even
as at this time designing another medal on the
union of France and Austria.* But what are the
attributes which adorn or make the artiste? Love,

* It was on receipt of this medal that Maria Theresa addressed a letter of thanks to Madame de Pompadour, beginning familiarly " My dearest sister."

faith, forbearance, quick perception, acute sensi-
bility, harmony, human sympathy.

She was so transcendent as artiste, that some
of her works are " priceless gems " (so confessed
and coveted by her enemies). She possessed, as
we have seen, the social principles of Art, working
in the equality of artistic brotherhood with those
whom she patronized, not only at Sèvres, but in her
own study.

These facts, as recorded by contemporaries,
disprove the envious slander before-mentioned,
that the haughtiness of the Marquise was so great,
that, sitting enthroned in state, she refused to
rise to any, even though the Princes of the blood.
She could not rise, for the hand of death often
pressed heavily upon her.

The autograph letters which have been transcribed bear painful evidence of the state of their
writer.

They are often almost illegible from the sudden
pauses produced by physical pain and anguish. Sad
memorials of their once active, animated, brilliant
writer ! That they ever were written at all is an
honour to woman's fortitude and devotion, and a
tribute to the power that works good out of evil.

The love of the Marquise for the Stuarts

showed her fidelity to misfortune, although, as we have seen, she had suffered much in their cause. The letter (autograph) has been already given where she mentions the Duc de Fitz James. When Fitz James was appointed to Languedoc, he wrote to thank her. In answer she writes : "You mock me, M. le Duc, with your thanks. There was a post vacant which suited you. I spoke of it to the King,—that is all. The service I have rendered gives more pleasure to me than it does to you. Depart then for the army, and be the friend of the Prince de Condé. I fancy that young man will honour his country; his family offers grand examples and he has the wish to imitate them. His talents for war will soon develope themselves. So much the better. . . . In France the race of great men is almost extinct. I hope that you will help to resuscitate it; and I wish with all my heart that Fortune may treat you in a way worthy of you."

But though the Marquise rebuked defection, and inspired devotion, as exemplified in her letters to the Ducs d'Aiguillon and Fitz James, she lived in hope of effecting peace between France and England.

English political intrigue had its share in

English rejection of Bussy's authorized peace proposals.

France, grieved by this rejection, lost no time in ordering fresh battalions, &c., as betrayed to England.* Treachery lurked beneath the palace roof of Versailles.

The King had been roused from the apathy which had become habitual to him, so as to decide him in the expulsion of intolerance. But English money was as fatal to France in war-time as had been Jesuit intolerance. Before the suppression of the Jesuits, the Marquise and the Duc de Choiseul had (as seen by her letter to him) meditated the peace treaty, afterwards known as the "Family Compact."

At first, as she herself says in that letter, England, although fearing, laughed at the rumour of this Bourbon negotiation. But, during the following year, it simply and naturally developed itself, and its result fixed the attention of Europe as a complement of the alliance with Austria (of 1756). A brief notice of this celebrated treaty must here be made, from the authorities conserved —quoting from her present historian—in the archives of France.

* See Appendix, "Secret Notices."

England, as the enemy and, at that time, the conqueror of France, ridiculed this treaty; but, having shown the necessity of France, it would be hard to say by what other means the peace she needed could have been effected.

" Hostilities," says M. Capefigue, " had been begun without cause or pretext by the English upon the sea, and by King Frederic in Germany. France had been obliged to defend herself. She did so by armaments and alliances. The war had been, as all wars, with its chances and reverses ; the alliances were fine and well concerted ; thoroughly understood by Austria, Russia, Sweden, and the German circles. That war of seven years was now crowned by the ' family compact,' one of the great ideas of the 18th century against English preponderance,* and which the latter attacked under all forms."   " The necessity of peace in the year 1763 resulted,—1st,† From the prodigality of English subsidies detaching successively from France, Russia, the German circles, and almost Sweden.

" 2nd.—The opposition of the Parliaments of France, which never permitted votes of money

* L'Histoires des Traités de Paix, M. de Garden.
† Archives. Garden.
20 *

considerable enough to develope the war in the midst of exhausted finances.

"3rd.—The calumnies of disaffected and so-called philosophic subjects, who had yielded to the interests of Frederic of Prussia. The Cabinet of Berlin had a great party in the army, in the Parliament, and in philosophy; through it the alliance of 1756 had been attacked, which only had permitted the sustenance of war against England; from it were cast the most odious calumnies against King Louis XV.; the refugees, encouraged by it, published pamphlets, in which Madame de Pompadour was even accused of carrying off young children, and of preparing famine for the people, and of having sold herself to the Empress of Austria for the flattery of the latter."

(The "Secret Notices" appended to this work, originally sent from France, through Prussia, to England, corroborate the 3rd Article of Peace Necessity. It is to the honour of England's present liberty of the press and liberty of the subject that these "Secret Notices" are transcribed herein for the confirmation of French Chronicles.)

The " Family Compact Treaty " was signed by all the members of the House of Bourbon.

" By this treaty Louis XV. became the head

and centre of an intimate alliance (external) which comprehended France, Spain, Naples, and Parma. The two great navies of France and Spain might thus unite themselves for the realization of a plan on the Indies and in America. From Dunkerque to Naples there were seven hundred leagues of coast. It seemed nearly certain that great material concessions would be forced on France by England, in India and in America; but, in the opinion of M. de Choiseul, these would be nothing if the projects of a young native of Provence were brought into play and realized. This young Provençal was a protégé of Madame de Pompadour, a new star of hope for France.

"His name was ' *Dumouriez.*' He was just 30 years of age, and was already made Chevalier de St Louis. Encouraged by the late Marshal de Belle-isle, he had declared aloud that it was essential to raise India against the English by means of the Mussulman race, the only Eastern one possessed of energy. And that, as for the Colonies of North America, they would emancipate themselves."

With this project upon America and India there was another to assure the preponderance of France upon the Mediterranean. It would appear impos-

sible that in a treaty of definitive peace France
could keep Minorca, ... the Cabinet of Versailles
therefore cast its eyes on the Isle of Corsica, that the
republic of Genoa had ceded in compensation for
the help which France had lent to it. The Isle of
Corsica was agitated by factions, and partly occupied by royal troops, first under the orders of M. de
Chauvelin,* and then of M. de Marbeuf, who belonged to a financial family devoted to the Marquise
de Pompadour. This M. de Marbeuf, in his correspondence with Madame de Pompadour, speaks of
his friendship for a certain brave young gentleman
named Charles de Buonaparte, and recommends,
through her, this young Buonaparte to the care of
the King of France.

At last the Treaty of Peace between France
and England was concluded, with indignation on
the part of the Pompadour at the King of England being titular King of France.† "This Treaty
is a truce." So considering this Treaty (the
work of her heart, head, and hands), the Marquise,
who was dying, every day sinking lower and lower

* The Marquis de Chauvelin, brother of the Parliamentarian Abbé Chauvelin.
† See Appendix.

into the grave, again exclaimed: " After us the Deluge ! "

The treaty was signed on the 23rd of April, 1763.

The Duc de Choiseul was decorated with the "Fleece of Gold," and with the "Order of the Holy Ghost." Madame de Pompadour was undecorated by outward signs of merit or of special favour, but as long as she lived she co-operated with de Choiseul for the aggrandisement of the French Navy and for the organization of Corsica, the cradle of the future French Conqueror. A new energy was needed in the Colonial system of France. France, although nominally at peace, was incensed by her losses in Canada, which she regarded, and still regards (whether rightly or wrongly), as the result of English piracy and of the misuse of English money.

The Count de St Germain denied to General Yorke at the Hague that France was mourning for Canada. The interview between these two politicans is an illustration of how language in diplomacy is used to conceal thought. It is more than probable that Count St Germain was doing business at the same time for Versailles and for

Berlin.* Envoys of France in London, at the
Hague, and at Berlin, were charged to make
an end of and to destroy the Pamphlets that
Prussia had incited and fostered for political purposes. "But this," says France to-day, "increased the commerce of Calmuny. When a refu-
gee was without character or resources, he had
but to make a scandalous book, a pamphlet full of
lies." After England, the greatest enemy of
the Marquise de Pompadour was Frederic of
Prussia. The only woman to whom Frederic was
civil was Catherine of Russia, who he declared
was greater than Semiramis, and who was elected
one of the Academicians of Berlin after having
put her husband into prison.† "When Pamphlets against the enemies of England and
Prussia were made, the authors sometimes offered them for sale to French Ambassadors." If
so bought up for the sake of truth, peace, and
morality, they were suppressed. But if, as was
more likely, they were treated with contempt,
they appeared in all shapes and forms, to the great
hindrance of historical truth and of universal
morality. Some of them were a degradation to

* See Appendix, Holdernesse Dispatches.
† See Appendix, Autographs.

human nature.   "And yet it is from these,"
cries the living historian of France, " that men of
the 19th century, out of France, judge of those
of the 18th century in France. Is this the way to
teach new generations?"

Is this the way to advance the cause of peace,
of progress, and of European prosperity ? Is the
cause of virtue advanced or religion vindicated by
debasing human nature ?

The conflict of party-spirit raises a blinding
dust through the highways and by-ways of last
century France. For example, it has been said
that Rousseau spurned the bounty of the Marquise
de Pompadour, although she first, by her admirable
acting, had brought his celebrated *Devin du Village*
into fashion. We have seen Rousseau at the Opera
the night of his *Devin's début.* The reader may
remember the Royal bounty to the astonished
rustic, who woke up and found himself famous.
Here is the autograph letter from Jean Jacques
Rousseau, dated,

"Paris, 1763, 7th March.

" Madame, in accepting the present which has
been remitted to me from you, I believe to have
testified my respect for the hand from whence it
comes, and I dare to add for the honour that you

have done to my work. Of the two proofs to which you have submitted my modesty, interest is not the more dangerous.

" I am, with respect, your very humble servant,
                                    " J. J. Rousseau." *

Invention need be at no pains to forge insults for the Pompadour. She had griefs enough at the last, of what she calls, in one of her autograph letters already here transcribed, her " *longue et douloureuse maladie.*" She had no home consolation. She knew that even her coadjutor de Choiseul had a sister by whom he desired to supplant her in the King's favour directly she was dead. With de Choiseul's wife she could have little sympathy. What had she, with the shadow of death upon her, to do with that charming little woman who rejoiced in her white spaniel, her black negro, and her African baboon, at whose " small white feet " the young Abbé, author of the " Jeune Anarcharsis," was sighing, and who collected around her all the new school of fashionable *philosophes*, whose puerilities were contemptible to her, the pupil of Montesquieu ? Looking back from the brink of the grave, the Pompadour yearned for old friends, even for Voltaire.

* Bib. Imp.

She entreated the King to permit Voltaire's return to Court.   But upon this point the King
was inexorable, knowing that the philosopher of
Ferney was in correspondence with Frederic of
Prussia.   Voltaire requested a favour of the Marquise at this time, which she gladly granted.* Five
years afterwards Voltaire declined returning to
Paris in answer to Richelieu's persuasions.† But
the Pompadour sealed her peace with Voltaire, her
confidant of 20 years before.

Her destiny was fulfilled, but in a manner
which she had not foreseen. Through sickness,
and much suffering,—through evil repute, ingratitude, and public injustice,—through the death
of her child, the storms of circumstance, the pangs
of conscience, the lonely hours of languor, and
through reconciliation to the faith of the Cross.

Her successful opposition to the Jesuits, however, deprived her at the last of the sympathy of
those who shared her faith, and whose respect she
had previously won, viz. of the Queen and the
Dauphin, who were partisans of the Jesuits. Thus
all her efforts for France and for the King were
agonizingly inverted to pierce her own heart.
Her only hope now was of Heaven, but, having

* Appendix, Letters.   † Ibid.

attained this hope, she beheld the King striving to drown the pangs of his conscience in sin. Alone, conscious of human insufficiency, and looking back upon her life as the baseless fabric of a vision, she saw, with the prophetic inspiration of death, that the Revolution was at hand.

When the people began to bless the "King's Favourite" for peace, liberty, and national prosperity (which glimmered for a time), the "Favourite" was seen by them no more.

So much for the "Destiny" of this woman who had had such faith in herself, the once radiant centre of literature and art, the consummate actress, the brilliant talker, the leader of fashion, the fascination of the King, the boast of French chivalry, the poetess, the musician, the songstress, the splendid Diana of the Hotel de Ville. And what remains of all her gifts? Helplessness, prostration, emaciation : a soul weary of imprisonment, longing for rest, and for the realization of a new hope, a new destiny. Destiny had only cheated her in this world.

She shrank from the light of day, just as the people began to bless and to praise her. They had often, urged by her enemies, insulted her as she had driven down the Boulevards and through the

Champs Elysées, which she had planted, but now, if they could have seen her, to make amends for their injustice, the people would not have known her.

She had long foreseen her fate. One night long before this, when still seemingly well, she had entertained the King at supper, and with him the Prince de Soubise, whom she had urged on to deeds of heroism. After supper she drew de Soubise aside, and placed her will in his hands. The Prince was shocked, but the Marquise was gay; she could see no horror in death, even in the midst of a Royal feast, and she would not allow her friend to sorrow or to wish her long life. The Prince de Soubise told this of her whom he had loved and revered, after she was dead.

The Prince de Soubise was not the only one who never forgot those suppers at which the Marquise, to the last, entertained the King, and those of his court most distinguished by sword and pen. They were the *réunions* of the old and the new chivalries, of courage and of learning. Feasts of reason and flows of soul have been horribly vulgarized since, as France declares, Europe has become a booth of wandering Jews;

but all that the fastidious assume at their tables to-day was originated by the Marquise de Pompadour, whose boast it was to have everything beautiful in nature and in art before her at those suppers, and nothing degrading to human nature beside her. At these hours, which became fewer and more far between as the life of the illustrious hostess waned, the King used to rally, for the moment, from the lethargic apathy that was for ever increasing upon him, and from which others sought to wean him by vice. Observing that Louis was still happily susceptible of good influences, the Marquise strove to inspire the Duc de Choiseul, the talented de Soubise, and a few others, with devotion to their master and with tact in his service, which might survive her.

Her love for music encouraged Glück (the composer who, notwithstanding his genius, had previously failed in England for want of patronage and sympathy) to write his opera of 'Orfeo,' familiar to Paris and London in the present day. Her perception of genius had drawn Pigalle the sculptor from obscurity, to execute her drawing of the King, as Louis appeared when aroused to intellectual consciousness.

Sometimes the mystic Count de St Germain

was admitted ; that " Phenomenon," (as General
Yorke called him,*) who was, by turns, spirit-
ualist, magician, virtuoso, political *employé*, and
who may throw light upon the origin of to-day's
occult pretensions. The common talk of Paris
was that St Germain had given the Duc de
Richelieu the elixir of life, love, and youth, to
drink. We have seen how the gallant Richelieu
submitted to St Germain's treatment of raw veal.

The King was amused by the tales of this
wonderful traveller, whose beginning and whose
end nobody knows ; neither the origin of his
vast fortune. He was supposed to have been the
off-cast of some royal house in the centre of
Europe. Certain it is, he preserved his own
apparent youth to a fabulous period (being seen a
generation afterwards still young). He was the
antetype of mysticism in London and Paris at
the present time. " Sire," said he to Louis XV.,
" to have some esteem for mankind, one must neither be confessor, minister, nor lieutenant of
police."

" Count," replied Louis, " add, nor King."
" Do you know why, Sire ? " answered St Germain, " did your Majesty see the thick fog over Paris

* See Appendix, Holdernesse Secret Dispatches.

yesterday? Very well! the fog that false friends, flatterers, and ministers throw round the King is far more dense than that."

At these suppers, at which the Marquise exerted herself painfully to entertain the King to the last, she beheld, as in the Egyptian feast, the skeleton of her own destiny. The King, and the guests invited to meet him, chosen for their genius, heroism, or wit, could not believe at the last that the hostess would be dead before the flowers upon the table were withered.

Artists, with whom she had been a fellow-worker, conscious of her increasingly fine perception, asked her criticism as a boon to be the more valued as she was gradually withdrawn from the world upon which through her they strove to catch the reflection of another.

Philosophers, for whose liberty of press and speech * she had forced open the doors, were

---

* A curious book (on similes) published in 1757, and dedicated to the Marquise, "Dame de Palais de la Reine," has a preface in which the Publisher (David) ventures to point out to her the fulsomeness of flattery, but at the same time is enthusiastic on the enlightened protection "she accorded to Literature, and on her favourable reception of those who cultivated it." The preface ends with—"I wish to make known to all the world that I owe much to your justice

(though aped by Charlatans) growing in European reputation. In 1762, the Empress of Russia had written to d'Alembert (he who had made the Elegiac Oration on Montesquieu) to come and superintend the education of her son. D'Alembert refused.

" Mons. d'Alembert," wrote the Russian *Legislatrice*, "you refuse to transport yourself here to contribute to the education of my son. Philosopher as you are, I understand that it costs you nothing to despise what are called the honours and grandeurs of this world. . . . I know you too well to attribute your refusal to vanity: I know that the cause is but the love of repose, to cultivate literature and friendship. But what matters it? Come with all your friends. I promise to you, and to them also, all the happiness and ease which may depend on myself. . . . You do not lend yourself to the representations of the King of Prussia, and to the gratitude which you owe to him; but that

and goodness. My voice is too weak to make itself heard, but this book will carry it to all times and places. . . I choose it as a monument that centuries will respect, and upon which will be eternally engraved the public proofs of my gratitude." A presentation copy (in the Author's possession) is endorsed with an autograph satire peculiar to the Pompadour,—" Contraband in England. To—An honest man, although a Scotchman."

Prince has no son. I confess that the education of this son of mine is so near my heart, and you are so necessary to me, that perhaps I press you too strongly. Pardon my indiscretion in favour of the cause, and be assured that it is esteem which has made me so selfish." Signed: " Catherine."

Dated, " Moscow, 13 Nov., 1762."

On the 5th April, 1764, superficial gossip records : " M. Palissot, from his exile of Joinville, has prematurely celebrated the convalescence of Madame la Marquise de Pompadour, thus :

> ' Vous êtes tros chère à la France,
> Aux Dieux des Arts, et des Amours,
> Pour redouter du sort la fatale puissance.' "

On the 13th of April: "Madame de Pompadour has presented to M. de Saverdy, Controller-General, from whom so many wonders are expected, a box enriched with the portrait of Sully . . . . with all the grace of which she is capable. Inside the box were these verses :

> ' De l'habile et sage Sully
> Il ne nous reste que l'image,
> Aujourd'hui ce grand personnage
> Va revivre dans Saverdy.' " *

For three weeks before this the death of the

* Mems. de Bachaumont. Pub. à Londres 1777.

Marquise had been momentarily expected. When she slept, feverishly, for five hours together under opiates, it was recorded as a miracle. She who had helped to build the Military School at her own expense, — she who had sacrificed her wealth to the public weal, was tormented upon her death-bed by private pecuniary anxiety. " Who would have thought," taunts one of her enemies, " that the Favourite at her death would have left but 30 Louis-d'or in her writing table?" And for these she was indebted to the love of her faithful servant, Collin.

Her sense of harmony and of form growing keener and rarer the more she suffered, the Marquise must have felt more than the usual anguish of woman in seeing herself deprived, by her insidious malady, of outward beauty.* A woman soothed by domestic love, could never incur the agony of this one who had been a King's mistress, and who had buried her husband's child. With perception exquisitely sharpened by suffering,

---

* She was outraged by the foul pasquinades and gross carica-
tures which in every country find popular favour; irreverent
publications, full of the marvellous, for the morbid delectation
of those whose social position removed them far from the
Court. Was it for this the Marquise had toiled for liberty
of press and of speech?

with an organization rendered morbidly sensitive
by disease, and by the consciousness of her peculiar
position, the Marquise, at a time when other women are in the pride of life,—honoured wives
and mothers,—was a martyr to the destiny she
had craved.   At Versailles she lay dying ;—Versailles, which she had adorned by everything
beautiful in art and nature ; — Versailles, where
she had played at tragedy in festival time with
the laurel-crowned King, the idol of his people,
in the days when Voltaire wrote plays at her
command ;—Versailles, where she had guided
the fate of Europe.

She knew that she had become a necessary
appendage to the King's Council, but that was
cold consolation to the heart that still beat quick
with human sympathies, and to the soul which,
as eternity dawned, felt the insufficiency, the
instability, of all worldly things,—peace—politics
—philosophy.

The Marquise never complained to the King.
She had long feared to disenchant him by the
wearisome sight of her suffering. With her, to
the last, " the King talks."   But she felt the
coming storm, and, in the physical depression of
death, she had not strength to foresee that her

works would survive the century, over which hung the dense cloud of corruption accumulated by former ages.

New combinations are only old ones remodelled, having survived, like the Pompadour's plans for the public buildings of Paris, the chaos of the Revolution.

" The Deluge " she prophesied came — in blood. This woman's life is a type of her time, showing the evil of the old things, which called for vengeance, and the yearning for something better.

On the 15th of April, 1764, the Marquise de Pompadour sent for the Curé of the Madeleine (the Magdalene), because she knew she could not live through the day. The Curé went to her, and received her last confession, and administered unto her the consolations of her religion.*

For a short time he remained by the side of the dying woman—he, the appointed minister to the Magdalene,—and then, believing that she

* It was at Choisy, three weeks before, when she had risen from her bed to receive the King at a Fête, that the Marquise found herself vanquished by death. During the last few days she had, by her own wish, been removed to Versailles ; Choisy was unendurable as the scene of her early life. At Versailles she was with the King to the end.

21 *

slept, he was about to pass noiselessly from the chamber. He was startled by a voice, and still more by the words : " Wait, let us go together."

A few minutes afterwards, and nothing remained of the once brilliant and life-loving Marquise de Pompadour but an emaciated corpse.

Before her death, she, the " King's favourite," had caused herself to be dressed according to the third order of the Capuchines, in coarse serge, with the chaplet of St François round her waist, and a cross of wood upon her breast. She was carried to the grave, according to her wish, by the Capuchin Brothers (a pauper burial), and laid in the tomb she had chosen for herself, by the side of her daughter, in the Convent Church of the Place Vendôme. She was 42 years old when she died. The King had shown extreme grief when told she was dying, although he strove to disbelieve the fact as impossible. When she was dead, his melancholy became morose. From a high balcony at Versailles the King saw the pauper funeral of the woman he had loved pass through the palace gates. He did not shed a tear. He often had talked to her of death even in the midst of fêtes, and now he seemed to say, " Behold the Destiny of us all."

Two days before, on the 13th of April,* she had with much difficulty dictated a codicil to her Will. Here are the Will and the Codicil. (The former, it will be remembered, she had given into the keeping of the Prince de Soubise years before at one of the gay suppers at Choisy.)

" In the name of the Father, of the Son, and of the Holy Ghost ; I Jeanne Poisson, Marquise de Pompadour, wife (*séparée de biens*) of Charles Lenormand d'Etioles, have made and written this, my Will. . . .

" I recommend my soul to God, and pray Him to have pity on me, and to pardon my sins, hoping to appease His Justice by the merits of the Body and Blood of Our Lord.

" I desire that my body be interred at the Capuchines of the Place Vendôme in Paris, in the tomb I have chosen for myself, and that this burial be made without pomp, and without ceremony.

" I supplicate the King to accept the gift that I make to him of my hôtel in Paris : I would desire that he bestow it on M. le Comte de

* The very day on which she had sent her present and verses to the Finance Controller. (p. 322.)

Provence.* I also pray his Majesty to accept my stones engraven by Leguay, seven bracelets, rings, and seals, to augment his Cabinet of fine engraven stones. I constitute as my heir universal, my brother the Marquis de Marigny.

"I name for my testamentary executor, the Prince de Soubise; however afflicting to him may be this commission, he ought to regard it as a certain proof of the confidence with which his honesty inspires me: for himself, I beg him to accept two rings, the one containing a large diamond, colour Marine, the other an emerald engraven by Leguay representing Friendship; I dare to hope he will not part with this; it will recall to him the person who in the world has had for him the most profound esteem, and the most lively friendship."

" Done at Choisy, 17th November, 1757."

" Codicil:

" My wish is to give to the persons named beneath the following, to make them remember me, I who have loved them:

" To Madame de Roure, the portrait of my

* The Count de Provence, the second son of the Dauphin, a serious, studious child.

poor dead daughter, and a box with the portrait of the King. To Madame de Mirepoix, my watch ornamented with diamonds, and a box with a portrait of the King. To Madame de Grammont, a box with a diamond butterfly.* To M. de Choiseul a diamond ring. To M. de Soubise, a ring engraved with Friendship; for the 20 years I have known him, it has been his portrait and mine.

"This codicil I cause to be written by M. Collin, having only the strength to sign it. April 13, 1764."

The most valuable property left by the Marquise was her library, so that a female court scoffer declared that, after all, the Favourite had only left "Moveables." The day after her death, Collin (Maitre d'hôtel) legally certified the last verbally expressed testamentary wishes of the Marquise, which were executed in favour of the Poor.

In 1764, after her death, the Brothers Herissant, printers for the King's Cabinet, published a volume under the title of:

* Madame de Grammont, sister of de Choiseul, was intended by him to succeed Madame de Pompadour. The legacy of the Diamond Butterfly (Hope, brilliant but volatile) was therefore as eloquent as the Friendship, bequeathed to de Soubise (Love without Wings), engraved on an emerald, emblematic of eternal constancy.

" Catalogue of Library Books, belonging to the late Madame, Marquise de Pompadour, Lady of the Queen's Palace."

Amongst these, Theology and Philosophy hold the largest number. " Scholastics, Polemics, and Mysticism, are placed by the side of Metaphysics." As her political position became more important and defined, the Marquise had added volume upon volume concerning the great questions of her day, of which questions those now agitating Europe are the echo.

The sale of Madame de Pompadour's library lasted six months. It was so rich in MSS. that the sale realized more than £40,000 sterling. One of the most precious articles in this sale was a small volume of sixty-three pages engraved by her during her later years of sorrow. A few copies were taken from this volume, and were presented as mementos to those who had esteemed the *artiste*. The MSS. not gathered into the royal library, but carried off to Holland and elsewhere, incurred sad risks of being tampered with, so as to suit the tastes of the times. The problems of Madame de Pompadour's day were not solved by the Revolution which closed the last century. The works of Madame de Pompadour's hands

form a history engraved on stones, of her own life,
and of France in her time. Amongst these works
is her design for the statue of Louis XV.* It has
been seen how Pigalle, the sculptor,—whom the
Marquise had raised from obscurity,—worked for
twenty years upon the statue of Marshal Saxe, without impressing the marble with aught but the me-
chanical perfection of Art. This marble coldness
was attributed to the late Marshal's want of Faith.
The statue of Louis XV., designed by Love, was
Pigalle's *chef d'œuvre*. It was an equestrian statue.
When it was set up in the Place Louis XV.,† and
uncovered to public view, the loyalty of the people,
which had waned so long, was re-kindled at the
sight of it. . . . Again they saw their " Well Beloved" as they had seen him twenty years before,
when he rode forth through the midst of them to
the war, in which he gave France glory. Again
he seemed to turn towards them, and smile. And
again the people rent the air with acclamations,
and cried " God bless the King." . . . The banners of France now hung, drooping, in the
Military Hospital hard by. The Church of the
Magdalene was rising from the ground. When

* Appendix Z. † 1765.

artists passed that statue of King Louis XV.
they saluted it.   The people's discontent was hush-
ed at sight of it.   Upon the base of that statue,
Revolutionary fury, at last let loose, wrote, in
characters of blood, its own satire :

> " Grotesque monument—Infâme piédestal
>   Les Vertus sont à pied, le Vice est à cheval."

APPENDIX

TO VOL. II.

Autograph Letters from Madame de Pompadour to her brother, the Marquis de Marigny, addressed to him in Italy.

The following Autograph letters from his sister to the Marquis de Marigny when in Italy have survived the Revolution which destroyed so many works in which they were mutually engaged for the glory and embellishment of France. The first * is endorsed by Marigny,

" Received at Rome the 31st March."

" If the letter which I had addressed to the postmaster of France at Turin did not reach you, my dear brother, it is but a small loss. The '*Infanta*' † has so many reasons for

---

* *Lettre Autographe de Madame de Pompadour. Collection of the late M. le Comte de Panisse.*

† The wife of Don Philip (son of Elizabeth Farinese) and the favourite daughter of Louis XV., King of France.

loving the King that I am not astonished at the eagerness
which she testified to hear tidings of him. It is difficult to
find a father so *unique* upon all points. . . . . . I have suffered in my head considerably; to-day my cold is better, and
I have been to the hermitage. Nevertheless you will hear
from Paris that I spit blood; that is as true as often as it
has been told. Madame la Dauphine is *enceinte ;* you may
judge of my joy. Good-night *cher bonhomme.* I embrace
you with all my heart."

Second Letter from Madame de Pompadour to her brother
the Marquis de Marigny, endorsed,

" Received the 6th of June 1750, *at Turin. "*

"My picture has surely reached you, my dear brother;
so there can be no more impatience but for that of the
King. I know not if you have given orders to the Sieur
Verney for the two that I ask of him. *

"The relation of Madame du Haussey† may by chance be
a man of merit, but there are few who can lay claim to that
distinction. . . Mons. de St Germain‡ has told me that Lefort
would arrive at Turin the 2nd or 3rd of June; thus, you

---

* Verncy, or Vernet, who afterwards became celebrated under
the patronage of Madame de Pompadour for his well-known sea
paintings, which he dedicated to the Marquis de Marigny.

† Madame d'Hausset, femme de chambre to Madame de Pompadour, whose MS., although bequeathed to M. de Meilhan, a friend
of the Marquis de Marigny, afterwards ran revolutionary risk of
being tampered with.

‡ Mystic diplomatist and picture collector, to be met with again
at the Hague, and elsewhere, in this volume.

ought to be upon the march. I hope that you will continue to do as well at that court as upon the first occasion. Present my compliments to my Lord 'Lismore.' I ought to go to-morrow to Crecy, but I have declined the journey, suffering in the country with sore throats like those I had a year ago in Paris. I am too much attached to the King to permit him to suffer from the slightest personal anxiety. I had wished to pass 24 hours there. His Majesty would not allow me to do so. Good-night, dear brother; the portrait of Van-loo" (of the King) "is not finished. He has had the scarlatina at his house. M. de T." (Tourneheim de Normant) "has not dared to see him to give his opinion."

Autograph Letters from Madame la Marquise de Pompa-dour to Madame la Comtesse de Lutzelbourg.*

(Some of them published, by permission, in "*Mélanges des Bibliophiles*, and in '*l'Isographie*' Fac simile.")

The following translations may be acceptable as an Auto-biographical commentary on the life of Madame de Pompadour and as a *résumé* of ten years in the narrative of this work.

In reading these letters it must be remembered, that the Dauphin and his party—political and ecclesiastical,—were at one time during these ten years fiercely opposed (as recorded in the narrative) to the Marquise.

* Madame de Lutzelbourg was a friend of Voltaire. Voltaire, lamenting his Prussian treachery, when too late, entreated Ma-dame de Lutzelbourg to procure for him a portrait of Madame de Pompadour. "Grande Femme" was the sobriquet by which the Mar-quise addressed the Countess.

" 27 Feby, 1749.

"I have been afflicted by the *fausse couche* of Madame la Dauphine,* but I hope that this misfortune will soon be found not to be irreparable. The King is wonderfully well, thanks to Heaven, and I am also. You believe that we no longer travel, but you are mistaken, we are always upon the road. Choisy, La Muette,—little château and sure hermitage near the gate of the Dragon at Versailles,—where I pass the half of my life. It is 48 feet in length by five in breadth ; judge of its beauty ! But I am alone there with the King and with but few people, so I am happy there. The world will have sent you word that it is a palace like Meudon,† which will have nine casement windows by seven. But it is the fashion just now in Paris to talk nonsense (*déraisonner*), and that upon every subject.

"Good-night, my *très grande femme,* I will prepare a room for you at Meudon, and I wish that you may promise me to come there."

"*23rd March." (Not dated as to place, probably Versailles.)*

"I hope, and I flatter myself strongly, *grande femme,* that my silence has made no impression upon you ; in any case, if it did, you would be in the wrong. The life that I lead here is terrible. Scarcely have I a minute to myself. Rehearsals and representations twice a week ; continual journeys to the

* In January, 1749. The second disappointment of the King in his hopes of a grandson.

† The little château occupied by the King, when engaged on the plans for the Sèvres work palace, and afterwards occupied by the Dauphin and his family.

little château and to La Muette, etc. Duties considerable and indispensable. Queen, Dauphin, and Dauphiness happily reposing upon their *chaises longues;* three girls (two infants); and judge if it be possible for me to breathe; pity me, and accuse me not."*

.... 1750.

" What you have been told of me is absolutely false.† I

* Nothing could be more lugubrious than the life led by the Queen, the Dauphin, and the Dauphiness. "The most innocent pleasures are not made for me," had long ago said the Queen, as reported by Marshal de Richelieu.—The *Mercure de France* of *August*, 1738, to this purport declares: "The rule of her Majesty's life and the employment of her days becomes more severe and more austere. Secluded, far from noise, far from commotion, she only sallies forth for state occasions, for purposes of charity, or for visits to the community of the Child Jesus, where are embroidered for her in gold, annually, in the fashion of Persia, robes of muslin which she likes to wear." "The mornings of her Majesty are passed in prayer or moral readings (*lectures morales*) ; mass ; after mass, dinner; after dinner, embroidery-needlework for the poor ; no music ; history is read until supper-time. After supper-hours her greatest delight is, in her own words, ' To be opposite to Madame de Luynes at the side of the table in the delicious elbow-chair, used by Madame de Luynes.' " Cardinal de Luynes was of this party, and a few other devotees. The Court ladies had permission to go and to amuse themselves at this hour in the little apartments. The Queen's party was somewhat somnolent. In the " *Mémoires of the Duc de Luynes* " it is said that the old dog of the Duchesse de Luynes grew fat by his uninterrupted sleep every evening in the Queen's presence, until the voice of the Cardinal proclaimed, with a thundering noise (*Tintamarre*), " The Chapter."—" *Qu'on assemble le Chapitre.*"

† Concerning her extravagance in fitting up *Bellevue*, which would prevent her paying her debts. See Narrative, Vol. ii. p. 81.

will cause you to be re-imbursed forthwith. I have all the furniture which is necessary for me at Bellevue, therefore I have no longer any need of Persian stuff (*Perse*). Embracing you, *grande femme*, I thank you with all my heart."

"3rd January, 1751.

". . . . You judge rightly that I have been enchanted to receive the King at Bellevue. * His Majesty has made three journeys there; he must be there again the 25th of this month. It is a delicious place to the sight. The house, although not very large, is commodious and charming, without any sort of magnificence. We shall play some comedies there. The shows (*spectacles*) of Versailles have not yet re-commenced. The King wishes to diminish his expenditure *dans toutes les parties*; † although that expenditure may not be considerable, the public believing that it is so, I have wished to be tender of its opinion, and to set the example. I desire that others may think the same. I believe you to be well content with the Edict that the King has given to ennoble military men.

"You will be still more so by that which is about to appear for the establishment of five hundred gentlemen, whom His Majesty will caused to be trained in Military Art.‡ This Royal School will be built near the Hospital of the Invalides.§

* See Narrative, Vol. ii. pp. 22, 23.

† The reader may remember that a popular cry had once arisen that the gaieties Madame de Pompadour inaugurated at Court were ruinous to the State.

‡ It is observable here that the Marquise, who was paying the workmen herself, and who had inaugurated this plan entirely upon her own responsibility (see APPENDIX TO VOL. I.), gives all the glory of it to the King.

§ See Narrative, Vol. i. p. 302.

This Institution is so much the finer because His Majesty has worked at it for one year, and because his ministers have taken no part in it, and knew nothing of it until it was all arranged according to his fancy, which was at the end of the Fontainebleau journey. I will send the Edict to you as soon as it is printed.

"That which you desire for your son does not appear to me possible. I have consulted experienced folks, who have told me that the officers of the Guards would regard it as if I had committed a robbery upon them; likewise that the 12,000 livres of augmentation would be certainly taken away; and indeed, 2000 livres would do no great good to your son, though they would do much to a Lifeguard. Seek some other thing which I may be able to obtain for your son; I will carry into the attempt to oblige you all the friendship which you know that I have for you."

"April, 1751.

"It is true, *grande femme*, that it is a long time since I have written to you. We were always in motion before Lent, and since then, laziness has overtaken me. Give me credit in overcoming it for you. I doubt not that you have been very pleased with Madame de Chevreuse.* She is a very good woman, and one of my friends since I have been the fashion.† The death of poor Madame de Mailly ‡ has caused grief to the King; I am sorry for her also; I have always

* The Duchesse de Chevreuse, one of the Queen's ladies, and one of the party in the apartments of the Duchesse de Luynes.

† Or, possibly, since all scandal had ceased in Madame de Pompadour's position at Court.

‡ The King's Mistress (before the Duchesse de Chateauroux, her sister), long a recluse and a penitent.

pitied her. She was unhappy.... Do not send to me the
Funeral Oration of Marshal Saxe. I cannot think of his
death without grief."

———

" September, 1751.*

" You may judge of my joy, *grande femme,* by my attachment for the King. I was so overwhelmed that I fainted in
the Ante-chamber of Madame la Duchesse. Happily, they
thrust me behind a curtain, so that I had no witnesses but
Madame de Villars and Madame d'Estrades.† Madame la
Dauphine is wonderfully well: M. le Duc de Bourgogne also;
I saw him yesterday, he has the eyes of his grandfather,
ce n'est pas maladroit à lui. I go on Monday to Crecy for
five days, then to Fontainebleau. I give a fête to the King. I
marry young girls in my villages. They come the next day to
eat and to drink in the court-yard of the Château. Those whom
the King has ordained in Paris are worthy of his goodness,
but in the provinces they will be still more so. Good-night,
grande femme. It is a long night to be eternally upon the high
roads, as we are here. At Choisy, 29th September, 1751."‡

* Upon the birth of the Dauphin's son, the Duc de Bourgogne.
See Narrative, Vol. i. pp. 298, 299.

† Dame de Compagnie to Madame de Pompadour. In league
with the Ex-Minister d'Argenson against her patroness, whom
d'Argenson wanted to displace in the King's favour, by a mistress
of his own. D'Estrades was eventually found guilty of a felony
in abstracting a State Paper from Madame de Pompadour, and
was therefore banished from the Court by a *Lettre de Cachet.* See
Note " *Ministerial Enchainement, &c.*"

‡ The close of this letter seems to show that marrying
young girls did not raise the spirits of the Marquise. Again
it is seen she gives the credit to the King for one of her best in-
spirations (see Narrative, p. 299, Vol. i.). In the schedule of Madame

"5th November, 1751.

" I feel but too keenly the misfortune of having a sensitive soul; my health has been deranged by the death of Madame de Tourneheim.*

" I am a little better since the last four days . La Sauvé " (nurse to the Duc de Bourgogne) "has been nothing but a madwoman in putting a 'frightful packet' in the bed of M. le Duc de Bourgogne; she thought that in pretending to save his life her fortune and that of her family would be made. Observe, there was nothing in the packet but what would burn the sheet, ... her pretended poisoning was *en suite ;* what she took and vomited was proved by the tin plate behind a looking-glass. She is in the Bastille, where she will remain until she will tell her motives ; but there has been no anxiety for the prince; he is charmingly well. We are so often upon the road, that I have not been to the chase for three years." (Madame de Pompadour, surrounded by enemies, here shows a feminine doubt of the sincerity and sympathy of even her "*grande femme,*" by concealing the fact of her ill-health, which did not allow her to take unnecessary exercise) "I have not been to the chase for three years. It is well to give one's self time for thought. Goodnight, *grande femme,* I love you very truly."

1756. (*See Narrative,* Vol. ii.)

To the Countess de Lutzelbourg. (Friend of Voltaire).

" What — Whom — do you call the ' Solomon of the

de Pompadour's expenditure (by Leroy) is this entry, " Madame de Pompadour has made upon the two occasions of the births of princes 42 marriages. She has endowed husbands and wives at the rate of 300 livres and 200 livres for clothes."

* A relation to her husband, and a friend of her youth.

North,' *grande femme?* Say, The Tyrant. . . . . I mortally abhor your Lutherans for loving the King of Prussia, and were I at Strasbourg I would fight all day." *

(*See Narrative*, Vol. ii. Chapter 7.)

"28 November, 1757.

"M . . . . is no longer unhappy, my poor Countess, but in retaliation, M. de Soubise is so to the last degree. You know my friendship for him; judge of my grief, by the enormous injustice which they have done to him in Paris; as to his army, he is beloved and admired by that as he deserves to be. Madame la Dauphine is in the greatest affliction for the death of her mother.† She is one of the Victims of the King of Prussia. Why does Providence leave to him the power of making so many miserable? I am in despair. Good-night, *ma grande comtesse;* I wish not to talk to you longer of the griefs which you share by the friendship that you have for me, and which I reciprocate."

---

* The Prussian ambassador, Baron Kniphausen (says Valory, French Ambassador at Berlin), is the only one who, by command of his master, does not see Madame Pompadour, while the Empress Queen writes her the most flattering letters.

Mitchell, British Plenipotentiary at Berlin, further relates : " In 1754, a proposal was made to the King of Prussia to yield the principality of Neufchâtel to Madame Pompadour for life, she to be created a Princess and to have the revenues, and the King to receive in lieu of them a gratification from France equal to them. This he rejected with disdain, and it is perhaps one reason of her hatred to him."

† Wife of King Augustus, Elector of Saxony. See Narrative, Vol. ii. Chapter 7.

1758. *

" I have received your letters, *grande femme*, and those of
your son; they have given me great pleasure, I seek a half
(*moitié*) for him, and I wish well that the winter may not pass
away without my putting him into housekeeping. I thank
you for your stuffs; I am under reform, and of a sobriety
which surprises me myself. I have sold my knot of diamonds
to pay some debts. Is not that grand? You will say I am like
Cicero, who did not need others to proclaim his own praise.
I tell you, nevertheless, frankly, that I merit no praise, for
this sacrifice has cost me little. Good-night '*grande*.' I embrace you with all my heart."

" 6th May, 1759.

"The useful arrangement which has just been made for
the service of the King,† *grande femme*, deprives your son of
a decent revenue, but His Majesty gratuitously permits him
to await other favours, which is a very flattering mark of
goodness. The Marshal (Richelieu) cannot do what you
desire for your nephew. Concerning the waters," (probably
those prescribed as the 'golden elixir of life' by the Count
St Germain to de Richelieu himself,) "the Marshal has
assured me that you should have them, without their costing
you anything. . . . The battle has given me great pleasure.‡
M. de Soubise had arranged his quarters, and had chosen so

---

* *War-time. Personal sacrifices.* See Chapter 7, Vol. ii.

† Silhouette's system of suspending Court sinecures pro tem.
Vol. ii. Chapter 6, p. 267.

‡ The battle of Berghen, where the Duc de Broglie triumphed over
the Hanoverians. Letter of the Duc de Broglie. Vol. ii. Chap. 7, p. 301.

fine a battle-field at Berghen, that we could not be beaten. My only regret is that he " (de Soubise) " was not there, and that the King had retained him near his person. Torment not yourself concerning the journey to Lyon.* There is no risk for me. If the confidence with which the King honours me were unsheltered by a fortnight's absence, such confidence would be very badly placed, and I could not be flattered by it. I shall go during that time to rest in *my stable of Saint Ouen* (into retreat). You will not have that portrait for some time " (of the King), " Vanloo decorates it for the Salon of Saint Louis, and that is not a small matter. Good-night, *grande femme*. I embrace you with all my heart."

TWO AUTOGRAPH LETTERS OF LOUIS XV.†

" A Mademoiselle de Roman, Grande rue de Passy, à Passy. Dated,
" At Versailles, this 8 December, 1761.

" I saw very well, *ma grande*, that you had something in your head when you departed from hence, but I did not exactly guess what it could be. I do not wish that our child be registered under my name in his church register, but I wish none the less to be able to identify him in the course of years, if such be my pleasure. I wish then that

------

* A King's journey, concerning which the *grande femme* had tried to incite jealousy on the part of the Pompadour, for which the *grande femme* may be forgiven when it called forth the response of the Pompadour above recorded.

† The first was in the collection of the late M. de Panisse. The second in that of M. Chamboury. Quoted by MM. Goncourt, as also the foregoing.

he may be entered '*Louis Aimé*' or '*Louise Aimée ;*' son or daughter of Louis the King or of *Louis Bourbon*, as you will; provided there may be no (*blame*) upon your side, you may put there what you will. I wish also that the Godfather and the Godmother be from the poor, or from domestics, excluding all others. . . . "

Second Letter.

" At Versailles, the 13th January, 1762,

At five o'clock of the evening.

" On my arrival here, I was apprized of your happy deliverance. I did not expect it so soon, it will be necessary to perform the baptism late this evening or to-morrow early in the morning. You will tell to the Curé, under the secret of confession, to whom this child belongs; he is never to speak of it, and never to show, nor to give certificate of this baptism but by my consent—if that be possible to him, as I believe it to be; the Godfather and the Godmother, two domestics, of whose secresy you are certain; the name *Louis Aimé*, son of Louis de Bourbon, and your name *Dame de Meilly Coulonge*.

" Louis."

The son of Mademoiselle de Romans was baptized under the name of Bourbon, "son of Charles de Bourbon, Captain of Cavalry."

If Louis XV. had then been so familiar with such events as revolutionary records declare him to be, would he have been so scrupulous in baptismal directions, or have so much feared notoriety in this instance ?

French Finance and Philosophy.

To say nothing here of Paris Duverney, the friend of Madame de Pompadour in her childhood, who provided largely for the exigences of war, there was M. Silhouette, Financier, who showed, as did many a French Crœsus in the last century, that the gain of gold by no means necessitates the old gold-fable's pair of ass's ears ; nor restricts the man who has it to the exclusive worship of the molten calf. Silhouette was the friend of Helvetius, who was consulted by Montesquieu on his " Spirit of Laws " in MS. Helvetius, however, having his own " Spirit of Man" in foolscap, did not duly appreciate Montesquieu's " Spirit of Laws ; " Helvetius even advised Montesquieu to burn his " Spirit of Laws," but Montesquieu took his MS. in his hand, and said, " *Protem fine Matre Creatam*," and forthwith sent it to the Geneva press, (the self-confidence of genius he praised!) Helvetius[*] brought forth his " *de l' Esprit*," and it was condemned to be destroyed with his other books as blasphemous. Helvetius retracted, but after Madame de Pompadour's death he sheltered himself and his book with Frederic of Prussia.[†] Montesquieu had dedicated one edition

[*] Helvetius the Philosopher was the son of the late King's physician, also an author ; Dr de Quesnay introduced Helvetius the younger to Madame de Pompadour. Helvetius was more welcome to the King of France than was Diderot.

[†] " Religious toleration and the liberty of the press were greater in Prussia than in most of the European States, but by no means unlimited," as Lessing has justly observed. " In particular, public censures on measures of the government would not have been tolerated, so much as attacks on opinions relative to the church and to religion," (observes the English translator of Von Raumer) . . . . " The manner in which the dogmas of Protestantism had been forced upon Frederic in his youth, and what he had seen of Catholic intolerance, for instance, in France, could not satisfy Frederic's mind, nor

of his "Spirit of Laws" to Madame de Pompadour. Helvetius, it is said, wished to place his "Spirit of Man" under the Pompadour's protection.* But, though Helvetius was the friend of Silhouette, Court and Cabinet finance-finder, the Pompadour wisely passed on his "*de l'Esprit*" to the Duc de Choiseul, and thus evaded the encouragement of Helvetius, the author's, materialism, or the discouragement of Helvetius the financier's money.

As financiers thus made themselves doubly felt in France in the 18th Century, it may not be uninteresting to peep into the coffers of some of these men of metal :

Helvetius, Financier and Philosopher ..	10,000,000
Popelinière (whose wife the Duc de Richelieu had scandalized)	15,000,000
Lenormand d'Etioles (husband of the Marquise de Pompadour) and his uncle de Turneheim	30,000,000

---

was genuine Christianity manifested in either. Concerning Diderot Frederic said : 'There is in the works of Diderot a tone of self-sufficiency and of arrogance, which offends our sense of liberty.'". . . . . .

Again, "I am persuaded that a fanatic philosopher is the greatest of all possible monsters." (*Œuvres*, Posth., Vol. ix.) In speaking of religion, Frederic said ; "The law ought never to be confounded with the abuse. If I defend the moral doctrines of Christ, I defend that of all philosophers, and I give up to you the dogmas which are no part of it. . . . . When people exclaim against this religion, they ought to point out the time of which they speak, and distinguish the abuses from the institution."

* In 1758, Helvetius published his "*de l'Esprit*" in 4to, anonymously, with this motto :

> . . . . " Unde animi constet natura videndum
> Quà fiant ratione, et quà vi quæque gerantur
> In terris . . . . "

> *Lucret. de Rer Naturà*, lib. 1.

Delaporte (*chargé du Syndicat des Fermes*)   15,000,000
Savalette (guard of the royal treasure)   ..   10,000,000
Bourret (at one time supplier of corn)   ..   30,000,000*

With fourteen others of average revenue, holding posts of no
interest to the English reader.   It has been illogically urged
against Madame de Pompadour, "In her passion for buildings
and for acquisitions of every sort, the favourite had expended
much beyond her revenues and the *bénéfices de sa place*. At
every moment she was obliged to resort to expedients, though
nothing corrected her of acquisition and of labouring to
possess more. The pension that the King gave to her in 1746,
that pension of 2400 livres a month, which the King scarcely
reckoned in the first moment of passion, in the generosity
with which he overwhelmed his mistress, regulated itself
with the habit of the tie, and did not exceed 4000 livres
a month.   Also the gifts of the King, which, in 1747,
amounted to 50,000 livres, soon diminished to 20,000 livres ;
and in 1750, they ceased entirely."†

(The very year, be it observed, when she undertook to

---

* The English reader must remember to calculate most of these
French Financial quotations by Francs, although money in France
was, in the reign of Louis XV., sometimes reckoned by *écus* (4s.).
When the original extracts ('*Relevés*') are undecided, as in the
above case, by French writers, the English reader is requested to
judge for himself upon this subject.

"The farmers-general, taking borrowings to their account, made
all necessary anticipations at 4 or 5 per cent. interests, with the
certainty of a receipt of Taxes which would cover their advances."

† Lotteries were the custom of the time. Funds were raised by
Lottery before Madame de Pompadour's time, even for the building
of churches, as now such funds are raised by Fancy Fairs, Fancy
Balls, &c., the end justifying, as is supposed, the means, but for
these, as for all other evils of her day, the Pompadour is reviled by
her enemies.

defray the cost of building the Military School.   See Appendix to Vol. I.)

From this it appears that the soul of Madame de Pompadour (if it will be allowed that she had one) struggled for liberty—liberty of faith—in proportion as her health of body decreased, and as her pecuniary means became precarious. But to the materialist, Helvetius, sceptical amidst a heap of gold, is applicable the following saying of Voltaire addressed to the Marquis d'Argeus : *

"My dear Friend,—When at night, crowned with flowers, you are seated at the feet of your Mistress with a glass of *Aï* in your hand, you believe not in God, what care I ?   But if at night I met you, famished, believing not in God, and with a gun in your hand, I should not have legs fast enough to fly from you."

It is strange that Voltaire, who thus rebuked d'Argeus, prime favourite of the Protestant hero, should be traditionally loathed in England as the incarnation of unbelief, by those who are the first to clamour against the abuses of that Church at the temporal assumption of which Voltaire's satire was aimed.

Ministerial Enchainement and Intrigue.
The Duc de Mirepoix.   The Count de St Séverin d'Arragon. The Cardinal de Bernis.   The Duc de Choiseul.   The Duc d'Aiguillon.   The brothers d'Argenson.   Madame d' Estrades.

----

* The Marquis d'Argeus, " the most impious of all philosophers," who had become Chamberlain to Frederic of Prussia ; and was appointed by him, Director-General of Belles Lettres at the Berlin Academy.

Original Letters de Cachet.   Taxation and retrenchment.   Expenditure of Madame de Pompadour.

" Monsieur de Mirepoix," it was said, " is neither supple nor affable enough for the English. Moreover, he has a great defect for an Ambassador; he is too honest. M. de Mirepoix has passed his youth in pleasure and his manhood in war. The art of negotiation is neither learned at the theatre nor in battles."

Foreign affairs at Versailles had ceased to be really in the hands of M. de Puysieux, "whom the King called an honest man,† since the Cabinet within the Cabinet," under the advice of Dutheil the King's private Counsellor, had influenced the treaty of Aix-la-Chapelle. When M. de Puysieux found that the Ambassadorial correspondence arrived direct to the "*Secrétariat*" of Versailles without intermediary assistance, he resigned, and was succeeded by the Count de St Séverin d'Arragon, "whose common sense supplied his want of genius, and who submitted himself to that subordinate position of a title without functions." St Séverin d'Arragon's common sense was useful to the French Cabinet of " Ideas," although French vivacity was rendered sometimes impatient by the geometrical exactness by which St Séverin curbed all impulse. " Anger, passion, party-spirit, and small preventive minutiæ were unknown to him." He called all that (*tout cela*) "the reverse of the medal plenipotentiary." M. Dutheil had been offered the official department, but he replied, " I shall be more useful as I am ; while serious affairs definitively pass through my hands, to

† See Appendix, Vol. I. " Original Narrative, between the Maritime Powers."

what use a title?" It was afterwards that the Portfolio was confided to the Abbé de Bernis.

The Duc de Choiseul (Stainville) once envoy to Rome, and afterwards the favoured Ambassador at Vienna, the friend of philosophy and the advocate of the Austrian Alliance, received the Portfolio from de Bernis, when de Bernis was made Cardinal. Subsequently de Choiseul transferred the Portfolio, nominally, to his cousin (Praslin Choiseul), whilst he retained the Ministry of War, which necessarily included the supervision of Foreign affairs.*

The death of the Duchess of Parma, in 1759, after de Bernis had the Cardinal's hat given to him in exchange for his portfolio, was another blow to the Choiseul Ministry, as she had been one of the Intermediaries of the Austrian Alliance, which it was now to the interest of Versailles to maintain and to strengthen at all costs. The Duc d'Aiguillon was fiercely opposed to the Duc de Choiseul, on the grounds of political enmity and of ecclesiastical party-spirit.

The scandalous chronicle is notorious that the Duc de Choiseul (Stainville) originally ingratiated himself into the favour of Madame de Pompadour by handing over to her a letter which had been intrusted to him by his cousin,

---

* FAMILY OF DE CHOISEUL IN THE MINISTRY.

"César Gabriel, Count de Choiseul, born in Paris, the 15th August, 1712, replaced, in 1758, his cousin the Duc de Choiseul Stainville at Vienna; he the Duke being then called to the ministry of Foreign Affairs in the place of Cardinal de Bernis. When the Maréchal de Belleisle, minister of war, died in January, 1761, the Duc de Choiseul reserved to himself this ministry with that of the Marine, and gave that of Foreign Affairs to the Count de Choiseul. A little later in 1763, he took again the ministry of Foreign Affairs, and gave that of the Marine to his cousin, created Duc de Praslin and peer of France."

the Countess de Choiseul Romanet,* wherein—urged by the
faction of d'Argenson—the lady not only exposed her hopes
of supplanting Madame de Pompadour in the King's favour,
but even stipulated for the dishonourable privileges which
were to be allowed to her by his Majesty as " *Maîtresse en
titre.*" That the faction of the Marquis d'Argenson was
unscrupulous, cannot be doubted, but the friendship of
Madame de Pompadour with Stainville Choiseul was ante-dated
to de Choiseul's embassy to Rome. This friendship was ce-
mented by identity of hopes as to the Austrian Alliance, and
by his chivalrous protection of her, as told in the narrative
against the Jesuit scheme of getting rid of her from Court
and Cabinet by excommunication from the Church until she
was reconciled to her husband.

Madame de Pompadour valued the friendship of the Duc
de Choiseul still more, because, he being a connection of
de Maurepas (late Minister of Marine), his avowed adhesion
to her interests and his open respect for her were public re-
futations of the calumnies against her with which de
Maurepas amused and revenged himself in his exile.

Count d'Argenson and his brother the Marquis (who
wrote his dispatches in the trenches after the battle of Fontenoy) were fiercely opposed to the Marquise de Pompadour, although the unedited 19th century "Mémoires
d'Argenson" must be received with caution for obvious
reasons. On the other hand, the conduct of the Marquise de
Pompadour, as proved from even invidious 18th century
Mémoires, was courteous and forbearing. She not only, as
we have seen, soothed the dismissal of the Marquis d'Argenson, and did full justice to the ministerial ability of Count

---

* Mémoires de Duclos, p. 499, tom. ii. 1791.

d'Argenson, but when the latter was dismissed from office, after the attempted assassination of the King by Damiens, his nephew Paulmy d'Argenson was taken into Cabinet confidence, and the *Lettre de Cachet* to d'Argenson is couched as we shall see in terms of singular clemency, and with personal consideration for the offender against the policy which was then the interest of France to maintain.

In the Mémoires d'Argenson above alluded to is the following confession quoted by MM. Goncourt, the historians in France now most opposed to Madame de Pompadour.*

"Madame de Pompadour had then about her a cousin very ugly, very wicked, very avaricious, but to whom must be awarded both wit and intelligence. This companion, this obliging friend, had acquired a great ascendancy over the favourite, over whose wishes she domineered by caresses. . . . This relation and this friend, Madame la Comtesse d'Estrades, nourished against the position and the fortune of Madame de Pompadour one of those savage and profound jealousies peculiar to women in subordinate positions. . . . . . D'Argenson, one of whose means of power was a system of perfectly concocted *espionnage*, had taken note of the dispositions of Madame d'Estrades." . . . . Together they had incited Madame de Choiseul Romanet to try to supplant the favourite,—ineffectually. Madame de Choiseul Romanet was henceforth excluded from the royal *petits soupers*, but "Madame de Pompadour was not ignorant that all that intrigue had been conducted by Madame d'Estrades, aided by the counsels of d'Argenson, but she did not feel herself strong enough to send away her old friend. She contented herself by ostensibly showing her displeasure towards her. Nevertheless

* Mémoires de Duclos, tom. ii., p. 517.

d'Argenson, who by skilful manœuvres repaired d'Estrade's
credit, drew to his party all the friends of Madame de Pompadour, who were chilled towards her, Boulogne, Rouillé,
Puysieux, St Séverin, &c. . . . . More solidly established
than ever with the Queen, and in the pious societies hostile
to Madame de Pompadour, d'Argenson was closeted four hours
a day with Madame d'Estrades. . . . "Everything seemed to
be leagued together against Madame Pompadour, the interior
affairs" (of Court), "the Parliament pacification by which
d'Argenson regained credit with the King, and the reflections
of the King upon the luxury and expenditure of the Marquise—published, spread, and exaggerated by Madame d'Estrades; but the disappearance of a Letter changed the
aspect of affairs. Madame de Pompadour, ill and in bed in
the daytime, had received a letter from the King in which the
King spoke to her of the Parliaments. The letter was
placed, open, upon a little table near her bed. The Comtesse
d'Estrades had been in to pay her court to Madame de Pompadour; the Comtesse went out, and the letter was nowhere to be
found." . . . . After that, Madame d'Estrades was served
with a *Lettre de Cachet*, but her "disgrace did not intimidate
d'Argenson, who, whilst he redoubled his assiduities to the
King, had passed the evening with Madame d'Estrades, the
very day of her dismissal, and afterwards rented a house for
her, &c. &c., although he pretended to have been directly
insulted by Madame Pompadour, because she had sent away
d'Estrades, his friend! With such treachery beneath her roof
as this, and with such opposition in the Cabinet, Madame
de Pompadour might well exclaim, as she did then, and often
afterwards, "Alas! my life is one perpetual combat." At
last, as seen in the narrative, Count d'Argenson's dismissal

came, with that of Machault, in the following original *Lettres de Cachet.*

" Your service is no longer necessary to me : I command you to send to me your resignation of War Secretary of State, and of all the Offices joined thereto, and to retire to your estate at Ormes."

(The harshness of this "Lettre" was modified directly afterwards by the appointment being transferred to Paulmy d'Argenson, the exile's nephew.)

The Lettre to M. de Machault, the Chancellor, was modified by memory of his services to the State, and of the time when he worked at finance with the Marquise, as told in the narrative.

"A M. de Machault d'Arnouville, &c.

" Present circumstances compel me to demand the Seals of you, and the resignation of your charge of Secretary of State for the Marine. Be always certain of my protection and of my esteem. If you have favours to ask for your children, you may do so when needed ; it suits that you remain some time at d'Arnouville. I conserve to you your pension 30,000 livres, and the honours of keeper of the Seals."

The King, as told in the narrative, reserved the present use of the Great Seal to himself ; fearing its abuse.—The dismissal of MM. d'Argenson and Machault proved that for a moment he suspected the Parliamentarian party to which they belonged of his attempted assassination. Their names were in the Secret Notes, which formed a basis for Damien's examination, but that by no means proved them guilty. The doubt was painful to the King ; the more so, as he remembered the past services rendered to himself and his people by Machault in the matter of Taxation, which matter at the present war-time was one of continual trouble] to the Monarch, and, necessarily, an ever-increasing burthen to his people. At the beginning of this war, Louis XV. retrenched his personal and household expenditure. The following original note has survived the vexation of an over-taxed] people, which vexation culminated in revolution.

1755—1757. "Le Roy diminue une partie de sa maison, réforme plusieurs équipages de chasse, et un grand nombre de Chevaux de Course des deux Ecuries. Il y a aussi des règlemens sur les petits voyages pour les rendre moins dispendieux ; il est décidé qu' à la cour il n'y aura point de spectacle, et l'on suspend les travaux du Louvre."

The Marquise de Pompadour, between the years 1762 and 1763, after she had sent her plate to the Mint, was accused of lavish expenditure. This seems chiefly owing to her patronage of art and works of industry by which she strove to beguile the people's growing discontent under the war taxes. By her position, also, luxury and elegance were centralized in her abode long after she had ceased to value them for herself (to witness, date of accusation). Everything was brought to her in art and manufacture, which, for the sake of France, must in nowise be repudiated. At the time she had willed away all she possessed, and had even arranged her funeral toilette, her wardrobe was valued at 350,000 livres, her china (the models for Sèvres) at 101,945 livres, and at Bellevue, where the poor Capuchins shared her gardens, 3,000,000 were expended. This anomaly is a bitter homily on her position, in which she was crushed beneath the goods she had desired the gods to give her.

The following account may not be uninteresting of Madame de Pompadour's Expenditure at Versailles, extracted from *Relevé des déspenses publié par M. Leroy.*

	LIVRES.
Nesmes, 1st Steward	8000
Collin, *Maître d'Hôtel.* Occasional Secretary *	6000
De Quesnay, physician,† (*entretenu de tout*)	3000
Sauvant	2000
Gourbillon	1800
Annay	200
Tréon	150
La du Hausset, (*femme de chambre*) ..	150
La Neven	150

("No doubt," says Leroy, "the second *Femme de chambre*, a lady of quality, who so well concealed her real name that even du Hausset did not know it.")

Jeannetors (*femme de charge*)	400
La du Quesnay, Wardrobe woman ..	100

* Collin wore the Cross of St Louis. Collin is mentioned in the Codicil to the will of Madame de Pompadour. Collin borrowed 70,000 livres when his benefactress fell ill. It was Collin who from time to time was commissioned to raise money upon her jewels, &c., after she had impoverished herself in the seven years' war, so as to incite the loyalty of France by contribution to the Mint of household treasure.

† De Quesnay, although a resident beneath the roof of Madame de Pompadour (like many others maintained by her gratuitously), had other appointments under the Crown. One day when Louis XV. found de Quesnay with Madame de Pompadour at Versailles, the King, grateful for de Quesnay's public services, took from a vase of flowers a heart's-ease, and, presenting it to the great physician and political economist, begged him to regard that flower as his badge. From hence the well-known armorial bearings.

			LIVRES.
Lignes, Maître d'Hôtel	..	..	600
Benoit, Chef de Cuisine	..	..	400
Charles, Aide de Cuisine	..	..	400
Deux Garçons du Cuisine	..	..	400
Pâtissier	..	..	400
Rôtisseur, (public cook)	..	..	400
Garçon	..	..	200
Deux Garçons de Cuisine	..	..	400
Chef d'Office	..	..	400
Autre Chef d'Office ..	..	..	400
Aide d'Office	..	..	200
Garçon d'Office ..	..	..	150
Butler	..	..	400
Garçon Tommelier, (Butler's boy)		..	150
Huntsman	..	..	800
Swiss	..	..	600
Four Lacqueys ..	..	..	1800
Torch Bearers ..	..	..	300
Two Negroes	..	..	1800
One Concierge ..	..	..	400
One Porter	..	..	400
Two Sedan-chair bearers	..	..	1118
Two Boat-rowers ..	..	..	768
Three Postilions ..	..	..	1566
Four Grooms	..	..	1766
Three Embroiderers ..	..	..	1500

CAUSES OF WAR.

FROM ORIGINAL MS. NOTES OF THE DISPUTE BETWEEN THE COURTS OF GREAT BRITAIN AND FRANCE, WITH RELATION TO THE LIMITS OF NOVA SCOTIA, &c. &c.

(The following extracts have been sifted from a heavy volume of MS. Documents now placed in the British Museum. The research has been impeded through some pages by the MSS. being stained so as to be almost illegible, and by many passages in other pages being quite obliterated. Without fatiguing the reader to wade through the diplomatic prolixity which is tedious, the following passages have been deciphered and translated as literally as possible, so as to help to convey a notion of the way in which the seven years' war was inaugurated, suspicion being secretly fermented by anonymous notes of Intrigue from France.*)

The correspondence between M. Rouillé, Minister of Marine, at Versailles, with M. le Duc de Mirepoix, Ambassador from Versailles at the Court of St James's (following) is preceded by

"*Narrative from* 1754 *of the Hostilities committed by the French upon the Ohio, &c. &c.*

"The pretensions of France seem to be founded" (this is in English) "upon the prior Discovery of the Mississippi by M. de la Salle in 1684, a constant and uninterrupted Navigation and Commerce carried on in the neighbouring Lakes ever

---

* See Appendix, Vol. I. Canada, Louisiana, Secret Note of *Intrigue.*

since that time, and in consequence thereof a pretended title
set up to the Spring Heads of all the Rivers and Waters
falling into the said Lakes and River Mississippi, but no
actual Possession by erecting Forts, Culture, or Plantation is
Pretended, at least to the Territory in Question, till the present settlement.

"The title of the Crown of Great Britain may in like manner be founded upon Discovery, Charters, and Grants from
the Crown, previous to any Discovery on the Part of the
French, &c. &c."

So the dispute continues—France continues to build forts,
&c., with a view to connect Canada and Lousiana—mutual
suspicion is fostered and fermented. In 1755 England cap-
tures French ships. * The following letter preserved among
these MS. Documents by England may help to refute the
slander that to the woman in the French Cabinet and to the
woman in Austria the seven years' war was due.

"*From M. de Rouillé, at Versailles, to M. le Duc de
Mirepoix, at St James's.
"27th March, 1755.

"To attain to the desirable end of peace it will be necessary to weigh the nature and the circumstances of the engagements which will be in themselves of consequence to
contract, and to combine reciprocal rights and proprieties
(*convenances*.) A labour so important will demand much
care and much time. And what use in the mean
while of the Armaments which have been prepared on either
side? How will it be possible to negociate with effect
(*avec Fruit*) if active measures continue in America, and

* List of these ships from French Chronicles. Récit Contemporain, &c.

if they begin upon the high sea?* Will not these, upon
one side or the other, be in themselves a motive to mul-
tiply pretensions, and will not such difficulties become new
obstacles to pacification. It must be necessary, therefore,
to prevent this inconvenience, and that can only be done by
giving to the respective Governors in America uniform
orders . . . . which will interdict to them all acts of hostility
upon any pretence whatever. . . . . I have already so inti-
mated to you, Monsieur (*je vous l'ay de ja mande*), and, as
the truth is always the same, I shall constantly maintain
the same language. Sincerely to wish for peace, and not to
cause" (hostile) " active measures to cease, are two incom-
patible things."

To which this is the answer :

" The Court of London will concur with all possible haste
to conclude a definitive agreement which will embrace all
the Parts in America disputed between the two nations, as

---

* " Etat des Bâtimens capturés par les Anglais avant la déclara-
tion de Guerre.

Venant des îles	74
Négriers, chargés de près de 2000 negres	5
Bâtiments portant des Marchandises et des provisions à nos îles	26
Bâtiment allant en Guinée	1
Navires de la compagnie des Indes un allant au Sénégal et l'autre revenant	2
Bâtiments revenant de la pêche de la baleine	2
Terre Neuviens	66
Bâtiments portant des provisions à l'île Royale et au Canada, ou en revenant	22
Bâtiments faisant le grant cabotage	27
Barques, goëlettes et autres petits bâtiments faisant le petit cabotage	75
Total	300

has been insinuated by his Excellency M. le Duc de Mirepoix to be the good will of His Court (être les dispositions de Sa Cour). The proposal made by the Court of France, by the extract of M. Rouillé's letter, dated March 27, is the same which has been made before, and has for its object but a truce (*Armistice*) between the two nations. The Court of London finds therein the same difficulties which have presented themselves from the commencement of the negociation, and cannot regard it as a means which may favour conciliation (*comme un moyen qui puisse favoriser la conciliation, &c.*").

Afterwards comes,

" From M. de Rouillé" (Versailles) " to M. le Duc de Mirepoix, Court of London.

" . . . . The King would wish to carry his complacency further, but the proposals of the Court of London do not permit His Majesty to hope that the two Courts can attain to the termination of their differences by a just and proper conciliation.

"According to the Court of London the success of our negociation depends entirely upon the cession which the English demand not only of all " (effaced), " but also of Twenty Leagues upon the side of the French Country of the Coast of Canada. The Court of London proposes (*propose par rapport*) . . . . that the part of Canada situated above Quebec . . . . and all Montreal, that the River St Lawrence and the Lakes Ontario and Erie . . . serve as limits between the two nations.

"It is upon the settlement (*fixation*) of these limits that Messieurs, the English Ministers, pretend also to establish the basis of the negotiation.*   Very far, Sir, from the entering upon that Article, the King will never consent that the Sovereignty over the Southern Bank of the river St Lawrence, and over the Lakes Ontario and Erie be put in question, and that the parts which have always been regarded as the Centre of Canada become the limits of it.

" The preservation of Canada at all would become onerous and impossible after such dismemberment.

. . . . " We are disposed to enter into negociation upon all the rest and to lend ourselves even by sacrifices to all the *convenances* of England which can accord with the dignity of the King and with the safety of his possessions.

" We will willingly concert with Messieurs the Britannic Ministers upon the most efficacious measures to place the two Nations under shelter from all Invasion and from all constraint (gêne) on the part of the one face to face with the other.

" We have proposed to prevent ulterior deeds and acts " (hostile) " by the Orders that might be given to the respective Governors, and to the Commanders of Squadrons of Ships. A proposal so equitable and so moderate has been rejected."

Again from Versailles,

"*To M. le Duc de Mirepoix.*

" May 1755.

" The Court of France, in accordance with its principles of Equity and of Moderation, desires sincerely the mainten-

* See Narrative, Vol. I.   Madame de Pompadour to Marshal Belleisle after the Treaty of Aix la Chapelle.

ance of Peace and of the most perfect Intelligence with that
of Great Britain."

With such official documents as these to consider, and
with Madame de Pompadour's brisk letter of private instruction (Narrative, Vol. I.) in his pocket, it is no wonder that
when Horace Walpole met the Duc de Mirepoix, in Brentford Town, his Excellence was moodily considering his way
through the dust.

Afterwards comes a Memorial, drawn up by M. Mirepoix,
or presented by him, which Memorial is not to the credit
of England as a Transatlantic neighbour. Afterwards follows
the Answer of England, "La Reponse Angloise donnée à M.
le Duc de Mirepoix, 6th June 1755," which answer, like
the grievances of M. de Mirepoix, is voluminous and uninteresting, considering that England had then practically
illustrated her own views of the question.

The MS. which follows in succession is remarkable in
itself. This MS. is endorsed

*" Mémoire de Monsieur Rouillé, &c., avec des observations
from Lord H."*

FRANCE.	ENGLAND.
Upon one side of the paper is the	Upon the other side is
" MEMOIRE DE M. ROUILLE."	" OBSERVATIONS "
(By some strange accident, M. Rouillé's side in the MS. is so effaced as to render some of the following extracts difficult to decipher in the original.)	(on the part of England).
	(Lord H.'s Observations are also much obscured, but on the whole they are in a more legible condition than are those of M.

FRANCE.

Mémoire de M. Rouillé.

FROM VERSAILLES.

"It has not held to the King (il n'à pas tenu au Roy) that the Differences concerning America have not been terminated" (? word effaced) *" by the ways of negociation, and His Majesty is in a condition to demonstrate this to the whole Universe by Authentic Proofs.*

"The King, always animated by the most sincere Desire to maintain Public Tranquillity, and very perfect Intelligence with His Britannic Majesty, has followed with good Faith and with the most entire Confidence the Negociation relative to that object.

* Italics not in Original. The passages so marked here, are to facilitate the reading of both sides of the question.

(Six pages of blank.)

ENGLAND.

Observations.

Rouillé and four times more voluminous.)

FROM ST JAMES'S.

"Whatever may have been, and whatever may still be the Dispositions of the Very Christian King on the subject of the Differences concerning America, It is lamentable that the proceedings (*Démarches*) of the Court of Versailles have so little responded to the Intentions which the Memorial of M. Rouillé supposes on the part of His Majesty, and to the professions of good Faith, &c. *If it be from the course of that Negotiation Authentic Proofs are to be drawn, by which the Very Christian King is in a condition to demonstrate to the Universe that it has not held to His Majesty (qu'il n' à pas tenu à Sa Majesté) that the Differences in question have not been terminated by the ways of Reconcilement . . . the Facts will appear all in Favour of*

FRANCE.	ENGLAND.
Mémoire de M. Rouillé.	*Observations.*

the Moderation of the King of Great Britain.

" In the month of January, 1755, the Ambassador of France returned to London, and made great Protestations of the sincere Desire that his Court had to adjust finally and promptly all the Disputes which subsist between the two Crowns in America, and notwithstanding the extraordinary Preparations which were then made, actually, in the Ports of France, * her Ambassador proposed 'That before Examination of the basis (*Fond*), and of the circumstances of the Quarrel, positive Orders be sent previously to our respective Governors to forbid to them henceforth all new Encroachments and measures of fact, to prescribe to them, on the contrary, that things be restored without delay " (*que les Choses* soient *remisses*) . . . .

* See Narrative, Vols. i. ii.

FRANCE.

Mémoire de M. Rouillé.

ENGLAND.

Observations.

" and that the respective Pretensions be amicably deferred to the Commission established in Paris to the purpose that the two Courts might end their Differences by a speedy Reconcilement.

"England declared herself ready to consent to the proposed cessation of Hostilities . . . upon condition that all the American possessions be previously re-established upon the footing of the Treaty of Utrecht, confirmed by that of Aix-la-Chapelle. . . . That the possessions be restored actually in the same condition as they were after the Treaty of Utrecht.

" The assurances that the King of Great Britain and his Ministers renew incessantly by Word of Mouth (vive voix) and by Writing were so formal and precise upon the Pacific Dispositions of his Britannic Majesty, that the King would have re-

" The assurances that France received of the Pacific Dispositions of His Britannic Majesty were not less true and sincere than they were formal and precise, but His Britannic Majesty would be reproached to have pushed (poussé) such sentiments to

FRANCE.	ENGLAND.
Mémoire de M. Rouillé.	*Observations.*

proached himself to have had the least Doubt upon the Uprightness of the Intentions of the Court of London.

" It is scarcely possible to conceive how these Assurances could reconcile themselves with the Offensive Orders given in November 17*th* " (*? effaced*) " *to General Braddock, and in the month of April*, 1755, *to Admiral Boscawen.*"

(Three and half pp. of blank.)

" *The attack in the month of July last, and the capture of two of the King's Ships in full sea, and without Declaration of War, were a public Insult to the Flag of His Majesty. And His Majesty would have testified instantly* (sur le Champ) *all the just Resentment, with which such an irregular and unjust Enterprise inspired Him, had it been possible for*

the Point of risking the Rights and the Possessions of his Crown, and the safety of his Peoples.

" It is in vain that France qualifies as offensive *the Orders given to General Braddoudock, ... the Admiral Boscawen.*

" She " (France) " would be very glad to draw the Curtain over all the Hostilities commenced on her side in America since the Peace of Aix-la-Chapelle, until the Date of these Orders. From the Signature, so to speak, of that Treaty, and the Opening of the Commission which was established in consequence, in Paris for the Affairs of America,—France, mistrusting her Right in advance, and erecting herself as Judge and Client (*Juge et Partie*) in her own Cause, usurped the Province of Nova Scotia, and after a succession of Hostilities against the Inhabitants,

FRANCE.

Mémoire de M. Rouillé.

His Majesty to believe that the Admiral Boscawen had not acted but by the Order of his Court.

"The same motive had at first suspended the judgment of the King upon the Piracies which the English Ships of War had committed" (effaced) "for several months against the Navigation and the commerce of the" (? effaced) "Subjects of His Majesty in despite of the Rights of Peoples, of the Law of Treaties, of the Customs established" (effaced) "amongst Nations (*civilized*) governed by the Respect which they reciprocally owe to each other."

(Two pp. and half of blank.)

"The King had reason to expect from the sentiments of His Britannic Majesty, that upon his return to London *

* From Hanover, whither Bussy had been sent from Versailles to confer with him.

ENGLAND.

Observations.

subjects of the King, She erected Three Forts in the Heart of the Province, and if She had not been prevented was about to destroy the New Establishment of Halifax.

"Similar Hostilities were exercised at the same time against the Territories and the Subjects of His Majesty upon the Ohio, and upon the Indian Lakes.

"*Yet, notwithstanding the just Reasons which His Majesty had in coming to Extremities, his Majesty again added to a Patience of many years a strongly-marked Reticence even in the Modesty of that Succour which consisted but of two Battalions of 500 men each escorted by two Frigates, as also in the Orders given to the officer who commanded them, to dislodge the invaders from the Territories of the King. There is nothing in this Order irreconcileable with the assurances of*

Mémoire de M. Rouillé.   *Observations.*

He would disavow the conduct of his Admiralty and of his Officers of the Sea, and that he would give to His Majesty a proportionate satisfaction for the Injury and for the loss.

" But the King, seeing that very far from punishing the robberies of the English Navy, (his Britannic Majesty) encourages them, on the contrary, in demanding fresh succours against France, His Majesty would be wanting in that which He owes to his own Glory, to the Dignity of his Crown, and to the Defence of his Peoples, if He deferred any longer in exacting from the King of Great Britain a transcendant Reparation (*une Réparation eclatante*) of the Outrage done to the French Flag, and for the losses caused to the Subjects of the King. His Majesty believes, therefore, that he ought to address himself directly to his

the Pacific Dispositions of the King. It is the invasion on the part of France and all the Violences by which it has been accompanied which are offensive. And it has never yet been unlawful (illégitime) *to repulse an aggression.*

" . . . . How can that Court pretend to be surprised at the Ways of Deed, of which she complains (*les Voyes de Fait*), when, during *all* the course of the Negotiation, the Britannic Court constantly rejected the proposal of a suspension of Arms unless such suspension were preceded by Restitution of possessions, taken by open force (*prises a Force ouverte*) from England, a condition to which the Court of Versailles would never lend itself. . . . . .

" It is for Reasons so just and so valid that the King has rejected the peremptory Demand contained in the Mémoire of M. Rouillé . . .

Mémoire de M. Rouillé.

Britannic Majesty, and to demand from him the prompt and entire Restitution of all the French Ships, those of War as of Merchandise, which against all Laws, and against all Decencies (*Bienséances*) have been taken by the English Navy, and of all the Officers, Sailors, Artillery, Ammunition, &c., &c., which belong to those Ships.

" His Majesty will always like better to owe to the Equity of the King of England than to any other means (*moyen*), the Satisfaction which His Majesty has the right to reclaim. . . . .

" If His Britannic Majesty orders the Restitution of the ships (*dont il s'agit*), the King will be disposed to enter into Negotiation upon the other Satisfactions which are legitimately due to him, and will continue to lend himself, as he has done heretofore, to an

Observations.

To avoid all occasion of raising the Terms, ... His Majesty has caused a short and negative answer to be written in the Form of a Letter by his Secretary of State, Mr Fox. And his Majesty is still more determined not to admit what France demands as a Preliminary Condition which ought to precede all Negotiation, because it appears, even by this Mémoire itself, that they (*on*) would be as far off as ever from an equitable and solid accommodation upon the Griefs (*Griefs*) of which the King has had to complain since many years. And it is not seen (*l'on ne voit pas*) how they will be able to explain in France, the Resolution of His Majesty, to defend himself in America, and to prevent France from insulting his kingdoms, as a Refusal of Justice, and as a Design formed by the King,

FRANCE.

Memoire de M. Rouillé.

equitable and just agreement upon the Discussions which concern America.

"But if, contrary to all Hope, the King of England refuses himself to the Requisition which the King makes to him, His Majesty" (considers it—word effaced?) "by Justice as the Declaration of War the most Authentic, and as a Design formed by the Court of London to trouble the repose of Europe."

"At Versailles,
"This 21st Dec., 1755,
"ROUILLÉ."

ENGLAND.

Observations.

to trouble the Repose of Europe."

The foregoing Mémoire of M. Rouillé is accompanied by the following letter.

"A SON EXCELLENCE M. FOX.

"At Versailles, the 21st December, 1755.

"Sir,

"It is by the Order of the King my master that I have the honour to send to Your Excellence the subjoined for His Britannic Majesty. I profit with eagerness (*empressement*) by this occasion to offer to you the Assurances of the

distinguished consideration with which I have the honour
to be,

"Sir,

"Of Your Excellence,

" The very humble and obedient Servant,

ROUILLÉ."

Letter of Mr Fox to Monsieur Rouillé, "from Lord H."

" At Whitehall, January, 13, 1756.

" Sir,

         " I have received the 3rd of this month the let-
ter with which Your Excellency has honoured me, Dated the
21st of the month past, with the Mémoire by which it was
accompanied (*remis*) to Monsieur le Colonel Yorke by the
Secretary of M. de Bonnac, Ambassador of His Very Christian Majesty at the Hague. I have not delayed to place them
before the King my master. And it is by his orders that I
have the honour to inform Your Excellency that he continues
to desire the preservation of Public Tranquillity; but although
the King will lend himself willingly to an equitable and solid
arrangement, His Majesty would not know how to accord the
demand which is made of the prompt and entire restitution of
all the French Ships, and of all which appertained to them,
as a Preliminary Condition to all Negotiation.

" The King having done nothing in all his proceedings, but
that which the Hostilities, commenced by France, in Time of
full Peace (of which there are (*on a*) the most authentic
Proofs), and that which His Majesty owes to his Honour, to
the Defence of the Rights and of the Possessions of His

Crown, and to the safety of his Kingdoms, have rendered just
and indispensable.

" I am, &c.,

" H. Fox."

And then, sifted from a mass of Papers, in connection with
the foregoing, follow, as regards date, MSS., labelled,

"*Instructions and Papers with which M. Mitchell was furnished on his going to Berlin: some relating to American Affairs.*"

Sealed with the Arms of England.

Signed, in large straggling characters, GEORGE R.

" INSTRUCTIONS FOR OUR TRUSTY AND WELL-
BELOVED ANDREW MITCHELL, ESQ., WHOM WE HAVE
APPOINTED TO BE OUR MINISTER TO OUR GOOD BRO-
THER THE KING OF PRUSSIA, GIVEN AT OUR COURT
OF ST JAMES'S, THE TWELFTH DAY OF APRIL, 1756,
IN THE TWENTY-NINTH YEAR OF OUR REIGN.*

1. "Upon the receipt of these our instructions, and Our Let-
ters of Credence to the King and Queen of Prussia, and the
Queen Mother, Our Sister, You are, with all convenient
Speed, to repair to Berlin.

2. " Being arrived there, you are to demand an audience of
the King and Queen of Prussia, and of the Queen Mother,
wherein You are to deliver Our said Letters of Credence,
and to accompany the Same with suitable compliments in

* MS. 68. 62. Plut. clxx. i.

Our Name, and with the strongest Assurances of Our constant Friendship and Regard.

3. " In your Audience with the King of Prussia if it should not be attended with such Ceremonies as may make it at that Time improper, you are not to confine yourself to the above-mentioned general Declarations of Our Friendship and Regard towards Him; but to open to Him Our particular Views in charging you with this Weighty and important Commission. But, if you should find It unadvisable to proceed so far in your first Audience, Our pleasure then is, that you do desire as soon as possible to see the King of Prussia in private, and being accordingly admitted to Him, you will acquaint Him; That, from Our sincere Desire of giving Him all possible Proofs of our true affection towards Him, We have sent you immediately from Our Presence, fully instructed with our Sentiments and Dispositions upon the critical and delicate Situation of Public Affairs; And that as we have nothing more sincerely at Heart than to cultivate the most perfect and intimate Union with Him for the reciprocal Advantage of our Two Royal Families, and for the General Good of Europe, and That of the Protestant Cause in particular, so we are desirous to enter with Him into the closest Concert of Measures, for the obtaining the desirable Ends above mentioned.

5. " Whereas We have lately concluded a TREATY with Our Good Brother the King of Prussia, the principal Tendency of which (as will appear by the annexed Copy of it) is to preserve, if possible, the Peace and Tranquillity of the Empire, in the present Situation of Affairs; you shall upon your first audience, and upon all other proper Occasions, declare to the King of Prussia Our firm Resolution to maintain the

said Treaty, and our Readiness to concur in All such Measures as may be for the General Good and Welfare of Europe, and of the German Empire in particular.

5. " And Whereas The King of Prussia has represented to Us the Expediency of declaring, That the above-mentioned Treaty is not to take Place in Case of an attack upon The Low Countries, which Part of the Dominions of our Good Sister, the Empress-Queen of Hungary, is not comprized within the Treaties of Guaranty now in force between The King of Prussia and the Empress-Queen; Lest any doubt should hereafter arise, we thought proper to give way to these Remonstrances, and authorize Our Ministers to sign a Separate Article, a copy of which is hereunto annexed.

6. "WHEREAS certain Disputes had arisen, touching the Claims of several Subjects of Our Good Brother the King of Prussia, on account of Losses, supposed to have been sustained from the Capture of Their Effects made at Sea, by our Subjects, during the late War, in consequence of which the King of Prussia had neglected the Payment of Those of Our Subjects concerned in the Silesian Loan—and whereas this Affair is now finally adjusted, We have directed a Copy of a Declaration which has been signed by Our Orders, to be put into Your Hands herewith, for your Information on this subject.

7. " You shall diligently observe the Motions of that Court, and endeavour to penetrate their real Views and Designs from Time to Time for Our Information, and you shall particularly study the King of Prussia's Genius and Inclination, and endeavour to make yourself as agreeable to Him as possible, as well as to Those persons whom you shall observe to be in His confidence," &c. &c. &c.

Mr Mitchell is the bearer of three letters: one from King

George II. to King Frederic; another to King Frederic's mother, the Queen Dowager of Prussia, and another to the wife of King Frederic, which letter is here subjoined to remind posterity that that hero had a queen, although only a shadow of her remains in the blaze of his glory.

" Madame Ma Sœur,

"Le Sieur Mitchell devant se rendre à la Cour de mon bon Frère Le Roy Votre Epoux pour y resider comme mon Ministre, Je profite avec plaisir de cette occasion de renouveller à Votre Majesté les Profession de mon Amitié pour Elle. En me raportant à ce que mon dit Ministre aura l'Honneur de lui exposer à cet égard, je prie Votre Majesté d'y vouloir ajouter Créance entiere, et d'etre persuadée des Sentimens sinceres et parfaits avec Lesquel Je suis Madame ma Sœur de Votre Majesté, le Bon Frère.

George M.

" St James's, 12 Avril, 1756."

Secret Instructions.

Amongst innumerable other things, requiring of Andrew Mitchell the Eyes of an Argus, it is recommended by the Cabinet of London:—

" Not to open himself too freely." "To make a Discreet use of the ADVICES sent by Sir B. Keene,* relative to the supposed Transactions between the Courts of France and Vienna."

" To endeavour to find out whether the King of Prussia

* See "*Letter from Sir Benjamin Keene to Mr Fox, dated Madrid, July*, 1756," this Appendix, page 67.

may not think it advisable to enter into some immediate Concert with the King for taking proper preventive measures, upon the Advices which have been received of the Views and Intentions of the Court of France.

"The great point is to find out what the K. of P.'s future plan is, whether the late Treaty with the King was made singlely to avoid the consequences of our Treaty with Russia,* or whether the King of Prussia was unwilling to see a French Army in Germany, and might apprehend the power of France existed singlely against his Majesty might prove fatal to all Europe hereafter.

". . . . M. M. will occasionally find out His P. M.'s sentiments upon the present close connection between France, Sweden, and Denmark. Moreover "—(*and thus France would have been isolated, and thus her Alliance with Austria is vindicated as a stroke of policy,*) "as to the House of Austria the King" (of England) "can not depart from his Ancient alliance with them, if they by their conduct do not force His Majesty to it, which the King still thinks they will not do, that His Majesty is desirous to combine his engagements to the House of Austria with those he has entered into with Prussia, as there is nothing inconsistent, but the contrary in them, and it would be very happy for Europe if by His Majesty's means and in progress of time, the jealousies which have of late been between the K. of P. and the Empress-Queen could be removed.

"In all events his P. M. may depend upon the strictest and most cordial execution on the part of the King of all his

---

* See this Appendix, p. 66. "Letter from Sir Hanbury Williams from Petersburgh to Mr Fox, and Letters from the Grand Duke Peter and the Grand Duchess Catharine."

engagements towards His P. M., &c. &c.* . . . His Majesty is not unacquainted with the endeavours the K. of P. has used to make the Court of France easy with his late Treaty with the King, nor with the affectation of France in pretending to be so. The King also knows that his P. M. has offered to renew His late Treaty with France, which that Court at present declines.

" The K. of P. must see by this that the Court of France are inwardly highly exasperated against Him, and therefore His P. M. ought not to have his dependence upon them. . . . . . Mr M. will particularly inform himself unaffectedly of the K. of P.'s Views towards Saxony and Poland, the future succession to that Crown, and also towards the (torn) Elector of Bavaria " (rest torn off).

" Secret Note of Intelligence " from France
to England, and dated

" Versailles, 20th March, 1756."

(Two first words undecipherable) " Yesterday, that this Court have taken the Resolution and concerted the means of marching a great Body of Troops into the Bishoprick of Padesborn (?) as soon as they shall receive the news of the Death of the Landgrave of Hesse Cassell. The Pretence is to support the Hereditary Prince, if any attempt should be made to deprive Him of the Succession on his having changed His Religion. This is called supporting the Laws of the Empire, Protecting the Catholic Religion, &c., and

* " Treaties, their dates and subsidies," from Fol. 6816.—122, Mus. Brit.

being a very specious Pretext, it will be agreeable to some of the Electors and Princes of the Empire, and will give " (undecipherable) " an Opportunity of revenging Himself on the King of Prussia, and of beginning War in the Empire with great Advantage " (undecipherable). " The Court of Vienna have been sounded on the Affair ; and they have not shown any aversion to it, Tho' they wont chuse to appear in it at first. I know a person at Cassel hath Orders from this Court to dispatch an Express whenever the Landgrave is dangerously ill, and two by different roads, whenever He dies, and I believe more than He hath the same Orders. The Person who revealed This to me, observed it would be attended with great Advantage to France, make them received with open Arms by several Princes, coming as Protector of the Laws of the Empire, of the Catholic Faith, and that they will have whatever Assistance the Court of Rome can give them.

" Mons. Zuckmantel had orders when He went from Dusseldorf to Rome, to sound the Elector of Cologne's sentiments, and he found Him well inclined, and believes He will grant the passage to our Troops through the Electorate, and even give them quarters in the Bishoprick of Westphalia, so I thought no time should be lost in communicating this Discovery, that your Court may examine further into it, and take in time such measures as may seem prudent to them."

WRITINGS OF FREDERIC KING OF PRUSSIA.*

" Moyens dont la Grande Bretagne pourra se servir pour ruiner les projets de Ses Ennemis ou rendre la Guerre plus difficile."

"Sent in Mr Mitchell's * * * Letter of the 9th December, 1756, by Major.

1. "Puisque la France˙fait un si grand usage de ses Trouppes de Gene, tant en Bohème que sur le Rhin, il semble qu'il ne seroit pas impossible à la Grande Bretagne de donner aux Français quelque apprehension pour leurs Côtes de Normandie ou de Bretagne ce qui pourroit se faire par l'assemblée de quelques Trouppes et Vaisseaux de Transport sur leurs Côtes ; ainsi que par des démonstrations tant navales que terrestres, qui aboutiroient à cette fin.

2. "L'on croit qu'il seroit également de l'avantage de la Grande Bretagne de se prouver dans la Méditerranée un équivalent de la perte qu'elle à faite dans l'Isle de Minorque ; ce qui pourroit se faire par la Conquête de l'Isle de Corse, entreprise d'autant moins difficile que les Français y ont retiennent peu de Trouppes, et que les habitans, indisposés contre la domination génoise, favorisseront tous ceux qui y abordyeront pour les en délivrer.

3. "On ne parle pas dans ce Memoire des choses qu'on pourroit tenter en Afrique, en Amérique, ou en Asie, à cause du peu de connoissance qu'on a du local de ces pais eloignés, mais en se bornant à l'Europe, l'on croit qu'il y a de grands objets dignes d'interesser l'attention de la Grande Bretagne.

* British Museum.

Comme seroit celui de porter les Hollandois à faire une augmentation dans leurs Trouppes, objet dans lequel on pourroit réussir selon le sentiment des personnes qui commissent . . . . (?) la Republique, &c., l'Angleterre vouloit sacrifier des avantages passagers de Commerce à d' interets plus grands et plus permanents, desquels dependent la liberté et l' independance de l'Europe.

4. "Il est *seur* qu'en examinant les projets de la France pour la Campagne prochaine, que l'Allemagne aussi bien que particulièrement le Pays d'Hannovre ont tout à craindre de l'invasion des François, la Cour de Vienne et celle de Versailles, qui par leur puissance et leur liaison se croyent dans le moment présent à même de donner des loix à l'Europe, se trouveront confirmées dans cette esperances si personne ne se prépare pour leur resister. L'Electorat d'Hannover peut fournir 24m. hommes, la Hesse en fournit huit, mais elle en pourroit donner douze si l'on vouloit augmenter les subsides. Le Duc de Brunswick cinq, celui de Gotha trois, ce qui feroit 44m. hommes. Si les Hollandois n'en joigneroit que 20m. cela en seroit 64m., et si la Prusse se trouvoit seure de la Russie, elle pourroit ajouter quelque chose à ce nombre les Trouppes portées vers le Rhin au mois de Mai.

5. "Pour faire diversion à tant de forces, on croit que le Roy de Sardaigne ne seroit point inutile, ne put-on le porter qu' à faire quelque augmentation dans ses Trouppes ou à remuer de manière à donner quelque augmentation dans ses Trouppes, ou à remuer de manière à donner des inquietudes aux François et aux Autrichiens. Ce qu'on exige de ce Prince paroit entièrement compatible avec sa sureté d'autant plus que les François portant leurs forces sur le Rhin, et les Autrichiens dans la Bohème ce Prince est entièrement libre dans toutes ses actions.

6. " Comme la conduite de la Russie paroit très indeter-
minée jusqu'à présent, et qu'il ne seroit pas impossible qu'elle
se laissat entrainer par les idées de la Cour de Vienne,* et de celles
de Versailles à des demarches vigoureuses, et à des hostilités,
l'on soumet au jugement éclairé du Ministre Britannique, s'il
ne seroit pas nécessaire en pareil cas de se procurer une diversion de la part de la Porte, projet qui, s'il pouvoit réussir, mettroit le Roi de Prusse plus que jamais en état de seconder Les
Alliés. Ce qu'on croit possible, si Mr Porter, dont le crédit
est connu à la Porte, s'employe efficacement a demontrer
aux Turcs, combien dangereux est pour eux la liaison du
nouveau triumvirat qui vient de se former en Europe, consi-
dération qui leur doit paroitre d'autant plus importante, que,
si les Turcs agissent pendant la presente guerre, ils n'auront à
faire qu' à une partie des forces de leurs ennemis, au lieu que
s'ils attendent la paix générale ils dependront entièrement de
la discretion des Cours de Vienne et St Petersbourg. On
observe encore par rapport aux Turcs, que le commerce que
les François font dans les Echelles du Lévant est très important, et que ce seroit à présent le moment d'y apporter une
alteration considerable, à quoi la possession de l'Isle de
Corse pourroit beaucoup contribue. Au defaut d'une diversion il faudroit s'attacher à determiner la Porte de menacer
la France, le l'exclure totalement du commerce du Levant, ou
de la priver d'une partie des avantages et privilèges dont les
negocians y jouissent.

7. " Dans les lettres qu'on à du Dannemarc,† cette cour

* " In the Empire, the King of Prussia and the English excited
the Protestants, ... the Imperial army had for its General Prince
Hildeburgausen, an almost declared partisan of the King of Prussia.
Duclos, Mems. p. 526, Tome 2.
† " Denmark was always floating between jealousy against the

paroit dans les dispositions qu'on pourroit desirer si dans le moment présent la Russie se detache entièrement de l'alliance de l'Angleterre, et prend fait et cause pour la maison d'Autriche.* Il est probable qu'on pourra disposer de l'assistance et des secours de Dannemarc en lui promettant la garantie de Schleswig. L'Angleterre y gagneroit une Hotel dans la Baltique et des Trouppes qui pourroient servir à couvrir l'Electorat d'Hannover. Il seroit encore avantageux pour l'Angleterre, qu'on tâchat d'empêcher la sortie des Matelots Norwegieux qui vont servir en France, ainsi que l'exportation des Viandes Salées de la Norwegie, dont on se sert maintenant en France, au defaut de celle de Flandre.

Cette alliance entraîneroit necessairement la Suède,† qui, se trouvant isolé, se jetteroit entre les bras de l'Angleterre, ce qui formeroit un nouvel equilibre dans le Nord.

L'on croit que tous ces differents points méritent d'être examinés avec la plus scrupuleuse attention . . . . pour peu que le Ministère Anglais reflechisse aux veritables interêts de sa nation, ... sur tout lorsqu'on considère, que ce sera de la paix prochaine dont dependra le sort de l'Europe. . . . ."

Court of Vienna, the Catholic Powers, and disquietude concerning the King of Prussia." *Mémoires de Duclos*, p. 526, Tome 2. Pub. 1791.

* At the Court of Petersburgh were opposed political parties. The Grand Duke Peter, nephew of the reigning Empress who was in favour of France and Austria, secretly instructed the King of Prussia of all that was going on at Petersburgh. *Duclos*, p. 525, Tome 2.

† " In Sweden the King was governed by the queen, sister of the King of Prussia, and of the same character, who traversed all operations." *Mems. de Duclos*, 1791, p. 526.

" Mémoire Received by Mr Mitchell from the King of Prussia himself on the 26*th of July,* 1756, *and transmitted to Lord Holdernesse the* 30*th July,* 1756.*"*

*Addressed to " Son Excellence Monsieur de Mitchel, Ministre Plénipotentiaire de S. M. Britanique à Magdebourg." ***

" After all the good intelligences that we have received of the designs of the Austrians and of their intrigues as much in Russia as in France, no other part remains to the King for his safety than to anticipate (hinder) his enemies. The King is informed of the movements that the Russian troops have made ; by these news he believes himself to be in safety against all their bad will during the course of the winter. The King asks not any succour from the King of England, if that Prince will supply to him a squadron in the Baltic. This will be a new subject of gratitude that the Court of Berlin will have to that of London in the coming year. If the King of England believe that he requires his fleet elsewhere, especially for the defence of his (?), the King renounces this succour ; he will even, by friendship for the King of England, defer the commencement of his operations until the end, or about the 24 *d'Aut.* (August ?), so that the French may have this year neither the pretext nor the means of passing into Germany. The King of England is entreated to avail himself usefully of this time, in forcing the Dutch to make an augmentation of 30m. men of their land-troops, in drawing subsidiary troops 4m. from

* Large envelopes, sealed with the royal arms in red wax. The handwriting of King Frederic is so small as to be sometimes almost illegible. The French of his Prussian Majesty is often ill-spelt, and the royal disregard of punctuation adds to the difficulty of transcribing his documents.

Gotta, 6m. from Darmstat, 5m. b. (?), 8m. Hessians in giving subsidies to the Bavarians in joining to them the 3m. (?) in augmenting his troops of the Electorate 22m. men; the whole joined together would form an army of at least 74m. men.

"If that army, the spring which is coming, carried itself into the Duchy of (?), and holding itself on the defensive it found the means to stop the French quite short, be it in the Electorate of Cologne, be it in the Palatinate, it would cause to vanish (evanouir) all the designs of our enemies, it would cover at the same time the country of Darmstat, Hesse, Westphalia, and Holland; it would find itself in reach to succour whichever of these States, that might be menaced by the invasion of the French, and would put in safety the Electorate of Hanover (*'hannover'*), and all the possessions of the Princes of the Empire ; . . . if France strip her coasts along the English Channel, to form an army, the English fleet will be able to profit by it and to make descents upon the unfurnished coasts, to give alarms the length of Brittany and Normandy. If all those troops remain along the sea, France will not have upon the Rhine an army scarcely stronger than 50m. men. The Allies will have the superiority, and in holding her motionless (?) upon the banks of the Rhine, the common cause gains there as much in the crisis as by the gain of battles, the project merits attention, if it be wished to expedite it there is not a moment to lose, and it is necessary to work the accessories (?), to be ready by the beginning of the spring of the year 1757. It is the only way to continue the war and to assure a good issue to it. If we remain with crossed arms (*' brads croissez '*), we shall be crushed successively The one after the Other for want of having taken advantage of the benefit that time and our vigilance could give us, but there is not a moment to lose. The King, seeing the powerful league that is formed against him, is the first to oppose it ; his safety does not permit him to defer, and he hopes by that to find himself in a condition to serve his allies usefully in the course of this war."

"From the King himself, sent to Lord Holdernesse, 30th July, 1756."

" *Mémoire by the King of Prussia's own hand,*" 29th Octobre, 1756. " Sent in my *most Secret* 4th November to E. Holdernesse (by Goodall)."

" In the great crisis of the affairs of Europe, it is proposed to His Britannic Majesty to consider well the state of pressing things, and the remedies that may act without loss of time, and to take the necessary measures from the beginning of this winter to find resources in time against the misfortunes that may reasonably be foreseen.

" The Queen of Hungary has 90m. regular troops in Bohemia, to those she joins 10m. Hungarians," &c.

(After showing the momentous necessity of detaching Russia entirely from the Court of Vienna *)—

"But to the superior Lights (Lumières) of his Britannic Majesty are submitted all these cares (?) which certainly merit a very great attention for the consequence of the present war, and which would cause remorse for life if in this pressing time when there is winter to prepare one's-self something had been neglected, which inadvertence might cause the loss of Germanic Liberty, the Destruction of the

* See Secret Letters from Sir Hanbury Williams, British Ambassador at the Court of St Petersburgh, this Appendix.

Protestant cause, and the Peace (?) of the two only princes which can sustain it, without reckoning the total loss of the equilibrium of Europe, and the Despotism of the House of Bourbon and of Austria established in Europe, of which it is superfluous to consider the fatal consequences—de *faire envisager les suites funestes.*"

NOTE TO U. 3.

"Stetin, 1756.

"All this affair turns upon two points : the one is to gain Russia, which is what the King of England proposes to himself to do ; if he succeed, Germany will remain tranquil, and we shall have nothing to fear ; the other is (supposing that the news which has come from the Hague confirms itself, and that the Empress of Russia is persuaded to renounce her engagements that she has taken with England) to turn one's-self to the side of the Turks, and to scatter money to assure one's-self of a Diversion on their part, and at the same time to make on both sides, the King of England and myself, all those augmentations *specified* in the body of the Despatch, to put us in a condition to resist all the enterprises of our enemies. I believe that there is no time to lose for all this, and if measures are not taken in advance at Constantinople, in case that we miscarry at Petersburgh, it will befall us to take our measures too late. The best of all these means ('partis') will be that of peace ; in case there is no means of making it between this and the end of the year, it will be necessary to think in good time of the means of defending one's-self, and to neglect nothing for our mutual preservation. Say to M. Mitchell that it is not a question of

men, but of the gravest interests of Prussia and of England,
and that the least negligence in our pressing measures will
in time cause our mutual ruin.

"F." *

---

*" Summary of Arguments by which an Austrian Minister
may serve himself to draw Subsidies from England, the year
1764.* †

1. "He will mark in touching terms the regrets of the
Empress Queen to have abandoned the Alliance of England,
he will throw all the fault of it on the Count Caunitz,‡
whose credit and insinuations had forced the Queen to take
this part.

2. " He will adroitly insinuate that notwithstanding the
engagements that the Queen had had with France, she had
by preference served the King of England, and the inter-
position of her good offices to keep fair with the Electorate of
Hanover, which, without the Court of Vienna, would have
been sacked and burnt.

3. " That the Alliance with France had been but momentarily concluded in an instant of humour and spite, and sustained by necessity.

4. " That to re-establish the Equilibrium of Europe a return
must of necessity be made to the Ancient Engagements, that
England was more interested in them than the Empress

* Writings of Frederic of Prussia, MS. Mus. Brit.

† For the occasion of this Satire, see Narrative, Vol. ii. *After
the battle of Kölin, when King Frederic was lodged in the Bishop's Palace with Mitchell*, date 1757.

‡ Called by French historians " Prince Kaunitz," Austrian
Ambassador at Versailles.

Queen for the cause that to form a counterpoise to the too great Power of France, an ally is necessary to England possessed of great and very populated provinces, from which might be drawn a number of soldiers to oppose them to the Common Enemy.

5. "That England had made experience during the last war of her insufficiency to resist France by sea, that for interest sea-wars must be sustained by great Diversions on Land, of which no other power is capable but the Queen of Hungary.

6. "This Minister will enlarge much on the rambles of the human mind, and that there are certain faults which the common welfare demands to be mutually pardoned.

"He will add that it was happy for England that the House of Austria had connections with France, because now it was convinced by experience of the error and falsity of this system, and that having become wise to its cost it regarded as an invariable principle of Austrian policy never to depart at any time from the Alliance of England, and to sustain the interests of that Power as its own, and that it could boldly affirm that no Austrian Minister would ever dare to speak in a different tone to that of the Queen without running to his certain ruin.

"After having laboured a long time to produce opinions favourable to himself by such fine discourse, and being lavish of lamentations on the past blindness of his Court, he will insinuate *adroitly* to the Ministers, that the greatest reproach that Vienna made to itself was to have ceded (?) to the French, by the wrong that this port in their hands did to the commerce of the English; that it was known in London, that the Court of Vienna had constantly regarded Flanders and Brabant as provinces which were in its keeping, but that the sole interest that it took in the commerce of England makes it desirous of withdrawing that city from the hands of the French, as by that means it would be able to repair the wrong it had committed in a time of vertigo to .... and good allies, and to re-place things nearly on the footing as they ought to be.

"The Britannic Minister of the year 1763, touched by the sincere repentance of the Queen of Hungary, and by the interest that she takes in the commerce of the nation, grants to her yearly *a million of pounds sterling* to withdraw Ostend, Nieuport, Furnes, and Dunkerke* from the hands of the French, he promises to regard the past as though it had not happened, and agrees that England cannot find in Europe an Ally more zealous, more disinterested, nor more grateful than the Queen of Hungary."

"*Ipse Dixit.* Finis of the Professions
of Our Lady." †

"I will never see," writes Frederic, to the Marquis d'Argens ‡ at this time, "the moment which shall oblige me to make a disadvantageous peace .... I will either suffer myself to be buried under the ruins of my country, or if this consolation appears too much to fate which persecutes me, I shall know how to put an end to my misfortunes when it will be no longer possible to endure them. .... When everything is lost, when no hope is left, life is a disgrace and death a duty."

* Dunquerque, a town of French Flanders on the Calne, which here falls into the English Channel. Its government included some neighbouring villages.

† MSS. King of Prussia, Mus. Brit.

‡ See Voltaire's Letter to the Marquis d'Argens, this Appendix. "*French Finance and Philosophy.*"

" For nine months together," writes M. Mitchell to Lord
Holdernesse, " in consequence of the internal dissension of
England, the King has been answered with fair words.   But in
the situation his affairs now are in, there is no time to be lost :
if England will not endeavour to save him, he must save himself as he can."

On the 28th August Mitchell writes to Lord Holdernesse :
" England is cheated, and its Ministers duped by Hanover.
. . . . You know what has happened.   Why was not the
King of Prussia previously consulted ?   I can answer with
my head, he would have yielded to any reasonable proposal
for the safety of Hanover.   What will posterity say if an
administration that made the treaty of Westminster, for the
safety of Hanover, and suffered the Hanoverian Ministers to
say openly that they had no treaty with the King of Prussia,
. . . whose misfortunes are owing to his generosity and
good faith ?

" Let us have done with negotiating ; after what has happened no man will trust us.   I know not how to look the
King of Prussia in the face ; and honour, my lord, is not to be
purchased with money.   Nothing " (less) " than a miracle, or
an absolute submission to France, can save the King."

After the Battle of Kölin, the King of Prussia had said to
Mr Mitchell :—

" I will now speak to you as a private man.   You know
my aversion to all subsidies,—that I ever refuse them.   I
thought, and I still think, it is too mean a footing to put myself
upon ; considering the great progress of my enemies, I wish,
however, to know whether I may depend upon assistance."*

* Substance of this note, quoted from the Mitchell Papers by
the Translator of Von Raumer's " Contributions to Modern History," in favour of the K. of Prussia.

NOTE TO P. 153. NARRATIVE, VOL. II.

Copy of Convention between His Majesty and the K. of Prussia concluded, and signed at London the 7th Dec., 1758. (In Lord Holdernesse's of the 8th Dec., 1758.) *

" Be it Notorious (*Notoire*), &c. &c. That the onerous war in which His Prussian Majesty finds himself engaged, putting him in the necessity of making new Efforts to defend himself against the great number of enemies by which his States are assailed : And being thus obliged to concert anew with His Britannic Majesty . . . for their Defence and common safety : And his Britannic Majesty the King of Great Britain having made known at the same time the Desire which He has to draw closer the Bonds of Friendship which subsist between the Two Courts, &c. &c., the following articles are agreed :

" 1. It is agreed (*on est convenu*) that all the preceding Treaties (*précédents*) which subsist, between the Two Courts, of whatever Date and Nature they may be, and principally that of Westminster of the *16th of January of the year* 1756,† as also that the Convention of the 11th of April of the year current, shall be reputed, called over again, and confirmed (*censés, rappelles, et confirmés*) by the present Convention, in

---

* MS. 6816. f. 122. British Museum. Extracts literally translated.

† By this it will be seen that French chronicles (quoted in the Narrative) are wrong by 12 hours as to the date of the Treaty between England and Prussia. The Treaty of neutrality between France and Austria (signed by Count Stahrenberg, the Count de Rouillé, and the Abbé de Bernis) is dated the 1st May, 1756, four months afterwards. Wenck *C. Jur. Gent.* Amster., tome 3, p. 139.

all their points, articles, and clauses, and shall be of the same force as if they were inserted here word by word.

"2. His Majesty the King of Gt. Britain engages himself to make payable (*faire payer*) in the City of London, between the hands of the Person or of the Persons who shall be authorized to that effect by His Majesty the King of Prussia, the Sum of Four Millions of Crowns of Germany (*Quatre Millions d'Ecus d'Allemagne*), amounting to Six Hundred Sixty and Ten Thousand Livres (*Montant à Six Cent Soixante et Dix Mille Livres sterling*) ;   The which Sum shall be paid entire (*en entier et en un seul Terme*) immediately after the Exchange of the Ratifications, at the Requisition of His Prussian Majesty.

"3. His Majesty the King of Prussia engages himself on His Side to employ the said Sum for the maintenance and the Augmentation of His Forces, the which shall act in the manner the most useful to the common cause, and to the End proposed by their said Majesties for reciprocal Defence and for Mutual Safety.

"4. The High Contractors (*contractants*) engaging themselves moreover, *savoir* His Britannic Majesty, *tant comme Roy que comme Electeur*, ... and on the other His Prussian Majesty, not to conclude any Treaty of Peace, of Truce (*Trève*), or of Neutrality, nor other Convention or agreement *whatever* with the Powers who have taken Part in the Present War, but by Concert and by a mutual agreement.

"5. This Convention will be ratified, and the Ratifications exchanged upon one part and upon the other in the term of six weeks, to count from the date of the Signature of the present Convention, &c. &c.

"Done at London, the 7th Day of December, the year of Grace, 1758."

Signed on the side of England :   On the side of Prussia :

    Robert Henley, C. S.   Les Sieurs Dodo Henry.

    Granville —— P.   Baron de Knyphausen.

    Holles, Newcastle.   Louis Mitchell.

    Holdernesse.

    Hardwicke.

    Wm. Pitt.

Copy of a Letter from His Majesty to Monsieur Le Marquise d'Argens. Dated Hermansderff, near Breslau, 27th August, 1760.[*]

" . . . . Eh bien Mon Cher Marquis, que devient le *Pari* de la France? Vous voyez que votre Nation est plus aveugle que vous ne l'avez cru. Ces fous perdront le Canada et Pondichéri pour faire plaisir à la Reine d'Hongrie, et à la Czarine, vœuille le Ciel que le Prince Ferdinand les paye bien de leur Zele ! . . . . Adieu Mon Cher Marquis je vous embrasse."

(CYPHER.)

Copy of Secret Intelligence, Versailles, 3rd January, 1758. [†]

2993 2265 1637 786   1589   172   694   1821
"Our Minister at Vienna by Order of the Court has had

        2443   2796   8527   777   1068
a long conference with Count Kaunitz to be informed

1830 346   35,269 603   2404   803 2,917,360
from Him of the exact situation of the Empress's Army

---

[*] MS. 6843. f. 162. B. M.

[†] *British Museum,* MS. 6816. *Plut. P. L. X.* v. iii. 1.

2626,   1928.

and of her Finances.* He writes that Count Kaunitz told
him the Empress Queen wanted 100m. Recruits, 24m. Horses,
and that many other Things were equally necessary to
restore Her Army. He proposed Mortgaging the Remains
of the Pays Bas and Dutchy of Luxembourg for the
Security of the Money to be advanced. This proposal has
been examined in council ; if they refuse to lend the money it
will not be in the Empress's Power to act offensively,
and thereby they may lose the Object that induced them
to enter into war, but should the war after all prove unsuccessful, they are sensible they shall throw away this Treasure
all they know that neither the Maritime Powers nor the King
of Prussia will consent that any part of the Pays Bas shall
remain in the possession of France, as Her Imperial Majesty
has no Right either to give Mortgages or dispose of it. Count
Stainville † had assured " (satisfied) " the Court that think
very differently from Count Kaunitz. . . . I must remark that
Count Kaunitz assured Monsieur de Stainville that, Notwithstanding all the Victories of The King of Prussia, He
would be ruined at last for want of men, but his assertion is
not credited here, as the Court know His Prussian Majesty
intends to augment His Forces this Year.‡ Monsieur de
Stainville in His Letter gives such accounts of the misery
of the Austrian Troops that are returned in Bohemia, that
it is hardly credible, and He says there has been such a
Quarrel between Prince Charles of Lorrain, and Mareschal
Daun, that they can never more serve together.

* The Cyphers are interlineated through three parts of the letter,
but are not here inserted as rendering it tiresome to read.
  † Duke de Choiseul.
  ‡ See Treaty foregoing.

"I observe that the Ministers here grow daily more uneasy, and no one more so than Mareschal de Belleisle.* He
fears the King's Army will not be able to support Themselves in the conquered country. The Duke of Richelieu has
very lately represented to the King that his army daily
grows weaker, and his situation daily more critical, inso-
much that he advises saving the Remains of the Army by
retiring in Time,—If Prince Ferdinand should receive the
Succours from the King of Prussia, which he hears are in
March to join Him. I told you before that the Duke
of Richelieu had Leave to take such a Position as He
judged most advantageous, I now add that He has full
Powers to act as He thinks most for His Majesty's service
without waiting for farther Orders from Court.† I am informed that the Court have demanded of Monsieur d'Affri,
what Effect the Entry of our Troops into the Rest of the
Pays Bas and Luxembourg would produce in Holland. I
know that several of the Council are of Opinion to take
Possession of both, and I am informed Madame Pompadour approves their Sentiments, so I should not be surprised
to see it executed very suddenly, notwithstanding the
Opposition it has met with, and the more so as the Empress
now inclines to retire all Her Forces out of the Low
Countries and from Luxembourg, which will furnish this
Court with the Pretence of Lending the Empress Queen
Troops to garrison the latter and of defending the former."

* The Count de Gisors, Marshal Belleisle's son, was killed at the
Battle of Crevelt, June 13, under the Prince de Clermont.

† "The Duc de Richelieu was seduced and won over by the
King of Prussia, and allowed Madame de Pompadour's favourite
General (Soubise) to lose the Battle of Rosbach." *De Goncourt*
(*Historians adverse to Madame Pompadour*), 1860.

Extracts from an original Letter in cypher,* sent by Sir C. Hanbury Williams (British Envoy) to Lord Holdernesse (from Petersburgh), July, 1756.†

"Secret."

In the first part of this letter, Sir C. Hanbury Williams takes great credit to himself for having successfully prevented the presentation of a certain 'Douglas' at the Court of Russia, because the said Douglas "is not only in correspondence with our Enemies, but is actually in the service, and even wanted to bring over a French Marshal to Peters-

* *Mr Douglas, an English subject, arrived at St Petersburgh as a Spy for France. Fol. 3. Orig.*

Cypher (afterwards interlineated with different coloured ink), Quoted by Sir Henry Ellis.

351 219 1150 790 1836 1159 1490 1605 135
You may depend upon being informed of every thing that

1295 131, 1695 1840 1848 2528 349 373 1327 680
passes here, and I must begin with telling you that by the

1447,257 1461 178 1191 2111 262 1508 2404 787
ungratefull endeavours of the House of Austria and the Secret

1197 2324 1213 2687 831 768 2179 98
Intrigues of Mr Douglass the face of Affairs is totally changed

129 2586 788 2203 831 1884 1428 873 1945
from what it was a year ago. . . . . It is now eight months

23 82 1731 694 349 811 172 2113
ago since Mr Douglass came here for the first time. He

1145 662 768 2179 481 677 1121 2939 1476
made me a visit, but all his Discourses, and from many other

1211 611 1053
circumstances, I did immediately suspect him of being a French
439.

spy, &c.

† See Sir H. Williams' Letter to the King of Prussia (this Appendix), with Aut. Letters from the Grand Duke Peter, and the Grand Duchess Catharine.

burg. Such things, in my Opinion, Constitute him a Rebel."
Sir Hanbury informs that there are adverse political parties
at the Russian Court, then:

"The chief Argument made use of here, and which they
daily preach to the Empress, is that England has not yet paid
the 100,000 pounds, and that consequently the Treaty is broke,
and this I am well assured is the only Argument that has any
Weight with her Imperial Majesty. Our best friends here,
therefore, wish most ardently that, if possible, this money
might be paid, which They think might certainly prevent all
the malicious and ungrateful schemes of the House of Austria,
and most probably bring back this Court to their former
Right way of thinking.

"I am, &c.,

"C. Hanbury Williams."

This 100,000 pounds unpaid by England to Russia, affected
Spain; to judge from the following Letter (Extracts) of the
same date from the Court of Madrid, written by

Sir Benjamin Keene, to Mr. Fox,

Dated, Madrid, 14th July, 1756.

"Most Secret."

After expressing his hopes that "Spain still holds steadily,"
Sir Benjamin informs Mr Fox, that "They apprehend that
the Court of Russia, notwithstanding the opportune com-
munications I had his Majesty's" (Britannic) "commands to
make here, may be swayed from its good pretensions by the
Artifices of the Queen of Hungary and Her new Ally; but
if these Doubts may have their Inconveniency on one Hand,
they have probably had their Utility on another; for from

---

* See further notice of Sir B. Keene, British Plenipotentiary
at Madrid, by Lord Chatham—'Peace Proposals'—this Appendix.

hence it has been demonstrated to their Catholic Majesties
that in Case such a Misfortune should happen, the Crown of
Spain must make but a mean figure in the World. The junction of three such Powers as France, the Empress Queen,
and the Czarina would tempt and enable Them to give the
Law to all the rest . . . . . I may acquaint you in the greatest
Confidence that the Application His Majesty " (Britannic) has
made to the Court of Naples * to dissuade it from acceding

---

* Don Carlos, King of the Two Sicilies, eldest son of Elizabeth
Farinese, second wife to the late King of Spain, was half-brother to
Ferdinand reigning King of Spain. King Ferdinand was, by the
Savoyard blood of his mother (daughter of the King of Sardinia),
less inclined than were his late father or his brother to the House of
Bourbon. Also, the Dauphin of France had refused to wed King
Ferdinand's own sister, she being half-sister to the Dauphin's first
wife.† Nevertheless more *Cordons Bleus* (the mark of highest
honour) were sent from Versailles to Madrid than ever before,
and were reciprocated by orders from Spain to France. King
Ferdinand wished to maintain a just balance between France
and England, for the sake of Spain both in the Old and New
Worlds. But upon the representations of the French Ambassador
Spain armed herself in defensive preparation " (*il ne s'agit pas
encore de la guerre mais de s'y préparer*). " Armaments developed
themselves off Spain. England watched. England was informed
that France had stipulated to restore Minorca and Gibraltar to
Spain.‡ Minorca taken, France hoped to possess herself of
Gibraltar. With such an Admiral as Galissonière, what might not
France do ? But suddenly Admiral Galissonière, who had been summoned for Minorca honours to Versailles, died. With Galissonière
perished the head of the French Navy, and the hope declined of
advantageous conjunction of the navies of France and Spain.
Thus, England again ruled the sea; although, says Voltaire,
" *Dans ce pays ci il faut tuer un Amiral de temps en temps
pour encourager les autres.*"

---

† See Appendix, Vol. I.
‡ See Chatham correspondence, this Appendix, p. 97.

to that Treaty, has not been very pleasing here. The Independent Footing the King of the Two Sicilies pretended to put himself upon with regard to the King of Spain, when He gave Him that open Slur of refusing to accede to the Treaty of Aranjuez, will hardly ever be forgotten. The conduct of the Court of Naples in continuing affected Marks of the like Independency will not allow the elder brother to forget either the Offence or the Cause of it. From hence it follows, that the very Doubts of the Court of Naples, or Their seeming to consider for Themselves what Party they are to follow, except such a one as Spain shall point out to them, must give Disgust here. The King of Spain would have his Brother know there is no Security for Him but that which may be derived from His protection.* All steps, therefore, from the Friends of Spain that encourage Don Carlos (if I may use the expression) to make too much a king of Himself, are observed Here. . . . But I follow the Advice of Veracity Itself, and shall never suspect any base Proceeding at this Court as long as He † is in Power. It is true I do not so much as insinuate to Him the least Doubt about His intentions, the least sign of mistrust in me would be a calumny he does not deserve.

"For these Reasons, Sir, I will own that the sending of Eight Stout Ships into the Mediterranean gives me no pain. The design of Them is to support the Part Spain is acting with Dignity, and likewise to curb the Moors. Spain has no Reason to increase her Force to make Herself a more acceptable Gift to France, who will gladly accept Her as She is.

* Which justifies the Neapolitan King's nickname of "Baby Carlos."

† General Wall; of Irish birth, and Minister of Spain. Formerly Ambassador of England. See this Appendix, p. 98.

Upon the whole she need not be stronger to do us harm. They have been busy at Paris upon the Old Topick of Our Disputes in America. I lately wrote a Word to You upon the project of France to call Religion (without caring much for Religion itself) to Her Aid, in order to embroil the affairs of Europe more or less according to Her interest, for good, or bad success, . . . in Suspicion that this is the hidden foundation of the late Treaty invented by the Artificers of France, and consented to by the Bigotry of Vienna, both flattering themselves with the Improbability that Spain will ever join against Them in a Protestant cause.

" I am, &c.,
" B. KEENE." *

NOTE TO P. 201. VOL. II.

AUTOGRAPHS OF ROYAL LETTERS AND OTHER STATE
DOCUMENTS, LABELLED " OF SINGULAR IMPORTANCE."

1757.

" *Original Letters to Sir Charles Hanbury Williams from the Grand Duke Peter, and the Grand Duchess Catherine; afterwards Empress of Russia.* ('*Of Singular Importance.*') *With a letter from Sir Charles H. Williams . . . . . . explaining the manner in which thay came to be deposited with Sir*

---

* " The Queen of Spain, governing the King her husband, Ferdinand VI., prevents his declaring himself at the time his doing so would have been useful. The Duc de Choiseul afterwards engaged the King Charles 3rd, Successor of Ferdinand, by the ' Family Compact,' when Spain could no longer unite her weakness with ours and partake our losses." *Duclos*, p. 526, Tome 2.

Andrew Mitchell.* Also an original Letter from Sir C. H. Williams to the King of Prussia. And the Original Notification from the Court of St Petersburgh to Berlin, of the death of the Empress Elizabeth Petrowna, the ally of France and Austria."

It will be remembered that the Czarina of Russia, Elizabeth Petrowna, daughter of Peter the Great, was well affected towards Austria. (See 1st vol. of this work.) In the war of 1756 she joined Austria openly. In 1762, the Empress Elizabeth Petrowna died. She was succeeded by her nephew, Peter III. He began his reign by adopting liberal principles, but his people were too ignorant to appreciate these benefits, and his attempt to improve the army by the adoption of the Prussian Exercise gave offence to them. His Queen Catherine, to whom he had been unfaithful, gave her aid to conspiracies formed against him, and by the soldiery he was deposed and imprisoned the same year he began to reign; and Catherine, in 1762, was proclaimed Empress of all the Russias as Catherine II. These hints to the reader may help to interest him in the following correspondence, as characteristic not only of Peter and of the strong-minded Catherine, but as showing also the adverse current of their diplomacy in Russia, during the life-time of the Empress Elizabeth, and the effect of that diplomacy upon France and Austria.

Chevalier Hanbury Williams (Ambassador of Great Britain at the Court of St. Petersburgh) had, when recalled in 1757, succeeded in gaining the following letters from Peter and Catherine, which letters (being in favour of England and Prussia) so puffed up the Chevalier with hopes of reward,

---

* Mus. Brit. MS. 6864.

that he wrote thus, with quaint orthography, to his brother diplomatist : —

> " A Monsieur
> " Monsieur Andrew Mitchell,
> " Ministre de Sa Majesté Britannique
> " A Breslaw.

" My dear Friend,

"Such a Letter of four lines you never recieved soon after you recieved this, perhaps the same Day, certainly the next. What I have to say to you, is to insist that you tell me exactly what the King of Prussia says to my Letter; I will tell the truth, the whole truth, and nothing but the truth.

" I believe that you will find what He says will soon put me upon the highest footing of any man in England at this time. That may perhaps give me an opportunity of repaying you some of the great obligations I have to you ; whenever I am in that situation, command me freely, for I am your obliged and sincere friend,

" C. Hanbury Williams.

"Mr. Hecht has thought my Dispatches worth sending by a particular courier ; don't fail to answer me by return of the same courier."

Then follows, written upside down,

" I flatter myself you will also write to the King what the King of Prussia says :

" I fancy the letter I have wrote to the King will please you : He will undoubtedly show it to you, or I would send you a copy to the utmost efferts of those parts which God has given me."

In very large and highly flourishing hand-writing, the Grand Duke Peter addresses himself thus, in somewhat barbaric French, to the " Chevalier Hanbury Williams."*

" Sir,

"I regret infinitely not to have had the pleasure before your departure to tell you by mouth how much by your merit and by your conduct you have attracted my esteem towards your self. I thank you, and do not doubt of your attachment to my interests. They are bound to those of the King of England by more than one side. I hope that the Common Enemy of the two kingdoms (*s'en ressentira*) will feel this one day. I am very glad to see that you rendered justice to me upon that point. I pray you to interest yourself near the King your Master upon my part for (?). He is a worthy and faithful subject. I shall have towards you a very particular obligation, being with the very distinguished consideration,

" Sir,

" Of your Excellence,

" The very affectionate friend,

PETER."

"This 19th of August, 1757."

From the Grand Duchess Catherine :

(In a large bold handwriting.)

" Sir,

"I have taken the resolution to write to you, not being able to see you, to make my Adieux to you. The

* Autograph. Mus. Brit. MS. 6864.

most sincere regrets accompany him whom I regard as one of my best friends, and whose conduct has attracted all my esteem and my friendship. I shall never forget the obligations which I have to you. To recompense you according to the nobility of your sentiments, this is what I will do.

"I will seize all imaginable occasions to bring Russia to that which I recognise for her true interests, which is to be bound intimately to England, to give to the latter, by all human help, the ascendant which she ought to have for the welfare of all Europe, and more in particular for that of Russia. Over their common Enemies, such as France, of which the greatness is the shame of Russia, I will study to put in practice these sentiments, I will build thereon my glory, and I will thereby prove its solidity to the King your Master. I am very glad that the welfare of Russia compels me to acquit myself towards England of the personal obligations that I have to His Majesty, of which I preserve the remembrance with the most lively gratitude. I pray you, confidently, Sir, to arrange for the best that of which you are so instructed. Be persuaded that one of the things of the world I desire the most, is to bring you back here in triumph.

" I hope that one day the King your Master will not refuse to me the favour that I ask of him to see you again.

" Nothing to him will come of it but profit. I am with a consideration quite particular,

" Sir,

" Of your Excellence,

" The very devoted Friend,

" CATERINE." *

" This 19th of August, 1757."

* Autograph. Mus. Brit. MS. 6864.

To the Chevalier Hanbury Williams, Catherine adds :

" Monsieur,

" Je suis au desespoir d'être privé du plaisir que j'aurois *eue* a Vous voir a Vous parler en liberté. Votre amitié des-interressée pour moi et pour le G.D. est sans exemple. Mon Cœur est ulceré par la dureté du traitement que Vous essay*é*; Mais aussi ma plus vive reconnaissance pour Vous sera eternelle. Puissent des tems plus heureux me permettre de Vous la prouver dans toute son etendue ! Elle egale (et c'est tout dire) les obligations que je Vous ai, et l'estime infinie qui est due a la beauté de Votre Caractere. Adieu mon meilleur, mon cher.

" Ami." *

(Which shows that even the great Catherine, being woman, could not dispense with a Postscript, and that from her infirmity on this point, it was no wonder the Chevalier Williams had his head turned.)

The Chevalier Hanbury Williams, having caught the epidemic of flattery, writes, with a full puff of gratified vanity to King Frederic :

" Sire,†

" Since I have received the Letter that Your Majesty graciously ordered Monsieur Vierich to write to me, I have always floated between Modesty and Gratitude, without being able to decide upon the Means the most humble and the most proper to thank your Majesty, and it is but in prostrating myself before your sacred Feet that I ask of you Pardon for the Liberty that I take in

---

* Autograph. Mus. Brit. MS. 6864.

† " *Lettre du Chevalier Hanbury Williams à Sa Majesté le Roy de Prusse,*" MS. 6864.

addressing to you this Letter, very humbly to thank your
Majesty for having deigned to remember the Zeal of a
faithful Servant, and at the same time to forget the small-
ness of his Services. Even the Zeal which I bear to the
sacred Person of Your Majesty cannot add the least Merit
to my actions. I have always had much for my Religion
and for Liberty, and the effects of this cause will oblige
me in spite of myself to devote myself to their Defender,
Who sustains Justice by his two Companions, Prudence
and Courage; Who makes Antiquity blush, the Admiration
of the present Century, and Who certainly be the agreeable
astonishment of posterity, the which will without doubt
regard the exploits of FREDERICUS MAXIMUS in the year
(l'Année distinguée superieurement par son Hero 'sur toute
autre), the year distinguished by its Hero above all others,
1757, as the productions of an entire century, and, as the
perfect Statue Naked of Venus de Medicis above all ORNA-
MENT. He who will narrate them in the most simple
and Truthful Manner will write them best, and will render
most justice to His Hero. I know but of one Living who
is capable to do so, and it is with transport that I indicate
it is the immortal Production of the united Valorous blood
of the Illustrious Houses of Brunswick and of Brandenbourg,
it is the grandson of my Royal defunct Sovereign, it is the
Nephew, the Ally, the Friend of my AUGUST MASTER and
of my Country, and it is with Truth the most religious, and
almost with Enthusiasm that I declare it is HIMSELF.

"But, amongst all Great Authors who until this have
desired to attempt to praise or tell the Truth (for it is the
same thing) of *your* Majesty, I have met none, who in my
opinion has perceived the most brilliant Leaf of your two
Laurel trees. Deign, Great King, permit that a pencil as

unskilful dare to trace it to You. You are, Sire, the only Monarch who ever allied himself, and in consequence of that alliance, have acted in concert with the perfidious House of Bourbon. Who has known by his superior Foresight how to avoid that shoal (*écœul*) against which all the other Powers of Europe have, turn by turn, made Shipwreck? They have all began under the Title of Allies. They have all ended by that of Dupe, or of Slave; in the Front of that shameful Band the ungrateful House of Austria presents herself to-day for the twentieth time, and I dare to assure your Majesty that this Calculation is just. Your innate Dignity has guaranteed you from the last, and your Boundless Wit (*Esprit*) with which Heaven has endowed you, SIRE, has saved you from the First.

" Whereunto could I not pursue the noble subject which I fear has already carried me away too far? For I hear a voice which stops me and orders me to stop. It is that of a good cause. It scolds me (*gronde*) for the moments which your Majesty will lose in reading this letter, and reproaches me for them as for a Theft which I have made to him. I stop, then, Sire, for against You it is impossible for me to sin, as to add to the ardent Zeal, the inviolable Attachment, and the perpetual Gratitude with which I have the Honour, and shall never cease to be,

" Sire,

" Of YOUR MAJESTY,

" The very humble, very grateful,

" And very devoted Servant,

" The Chevalier CHARLES HANBURY WILLIAMS.*

"Hamburgh, this 8th Feb., 1758."

* MS. Mus. Brit. 6864.

As a solitary sample of his Prussian Majesty's politeness to the fair sex, Frederic writes to Catherine (when she has become Empress) in 1767.

"*Lettre du Roy de Prusse à l'Imperatrice de Russie de Potsdam.*

"Madame, my Sister,

"I ought to begin by thanking your Majesty for the favour you have done me in communicating to me your work upon the laws. The ancient Greeks . . . would have placed your Majesty between Lycurgus and Solon." . . . .

To a mutual diplomatic friend Frederic adds: "I have read with admiration the work of the Empress; I have not wished to tell her all I think of it because she might have suspected me of flattery, but I can say to you in managing her modesty, that it is a work masculine, nervous, and worthy of a great man. History tells us that Semiramis commanded armies; the Queen Elizabeth passed for a good politician; the Queen Empress has showed much firmness on the Advent of her reign; but no woman yet had been a she-lawgiver (legis-latrice); that glory was reserved for the Empress of Russia, who deserves it well.

"Signed, Fédéric." *

* MS. 6864.

Catherine was declared associate of the Academy of Berlin. In her address, which was read to that learned Assembly, she said: "Under the auspices of a King endowed with a spirit so sublime, so enlightened, and surrounded by so much glory, you are accustomed to judge of men and of things without prejudice and without illusion . . . . My science is limited to the knowledge that all men are my brothers. . . . I will employ all my life to rule my actions upon this principle. . . . . Sign, Caterine."

In 1762, just as Frederic declared that Catherine's right place

" Translation" (*into French*) *" Of the Emperor of Russia's
Notification to the King of Prussia of the death of the Empress
of Russia, the* 25*th Decembre. Vieux Stille,* 1761."

" We, Peter III. Emperor of all the Russias, to the
Most Serene Frederic, King of Prussia. It has pleased
the Most High " ('powerful' erased) " to call to Himself, on
the 25th of this month, after a long and painful malady, the
Most Serene Empress of all the Russias, Elizabeth Petrowna
our very dear Aunt. We have not wished to fail in informing
your Majesty of an event so sad for us, but by which we are
happily to mount, and to the satisfaction of all our Subjects,
upon the Imperial Throne of Russia, to the which we are called
by the right of blood and by a legitimate succession. Not to
flatter you, but by a Suite of friendship which has existed "
('*always*' erased) " between our predecessors and your Majesty,
you " (*elle-Majesté*) " will take not only some part in this
new event, but above all you will have the same sentiments

ought to be between Solon and Lycurgus, Horace Walpole asks an
Englishman (in reference to the marital conduct of the fair Imperial Legislatrix), " What do you say to a Czarina mounting her
horse, and marching at the head of 14,000 men, with a large train
of artillery, to dethrone her husband ? Yet she is not the only
virago in that country ; the conspiracy was conducted by the sister
of the Czar's mistress, a heroine under twenty ! . . . . The Czarina
has only robbed ' *Peter* to pay Paul. ' "
The letter of Frederic to Catherine was also the new era of a
revolution in his manners towards women. A few years later,
Thiébault the Frenchman (Professor of Belles Lettres at Berlin by
recommendation of d'Alembert) declares that Frederic gave a
general order that letters addressed to his Majesty from women
should be answered by his Secretaries with politeness. Experience
had compelled the great Monarch by that time to esteem the
feminine political importance of the 18th century.

and the same inclinations by which we are animated, to renew, to extend, and to *establish* ('to affirm and to confirm' interlineated above and half scratched out) in a durable manner the friendship and the good intelligence of" (word undecipherable) "which tends to reciprocal advantage. It is a care by which we will always occupy ourselves particularly in consequence of our distinguished sentiments ('*preferables*') towards your Majesty, and we will seize with pleasure every proper occasion to convince your Majesty more and more of our sincere and inviolable inclinations to attain to that end. Waiting (*en attendant*) we recommend Your Majesty to the protection of the All-Powerful, and are always ready to render to him all services.

"Given at Petersburgh the 25th Dec. 1751."*

In 1763, Augustus, King of Poland, died. Then did Frederic, the woman scorner, unite with Catherine the she-law-giver "greater than Semiramis" to effect the partition of Poland. Scenes of horror followed, although in the mean while the 'illustrious brigand' had indited this philosophic peace-poem, which Marshal Keith had forwarded to Mr Mitchell, the British Plenipotentiary at Magdebourg, by his Prussian Majesty's request.

NOTE TO P. 273.

Verses by King Frederic,
L'Origine du Mal. A.D. 1761.

"*Autograph writings of Frederic of Prussia.*" Mus. Brit.

"Ministre vertueux d'un peuple dont les loix
Ont a leur Sage frein assujetis leurs Rois,

* Copies of Royal Mus. Brit. Letters, MS., 6864.

Chez vous la liberte respire auprès du Trone
Sans qu'armé de son foudre un monarque l'etonne.
Vos Princes jouissants d'un droit vraiment Royal,
Sont puissans pour le bien, sans pouvoir pour le mal.
Que leur sort est heureux, qu'ils sont dignes d'envie!
Ils sont à la vertu soumis toute leur vie.

La justice est pour eux la regle du devoir,
Et leur caprice en vain reclame leur pouvoir.
Pourquoi, mon cher Mitchel, pourquoi l'Etre Suprême,
N'at-il donc pas daigné nous enchainer de même?
Nous porterions encore le Peau de la bonté
S'il nous avai ravi la triste liberté
De quitter la vertu pour embrasser le vice,
Pourquoi nous exposer au bords du precipice.

Moins libres dans nos choix nous serions plus heureux,
Si la necessité nous rendoit vertueux.
La haine, l'interest, l'orgueil, la jalousie
Des crimes corrupteurs la noire frenesie,
Loin (loing) d'entrer dans nos cœurs et de nous abuser
N'auroient plus le pouvoir de nous tiranniser.
L'innocence et la paix habiteroient la terre,
Et l'on ne verroit plus de meurtres, in de guerre, &c.

Dated: &c. (In small handwriting),
"Breslau le 28 de Decembre, 1761."
With large envelope attached, sealed with crown: addressed,
"Son Excellence Monsieur de Mitchel, Ministre
"Plenipotentiaire de S. M. Britanique
"A Magdebourg." *

* Sir Andrew Mitchell had become much attached to the King
of Prussia. When Mitchell was to leave Berlin, (25th of June,

NOTE TO P. 189, VOL. II.

"ROYAL LETTERS."

*Letter from the King of Poland (father of the Dauphiness of
France) to Frederic the Great, King of Prussia.**

" Monsieur Mon Frère,

"The minister of your Majesty at my court having
made requisition for the passage of your troops † by my
States to go into Bohemia, I have granted it to him, hoping
that your Majesty will cause an exact Discipline to be
observed. Also: I send to your Majesty my Lieutenant-

1765,) the King wrote to him : " I am very sorry, my dear Mitchell,
that your recall entirely separates us ; however, the memory of your
good conduct and of your merit will not be lost here." But even
Mon cher Mitchell testifies like Voltaire, " Frederick is very artful,
and possesses in the most eminent degree the talent of conciliating
those he has a mind to gain."

King Frederic writes in 1761 to M. Mitchell at Magdebourg with
his own hand (in reply to the letter of that functionary notifying to
him, Fédéric, the marriage of His Britannic Majesty with the Queen
his wife) : " I have but at this moment received your letter, you
will judge by that our correspondence is very interrupted" (by the
badness of the roads). " I am very afflicted to learn the bad state
of your health. Merit is not then an immunity against maladies (le
merite ne donc point de privilege Contre Les Maladies) ; I pray you
to employ all your care to re-establish yourself, and to remember,
sometimes, the absent   " Fédéric."

MSS. Mus. Brit. 6843.

* Mitchell Papers, MSS. Mus. Brit. 6864.

† In the originals, as in most such Documents, the second person
plural varies with the third person singular.

In reading these letters, showing the practical " *Origin of the
Evil*," remember Machiavel,—*Maxim* 3 (see Prologue) : " *By sudden surprisall and boldnesse, many times more is obtained than by
ordinary meanes can be gotten*."

General and Commandant of the Swiss corps, Sieur de Meagher, for the better to concert all that is relative to this march and to regulate the execution of it. I have otherwise been strongly surprised by some unexpected Declarations, and little conformable to the Treaty of Peace and to the Friendship which subsists between us, the Baron de Maltzhan has added in the name of your Majesty. But I hope that you will explain yourself favourably to the above-named Sr de Meagher in a way to re-assure me entirely thereupon. I await that explanation with all confidence, and am, with the most perfect esteem and consideration,

"Monsieur Mon Frère,

"Of your Majesty,

"The good Brother,

"Auguste Rex."

"At Dresden, this 29th of August, 1756.

"To the King of Prussia."

Then follows the answer from the King of Prussia to the King of Poland, as translated in narrative, Vol. ii., beginning with "The inclinations which I had for peace are so notorious," and ending with: *

"I have all my life made profession of probity and of honour, and upon that character which is more dear to me than the title of King which I hold but by the chance of Birth. I assure Your Majesty that when even at some moments, especially of the commencement, appearances will be against me, that your Majesty will see that his Interests will be sacred to me, and that you will find in my proceedings more consideration (*ménagement*) for your interests, and for those of

* Copie de la Reponse du Roy au Roy de Pologne. Mus. Brit. MS. 6864.

your Family, than some Persons may wish to insinuate to you, who are too much beneath me for me to deign to make mention of them."

Again, preceding this: "I shall have for your Majesty and for your family all the attention and the consideration which I ought to have for a great Prince whom I esteem, and of whom I only find to complain that he delivers himself up too much to the Counsels of a man whose bad intentions are too much known to me, and whose black conspiracies I should be able to prove paper upon table."

The King of Poland writes to the King of Prussia,
Au Roy de Prusse.

". "At Dresden, this 3rd September, 1756.

"Monsieur Mon Frère,

"The General Meagher has brought me the letter which your Majesty has written to me in answer to that with which I charged him for your Majesty. I am truly very sensible of the affectionate expressions with which your Majesty assures me of your friendship for my person; I flatter myself that you will make me constantly to feel the effects of those assurances which are very precious to me.

"The differences which have arisen between your Majesty and the Empress Queen do not regard me in any way. Moreover your Majesty has caused to be made, as you inform me, new representations to the Court of Vienna, and you will regulate yourself according to the answer which you receive therefrom. But I should have flattered myself that in taking the harmless passage by my States according to the constitutions of the Empire, known to your Majesty, that you would not occupy them, and that in conforming yourself to the Declaration which you have made public that you have no intention of making war against me, nor of treating my States as an Enemy's country, you would have acted contrary in them with the *ménagements* of a Prince, a well-intentioned friend: instead of that, the troops of your Majesty make exactions there, *s'emparent de mes caisses*, and carrying them away, have demolished a part of my fortress of Wittemberg, and arrest (*arrêtent*) my General Officers and others when they meet them. I appeal thereupon to the sentiments of justice and of probity of which your Majesty makes profession, and I am persuaded that you will not find that I and my States ought to suffer for the differences of your Majesty with the Empress Queen. I would desire for the rest that your Majesty would give me to know the black conspiracies of which you make mention in your letter, and of which I am ignorant unto this present time. I pray then your Majesty to attend to my representations and to evacuate my States, in making your troops to go out of them the soonest possible. I am ready, as I have already caused to be explained, to give to your Majesty all the sureties which you can exact from me, conformable to Equity and to my Dignity. But as time presses, and as in the violent position in which I find myself, I should not know how to see troops approach nearer who in some sort act as enemies, and who by that make me apprehend consequences still more disastrous, I take the part of repairing to my army to receive there at the soonest the ulterior explanations of your Majesty, protesting to you once more that my intention is by no means (*nullement*) to separate myself from a Convention of Neutrality with you, but that rather I will give hands to you (*j'y donnerai les mains*) with a perfect satisfaction. I place all confidence in the friendship of your

Majesty, reiterating to you the protestations of mine, and am with the most perfect consideration of your Majesty,

"The Good Brother,

" Auguste Rex."*

"To the King of Prussia."

On the 5th of September, 1756, the King of Prussia once more protests to the King of Poland (after expressing an " impossibility to evacuate his States, for a hundred reasons of war," a wish that the "road of Bohemia passed by Thuringia, so that I had not occasion to molest his Majesty's States ; " " my inability to employ miracles in turning the course of the Elbe, and to make troops to fly, &c. &c. &c.") : " That will never make me forget what I owe to Crowned heads, to a Prince my Neighbour, who is only seduced, and for whom, as also for all his Royal Family, I shall upon all occasions conserve, even were he himself my most cruel enemy, the highest consideration and the most perfect esteem. Those are the sentiments with which of your Majesty I am the Good Brother,

" Fédéric."

The practical sequel of these protestations is to be found in the Narrative, Vol. ii.

* MSS. Mus. Brit. 6864.

*Original Letter of the King of Prussia to the King
of England.*

" (Sent in my Secret Letter to Holdernesse by Roworth.)

" At Dresden, this 11th of March, 1757.

" Monsieur Mon Frère,

"The Communication which Your Majesty has had
the goodness to make to me of the unworthy Proposals
which the Austrians and French have made to you, has
caused me the most lively gratitude, I have been astonished
at the effrontery of our Enemies, in believing to be able
(*de croire pouvoir*) to separate the Interests of the Electorate of Hanover after that they would have crushed me
(*m'auraient ecrasé*), to avail myself of their favourite Expression.

"It is certain that the Intention of the French would be,
if it succeeded in subjugating me, to fall again upon the
German Possessions of Your Majesty, according to their
first Plan, by that means to force England to a Peace which
would be advantageous to them. This snare was too gross
not to be discovered at first, without reckoning that in
Politics it is not permitted to trust one's self to an irrecon-
cilable enemy. That which re-assures me is the character
of Your Majesty. You know that I have engaged in this
war but to take measures with you for the safety of your
States, and I am sure that far from abandoning me in the
pressing crisis, you will fulfil your engagements with this
good faith of which you have given so many splendid proofs

during your glorious reign. It is with this firm confidence
that I am with the highest esteem,

" Monsieur, my Brother,

"Of Your Majesty,

" The Good Brother,

" Fédéric." *

" To the King of England."

* Mus. Brit. MS. 6864.

CONVENTION OF CLOSTER-ZEVEN.

" The Duke of Cumberland appears to have quite lost his head or
his heart on this occasion. With an army of 38,000 men, consisting
of Hanoverians, Hessians, and other Germans, he offered the French
Marshal no resistance. But the tide of war had now rolled so near
to the Danish territory that the Court of Copenhagen became alarmed, and offered the intervention of the Count de Lynar, the Danish
ambassador at Hamburgh, who on the 8th of September signed the
singular convention of Closter-Zeven. According to this treaty all
hostilities were to cease in twenty-four hours or sooner. ' The auxiliary troops from Hesse, Brunswick, Saxe-Gotha, &c., were to be
sent home ; the Hanoverian army and its detachments, particularly
that at Buck-Schantz, were to retire under Stade, and to repass the
Elbe ;' but ' the French army were not to pass the river Oste in the
duchy of Bremen till the limits were regulated, and to keep all the
ports and countries of which it was in possession.' This convention
was neither a capitulation nor a treaty. The Count de Lynar who
negotiated it was a religious *illuminé*, who declared that the idea of
it was an inspiration of heaven, and that the Holy Spirit had given
him power to stop the French army, even as power had been formerly given to Joshua to stop the sun, that he might spare the precious
Lutheran blood which would otherwise have been shed. The Court
of France afterwards insisted on disarming the German troops, and
asserted that the Duke's army had ' laid down their arms.' The
consequence of all this was one of the most intricate disputes that
ever employed diplomacy. King George, to clear himself from the
dishonour of the convention, disavowed his son's authority to sign
it. The Duke of Cumberland tried to escape the odium of the con-

NOTE TO CHAPTER XII.

*French Colonies and old Chronicles, showing how France thought
to redeem her hopes.*

" The principal interest in this war of France" (declares
M. Capefigue in 1857 in paraphrase to the *Récit Contemporain*
of 1757)* "was not in the campaign of Germany, where she
acted as auxiliary of Germany in virtue of the treaty of Alliance; her real conflict for power and political preponderance
was upon and across the ocean. . . . In spite of an infe-
riority of numeric force, France triumphed in the dawn of the
struggle. Minorca was conquered. In India, Madras had
been taken. Calcutta had fallen to the power of Bussy.
Canada under the Marquis de Montcalm had received an immense development; conquests had added some English
possessions. So passed the three first years of the maritime
war. Afterwards, came reverses. Why is this? The Company
which had for a moment conquered Madras and Calcutta sees

vention by resigning all his commands, which his Royal Highness
did as soon as he returned to England. Upon his first appearance
at court the King never addressed a word to him, but said to those
about him, and loud enough to be heard by the Duke, ' Here is my
son who has ruined me and disgraced himself.' The Duke was
never again employed in the field, and died in 1765; a man of an
unfortunate military reputation, but not deserving, perhaps, *all* the
blame and odium attached to his character.''—*Sir Edward Cust ;
Annals of the Wars of the 18th Century.*

   * "*Les Colonies de l'Inde, de l'Afrique, et de l'Amérique.*"
" *Guerre Maritime entre la France et l'Angleterre.*" (Louis XV.)
Deuxième Période.

itself in turn besieged in Chandinagor and Pondichéry. These establishments fall to the power of the English. Canada, which had been moved by an impulse so great, is conquered by England. . . The causes of English success and the firm direction of English affairs were owing to William Pitt.* The ministry of Pitt ordered an active campaign against the French establishments of North America. . . . The Isle of Cape Breton was the finest establishment of the French Fisheries; defended by Louisbourg, it was necessary to seize that place. Three months' siege sufficed, and the fortifications were razed. The French defended themselves vigorously to the South and to the centre of the colony. It needed two campaigns to subject Canada to England. The courage of Amherst and of Wolfe found a worthy adversary in the Marquis de Montcalm, but he was deprived of all support, of all help, and even of all tidings from the metropolis. No fleet could pass across the British Squadron. All that could be obtained or received was transmitted by Corsairs.

"The following campaign opened fatally for the French in Canada. They performed prodigies, but English arms three times more numerous seized Quebec, capital, the central position of Canada, at nearly the same time that Pondichéry

* William Pitt had sworn to destroy the commercial elements of France.

"The sea was no longer free. . . . The system which seems to prevail in the mind of the English ministry was to make of France a continental power without Colonies, and therefore without commerce; it was not only military rivalry which caused fear, but commercial jealousies. . . . . France must be deprived of her colonial crown,—this was the end and aim of Pitt's system. To fortify the Navy and to subsidize the Continent, so as incessantly to keep awake the enmity of France, this was his view, *and the system has constantly since been that of England.*"

fell to the power of the Britannic forces in India. . . . .
Nevertheless, the Council at Versailles was not discouraged
at the moment. De Belleisle had conceived the vast and
bold project of a descent upon England. . . . Marshal Belleisle never renounced this project, deferred though it was. . . .
When the war of Germany became rather Prussian, Russian,
and Austrian than French, de Belleisle renewed with fresh
spirit his representations to the Council as to a descent on
England or on Ireland. . . . . At one time prisoner in London,
he had roused in his favour certain bold heads there and excited ardent imaginations." * (De Belleisle's plan for this
descent still exists . . . . though it is too long here to transcribe. The impulse of Belleisle's plan thrilled through
France, but gold was wanting in India as elsewhere.)

" The causes of decadence in the Establishments of French
India resulted principally from an Absence of Unity in the
principle of Administration. So many ideas originating from
a collection of individual interests by which the Company was
formed, were beyond the reach of the Council at Versailles.
. . . There was not, as in England, a sovereign Admiralty.
. . . These conflicts neutralized the measures for Coloniza-
tion in India. It was because MM. Dupleix, de Bussy, and
de la Bourdonnaye,† had strongly established the Dictatorship,
that they had had a brilliant administration and considerable
success. These men, despising the too-mercantile counsels
of the Merchant Company, had raised themselves to the true
French question of an Eastern Sovereignty. The financial
situation of the Company was not brilliant. This produced a
curious paradox—the French establishments in India (that

* See ' Secret Note of Intrigue' from Versailles to St James's.
Holdernesse Dispatch. This Appendix, infrà.
† Appendix, Vol. i.

country of gold and wonders) were so impoverished that the
money of Europe was sent out to them. They owed 14
millions of treasure to the King.*   The Company it was who
insisted on having the Count de Lally as chief of the Indian
expedition.   He was a brave general, appreciated highly by
d'Argenson (minister of war) and de Belleisle, but it was like
sending fire to fire.   He was a fine leader of obedient troops,
but was he calm enough for an effeminate Indian population,
and a company of speculators ?   De Lally tried to govern a
commercial régime by military rule.   He thereby created
hatred.   Bussy, whilst strong in conquest, had remained a
man of commerce and of the Company.   These internal
struggles struck the last blow at the French establishments in
India.   In the mean while the French Navy had dissensions
among itself.   This helped on the catastrophe that Canada,
the land so loving to France, should fall to England who
coveted her."

The greater were the Colonial losses of France, the more
she desired to revenge herself by a descent on Great Britain.
During Belleisle's imprisonment in England (see Vol. i.) he
had become acquainted with a Captain Thurot, who, transplanted to Versailles, at last in some sort executed the plan so
long devised there.

The Earl of Holdernesse " to Andrew Mitchell, Esq.†

" Whitehall, March 4th, 1760.

" Sir,

" I acquainted you by last post with the unexpected appearance of Mons. Thurot upon the North Coast of Ireland,

---

* For the advantage of Indian Import, Madame de Pompadour
dressed herself at one time in India muslins, whereupon female
envy immediately asserted that, by setting such fantastical fashions,
she—Pompadour—destroyed the trade of Lyons.

† *Vol. xv.   Fol. 58.   Orig. MS.*

and for further particulars I beg to be referred to what was printed at Dublin by order of the Lord-Lieutenant. The expedition is now totally at an end, Mons. Thurot being killed, and all his ships taken by three of His Majesty's frigates.

"HOLDERNESSE."

Extract from Dublin Gazette Extraordinary.

"Wednesday, Feb. 27th, 1760.
" Dublin Castle.

. . . . " It is conjectured that they landed about 1000 men altogether. . . . They were pickets of five different regiments, viz. the Swiss Guards, and four others. They had a few Hussars with them, of which nine were killed in the attack on the Town. Three of the officers were killed at Carrichfergus, one of them very richly dressed. An intelligent Person is sent to watch the motion of the frigates in the Bay. . . Major-General Strode had detached one Captain, three Subalterns, four Sergeants, four Corporals, and 100 private men, to take possession of the Castle and Town of Carrichfergus, and had also ordered a Detachment of the Austrian Militia to march thither." *

* This descent upon Ireland was preliminary to one for which larger preparations had been meditated by Marshal Belleisle, as seen in Narrative, Vol ii. " The Officers read the history of ' William the Bastard,'—and played pieces—*vaudevilles*—to celebrate the inevitable success of their expedition." " *Guerre Maritime et Coloniale.*" Récit. Contemp.

NOTE TO 264. NARRATIVE.

Copy of General Yorke's letter to the Earl of Holdernesse, Hague, March 24th, 1760. Secret, in Lord Holdernesse's of the 21st March, 1760." * *MS. Mus. Brit.* 6818.

" THE COUNT ST GERMAIN.

" My Lord,

" My present situation is so very delicate, that I am sensible I stand in need of the utmost indulgence, which I hope I shall continue to find from his Majesty's unbounded goodness, and that your Lordship is convinced that whatever I say or do has no other motive but the advantage of the King's service. As it has pleased his Majesty to convey to France his sentiments in general upon the situation of affairs in Europe, and to express by me his wishes for restoring the public tranquillity, I suppose the Court of Versailles imagines the same channel may be the proper one for addressing itself to that of England. This is at least the most natural way of accounting for the pains taken by France to employ anybody to talk to me.

" Your Lordship knows the history of that extraordinary Man, known by the name of Count St Germain, who resided some time in England, where he did nothing, and has within

---

* *The Duc de Choiseul wrote to M. d'Affry* at the Hague "that France is inclined to end the war both by sea and land, ... but if the King of England persist in including the King of Prussia in the peace, he would, to the great grief of his Most Christian Majesty, frustrate all these negotiations. . . . . . Lord Holdernesse desired General Yorke to say to M. d'Affry that under any circumstances the King of Prussia must be included in the negotiations and in the peace."

these two or three years resided in France, where he has been upon the most familiar footing with the French King, Madame Pompadour, Marshal Belleisle, &c., which has procured him a grant of the Royal Castle of Chambord, and has enabled him to make a certain figure in that country: if I do not mistake, I once mentioned this Phenonemon to your Lordship in a private letter. This man is within this fortnight arrived in this country. He appeared for some days at Amsterdam, where he was much caressed and talked of, and upon the marriage of Princess Caroline alighted at the Hague. The same curiosity created the same attention to him here. His volubility of tongue furnished him with hearers, his freedoms upon all subjects, all kinds of suppositions, amongst which his being sent about peace, not the last. M. D'Affry treats him with respect and attention, but is very jealous of him; for my part I took no notice of him, and did not so much as renew my acquaintance with him. He called however at my door. I returned his visit, and yesterday he desired to speak with me in the afternoon, but did not come as he appointed, and therefore he renewed his application this morning, and was admitted. He began immediately to run on about the bad state of France, their want of peace, and their desire to make it, and his own particular ambition to contribute to an event so desirable for humanity in general. He run on about his predilection for England and Prussia, which he pretended at present made him a good Friend to France. As I knew so much of this man, and did not chuse to enter into conversation without being better informed, I affected at first to be very grave and dry, told him that those affairs were too delicate to be treated between persons who had no vocation, and therefore desired to know what he meant; I suppose this still was irksome to him, for immediately afterwards he produced to me, by way of credentials, two letters from Marshal Belleisle, one dated the 4th, the other the 26th of Feb.; in the first he sends him the French King's passport *en blanc* for him to fill up; in the second he expresses great impatience to hear from him, and in both runs out in praises of his zeal, his ability, and the hopes that are founded upon what he is gone about. I have no doubt of the authenticity of those two letters. After perusing them and some common-place compliments, I asked him to explain himself, which he did as follows : —

" The King, the Dauphin, Madame Pompadour, and all the Court and nation, except the Duke Choiseul and M. Berrier, desire peace with England; they cannot do otherwise, for their interior requires it. They want to know the real sentiments of England, they wish to make up matters with some honour; Monsieur d'Affry is not in the secret, and the Duke Choiseul is so Austrian that he does not tell all he receives, but that signifies nothing, for he will be turned out. Madame Pompadour is not Austrian, but is not firm, because she does not know what to trust to; if she is sure of peace she will become so. It is she, and the Marshal Belleisle with the French King's knowledge, who sent St Germain as the forlorn hope. Spain is not relyed upon, that is a turn given by the Duke Choiseul, and they don't pretend to expect much good from that quarter.—This and much more was advanced by this Political Adventurer. I felt myself in a great doubt, whether I should enter conversation, but as I am convinced he is really sent as he says, I thought I should not be disapproved if I talked in general terms. I therefore told him that the King's desire for peace was sincere, and that there could be no doubt of it, since we had made the proposal in the middle of our success, which had much increased

since. That with our allies the affair was easy, without them
impossible, and that France knew our situation too well to
want such information from me. That as to particulars we
must be convinced of their desire before they could be touched upon, and that besides I was not informed. I talked of
the dependence of France upon the two Empresses; and the
disagreeable prospect before them, even if the King of
Prussia was unfortunate, but declined going any further than
the most general, though the most positive, assurances of a
desire of peace on his Majesty's part. As the conversation
grew more animated, I asked him what France had felt the
most for in her losses, whether it was Canada? No, he
said, for they felt it had cost them 36 millions and brought
no return. Guadaloupe? They would never stop the peace
for that, as they would have sugar enough without it. The
East Indies? That he said was the sore place, as it was con-
nected with all their money affairs. I asked him what they
said of Dunkirk? Made no difficulty to demolish it, and that
I might depend upon it. He then asked me what we thought
about Minorca? I answered that we had forgot it, at least
nobody ever mentioned it.* That, says he, I have told them

---

* In 1757 Mr Pitt secretly instructed *Sir B. Keene to sound the
Spanish Government concerning an exchange of Gibraltar for the
I. of Minorca.* (See p. 147, *Pitt's Correspondence.*)

(Sir Benjamin Keene, Knight of the Bath, was for many years Ambassador at the Court of Madrid, who died there just as he was about
to be made a Peer in 1757. William Pitt, Earl of Chatham, had a
high opinion of Sir Benjamin Keene, although the latter was
much abused by the Opposition in Sir Robert Walpole's time, under
the name of "Don Benjamin," for having concluded the Convention
with Spain in 1739. Ibid. pp. 50, 109, Vol. i.)

In reply "most secret" Sir Benjamin informs William Pitt that
he "had considered with more care than ordinary the most proper

over and over again, and they are embarrassed with the
expense. This is the material part of what passed in the
course of three hours' conversation, which I promised to
relate : He begged the secret might be kept, and he should
go to Amsterdam, and to Rotterdam, till he knew whether I
had any answer, which I neither encouraged nor discouraged
him from expecting.

"I humbly hope his Majesty will not disapprove what I have
done; it is not easy to conduct one's self under such circumstances, though I can as easily break off all intercourse as I
have taken it up. The King seemed desirous to open the
door for peace, and France seems in great want of it ; the
opportunity looks favourable, and I shall wait for orders
before I stir a step further. A general congress seems not to
their taste, and they seem willing to go further than they care
to say, but they would be glad of some offer, and H. M. C.
M. and the Lady are a little indolent in taking a resolution.

"I have the honour to be

"Your Lordship's obedient servant,

"J. Yorke."

manner of procuring an attentive reception of the insinuation he
had to make to the Spanish Minister." *   The answer was a charge
against England concerning the insults Spain had met with from
English (unchastised) privateers, "and the next point was what he
called our usurpations in America, when he ran out pretty largely."
Correspondence of the Earl of Chatham, Vol. i. p. 177.

This conversation therefore between General Yorke and Count
St Germain shows in diplomacy how the tongue is given to
conceal thoughts. Horace Walpole described Sir Benjamin Keene,
"as one of the best kind of agreeable men, quite fat and easy, with
universal knowledge."

---

* General Richard Wall, a Catholic gentleman of Irish descent,
for many years Ambassador of Spain at the British court, from
whence he was recalled to fill the office of Minister of Foreign
Affairs.

Lord Holdernesse writes:

"Whitehall, March 21st, 1760.

Secret.

"To the Honourable Major General Yorke.

"Sir,

"I have the pleasure to acquaint you that his Majesty entirely approves your conduct in the conversation you had with Count St Germain, of which you give an account in your Secret Letter of the 24th.

"The King particularly applauds your caution in not entering into conversation with him, till he produced two letters from Marshal Belleisle. . . . His Majesty does not think it unlikely that Count St Germain may really have been authorized (perhaps even with the knowledge of his most Christian Majesty) by some persons of weight in the Councils of France, to talk as he has done; and no matter what the channel is, if a desirable end can be obtained by it. But there is no venturing further conversation between one of the King's accredited ministers and such a person as this St Germain is, according to his present appearance. What you say will be authentic, whereas St Germain will be disavowed with very little ceremony whenever the Court of France finds it convenient; and by his own account his commission is not only unknown to the French Ambassador at the Hague, but even to the minister for Foreign Affairs at Versailles, who, though threatened with the same fate that befell the Cardinal Bernis, is still the apparent minister. . . . . It is therefore his Majesty's pleasure that you should acquaint Count St Germain that . . . you cannot talk with him upon such interesting subjects, unless he produces some authentic proof of his being really employed with the knowledge and consent of his most Christian Majesty; but at the same time you may add that the

King, ever ready to prove the sincerity and purity of his intentions to prevent the further effusion of Christian blood, will be ready to open himself on the conditions of a peace, if the Court of France will employ a person duly authorized to negotiate on that subject. . . . The Court of France shall expressly and confidentially agree that his Majesty's allies, and *nommément* the King of Prussia, are to be comprehended in the *Accommodement à faire*. It is unnecessary to add that England will never so much as hear any *Pour Parlers* of a peace which is not to comprehend his Majesty as Elector.

" I am, &c.,

" Holdernesse." *

Count St Germain called again upon General Yorke. Upon being asked for his credentials, he said that he had not authentic authority from de Choiseul, but from Madame Pompadour. " The Lady's credentials," however, he could not produce, which he, St Germain, accounted for by the fact that the Lady made it a rule never to *write* upon State affairs, but he did produce a letter from the Prince de Condé. . . . Whereupon England still proceeds cautiously, but advises General Yorke " not to offend St Germain because of the facility he had afforded to ' *that person* ' whose ' Secret Notes ' he, St Germain, had favoured. " Two of which " Secret Notes " now follow.

* MS. " Secret Despatch."

NOTE TO P. 259, VOL. II. NARRATIVE.

HOLDERNESSE DESPATCHES.* SECRET INTELLI-
GENCE FROM THE COURT OF FRANCE, A. D. 1760.
MS. (clear and cautious handwriting) *Mus. Brit.* 6818.

(The Earl of Holdernesse writes to Mr Mitchell at Berlin,
when enclosing to him the following Secret Note of Intelligence received in England from France. "I take this opportunity of transmitting to you copies of some Intelligence
that have lately been received here, but I am to desire you
would be particularly discreet in the use you make of them,
lest the Channel by which they are conveyed be discovered.")

Advices to Lord Holdernesse.
"Paris, 20th Feb. 1760.
"It is absolutely necessary to give your Court a small
sketch of the present disposition of those who have the greatest influence here, that they may not be surprised at the weakness, inconsistency, and discord that reign in the Council as
well as in the Court. The King changes so fast that I may
truly say, His Majesty grows old, lean, and melancholy, a
'*Vue d'œuil*' (?).
"The Dauphin amuses himself with singing Mass, Vespers,
and Litanies, with Madame de Marson, who by that means is

* Mus. Brit.—The anonymous writer of this Secret Intelligence,
alluded to in Lord Holdernesse's letter to General Yorke (preceding), concerning Count St Germain, the paid employé of Prussia
and of France. *See First Note of Secret Intrigue in France. Appendix to Vol. i.*

a great favourite : He is a declared protector of the Duc de
Broglio, and the head of his party. The Duc de Broglio
sends him duplicates of all the letters he writes to Marshal
Belleisle, and I leave you to judge how he resents this proceeding. Madame Pompadour continues as much in his
Majesty's favour as ever, and governs everything. Who-
ever opposes her will not long remain in power, except
Prince Soubise, whom the King honours with his friendship,
and Marshal Belleisle, who has a personal interest with his
Majesty, founded on a good opinion, as well as the esteem
the King has for him. Madame Pompadour continues to be
honoured with the Empress Queen's correspondence ; her
Imperial Majesty writes her such letters as are suited to
flatter her pride and vanity, and to increase the friendship
that so happily subsists between them for the good of the
two States ; this express word (I am assured by one who has
heard several read) is frequently used, and it pleases the King
as much as it does Madame Pompadour. By such means,
and by the servile court Count Staremberg pays her, she
still continues to be in the interest of that Court. I should here
tell you, Count Staremberg takes no steps without consulting
M. Pompadour, and is guided by her advice in everything.
Prince Soubise is *l'ami de cœur du Roi*, and he is very well
with M. Pompadour, but not so well as he was three months
ago. However, he cannot carry any point by his own interest, so he generally joins with the Duc de Choiseul. M. Belleisle stands alone : the King is persuaded of his capacity,
as well as his integrity, and that he has no views but what
tend to his Majesty's glory, and the good of his subjects.
This encourages M. Belleisle to speak his mind very freely ;
and the Cardinal de Bernis gives him an opportunity of representing to his Majesty the consequences that have arisen from

the unnatural alliance with the Court of Vienna. I know he told his Majesty very lately that the Court of Vienna desired that France should pay the Russians, and that the Russian and French troops should be employed in destroying the Prussians and the allied army, while the Empress preserved her own forces. He showed his Ministers the policy of the house of Austria had ever been the same in regard to all their allies, as his Ministers had seen at the battle of La Feld, and assured the King, the Court of Vienna espoused the Duc de Broglio, not from a persuasion of his being a great general, but because he was such a one as suited their views. M. Belleisle very lately gave a strong instance of his little regard, not to say hatred, to the Court of Vienna : Prince Charles of Lorrain wrote Count Cobenzel, that Monsieur Boccart, who was commandant at Ruremonde, had found means to render himself extremely agreeable to both those Courts, and they, in return, had solicited the Duc de Broglio to continue him there, after he was made a Lieutenant-General. The Duc de Broglio had given them a formal promise that it should be done without consulting M. Belleisle. But afterwards wrote the motives that engaged him to do it, on which M. Belleisle recalled Boccart, and sent another in his station, notwithstanding the representations of the Courts of Vienna and Brussels. There was a very indecent scene between M. Belleisle and Count Staremberg not long ago, in which they told each other, in the worst terms, whatever the most violent passion could suggest. M. Belleisle has since complained to the King ; Count Staremberg to his Court and to M. Pompadour. From what I have said, you will easily believe M. Belleisle will not study to make the Duc de Broglio shine at the head of the army : and you will be sensible that the Court of Vienna, the Duc de Broglio and his party, will leave no

means unattempted to ruin M. Belleisle.   But in that I think
I may say they will not succeed, for M. Belleisle's head appears to be as good as ever, though he is continually occupied
des minuties; so he really has not time to give himself up
à des Vuës plus etendues, and to follow them.   Besides which,
he is ill with Pompadour and the Duc de Choiseul, and not
well with Prince Soubise.   So he is sure of being opposed by
them, whenever he does propose anything out of his office;
and he has it in his power by his post to render ineffectual
most things they wish to have done.

The Duc de Choiseul is very well with the King, also
with M. Pompadour, and is not ill with Prince Soubise, he is a
friend to the Court of Vienna; and has all the qualities re-
quisite worthily to fill the post he enjoys.   His chief view is
to become prime minister, and he hopes, when M. Belleisle
dies, to succeed him; but if I am well informed he will be
deceived in this, the King having already promised it to Prince
Soubise.   He at present lives seemingly well with Prince
Soubise; but they do not love one another.   He is ill with
M. Belleisle, and does not conceal it; but as he does not
love business, and is very much at his ease, it would not be
surprising if he should be disgusted, and retire when he finds
he cannot obtain what he aims at.   Monsieur d'Estrées has
entirely lost his credit with the King, the Court, and the
nation.   However, he is still very well with M. Belleisle, he
also lately had a scandalous scene with the Abbé de Broglio
in the King's ante-chamber, in which they treated each other
like porters, and were laughed at by those who were the
spectators.   M. de St Florentine is taken up with his pleasure, and maintains himself in his station by voting sometimes
on one side, sometimes on the other, by paying his court to
M. Pompadour, and by being well with everybody.   M.

Puysieux is the honestest man at the Court, but the care he
is obliged to take of his health, and his love of peace and tranquillity, make him very much decline public business. M.
Berryer is as much declined as the fleet, and is very little
regarded by anybody. M. Bertim is a very honest man, but
has not the talents necessary for the Comptroller-general;
nor has he health. He only accepted the charge because the
King desired him. Mons. Pans de Montmartel and his commissioners do the business of the office. It was the reverse with
Mons. Silhouette, who was cried up for his talents; and if he did
not do the business of the State well, he did his own better
than any Comptroller-general ever did, for he has gained 50,000
French livres revenue in the short time he was employed. It
only remains to speak of the Duc de Broglio; I think, I may
say he has lost ground since he had the command of the army;
his keeping the troops so long in the field, and thereby sacri-
ficing such a number of troops to no purpose, proves that a
spirit of contradiction and not the King's service made him
alter the plan proposed by M. Contades. The affair of Dit-
tembourg and all that passed for twenty days before it, has been
severely censured by his enemies here, and cannot be justified
by his friends. M. Belleisle, M. Contades, M. d'Estrées,
and all the generals and officers who are their friends, have
spoken their minds very freely on the battle of Minden, and
by much the greatest part of the world are convinced Duc
Broglio did not do his duty there, and attribute the loss of
that battle to him. I am sure M. Belleisle has set this affair in
so true a light to the King, that his Majesty is persuaded M.
Contades had great reason to complain of him; and I am
informed Prince Soubise is not his friend. So it is not
easy to decide whether he will be able long to stand his
ground against M. Belleisle, who loses no opportunity to

lessen him in the King's favour. . . . This is a true picture of our ministry. By it you see everything is brought about by intrigues and cabals. Everybody thinks how to raise himself, or to destroy his enemies. Nobody has the public good at heart, and there is but one *Bon Citoien* in the Council. This may in some measure account for the vicissitudes, jealousy, and contradictions that appear to the world, and show why what is resolved one day is changed the next. It is said that the funds necessary for the campaign were found; but I am told it is not so, and I believe it. Your Court knows better than I whether the prospect of peace has produced the change in the army, that, I wrote you, was to be assembled near Liege. I can only say I believe the division between M. Belleisle and Duc Broglio has had some share in it, as well as the want of money. I find that the number of recruits that have been sent to Duc Broglio's army, are not yet very considerable, neither have the regiments yet received any part of the money necessary to make the repairs that are wanting. By this it will be the latter end of May before Duc Broglio's army will be in a condition to take the field. If your Court could profit by this delay, and fall on the troops that are quartered along the Rhine, they could not fail of success, as nothing is yet ready to oppose them; and the regiments in those quarters would be easily beaten or dispersed by the allied army's crossing the Rhine, which may now be very easily done, as I hear from the Generals who are lately come from those quarters. I cannot yet say with what number of troops the King's army or armies will be reinforced; by whom they will be commanded; nor when they will be assembled; but it is probable I shall be able to write to you with more certainty very soon. It does not yet appear plain to me that M. Soubise has renounced the command of the army that was intended to be assembled on the Maeze ; though the want of money, or the hopes of peace, have certainly suspended the assembling it so soon as was intended; and it is yet very probable Count Maillebois may be employed this year."

Endorsed " 1760.—*Advices in Lord Holdernesse's, of the 14th of March,* 1760."

HOLDERNESSE DESPATCHES — SEQUEL OF SECRET INTELLIGENCE FROM THE COURT OF FRANCE, FROM AN EMPLOYÉ OF ENGLAND AND PRUSSIA, FAVOURED BY THE COUNT DE ST GERMAIN, WHOSE DEFECTION WAS SUSPECTED IN THE BATTLE OF ROSBACH. MS. 6818.

" Paris, Feb. 25, 1760.

" When I last wrote, I saw there was something on the tapis that regarded the troops that were destined for Germany ; and I was not mistaken, as I am this morning informed. It was resolved yesterday in Council to fix the reinforcement at 36 battalions and about 42 squadrons. In the former are three battalions of French guards ; two of Swiss; four of Normandy ; four of Alsace ; three of La March ; three of Royal Suedois ; two of Vierset ; two of . . . ; five of Cambray ; and two Scotch regiments in all 30 battalions : But as the three battalions incorporated in the Alsace la Marche, Royal Suedois, make part of the Duc de Broglio's army, the augmentation is only 27 battalions. I could not learn from the person who told me this, the names of the other regiments, neither could he tell me the regiments of horse that were to march ; but I dare say, it will be impossible to send near such a number of cavalry as he mentioned, for horses are so scarce, that the Gendarmerie yet want near 600 to complete them, and I know M. Belleisle has hitherto objected to augmenting the expense of the army, as money is still scarcer than horses; besides, he is not without disquietude on withdrawing so many troops from the heart of the country, as he thinks we have as much to fear from a rebellion in some of the provinces as from descents on our coasts, for the people in the provinces are almost driven to despair by misery and discontent. I have since had a conversation with one of the most sensible men of this Court, who told me that the Courts of Vienna and Petersburg had used every argument to determine the King of Poland not to make his peace; assuring his Majesty, their measures were so well taken, and the campaign armies so superior to the King of Prussia's, that this year would infallibly finish the war, put his Majesty (indemnification proportioned to what his States had suffered) in quiet possession of his Electorate . . . . . He added, Those Courts have held the same language to our ministers at Vienna and Petersburg; and their ministers here strongly solicit the continuance of the war for the campaign. Count Staremberg went so far as to say, that if this Court would only stand in the defensive and prevent Prince Ferdinand from sending any succour to Saxony, it would be impossible for his Prussian Majesty to resist the force. The two Empresses, Swedes and the Empire would march against him, and that nothing but constancy is wanted to finish, with honour and advantage, what the King of Prussia had begun. He insinuated to me, that the Empress Queen, besides these representations, had taken a much more effectual way to secure Madame Pompadour in her interest. That the Duc de Choiseul still seemed rather inclined to favour that Court, though there was little reliance to be had on him, as he was the greatest *Fourbe* in Europe. But that the King and most of his ministers seemed inclined to a peace, if England would grant them such a one as they could make. He also informed me, there were great difficulties in raising the money for this year. That the parliament refused registering the new edicts. The King had sent them, because they knew there had been some overtures made for a peace; which in our situation they regarded as the greatest blessing France could enjoy. That once obtained, the great sums these new impositions were intended to raise, would become unnecessary, and the parliament suspected the ministers wanted to have the new edicts registered before the peace was made, being sure they would be so afterwards, and it was his opinion the minister could not, at this time, find means to oblige the parliament to register the new impositions, as people were really sinking under the load of taxes, and the provinces were depopulated beyond imagination, as has appeared by the difficulties the officers have met with in raising men to recruit their regiments; on this occasion, I asked how the additional expense of the reinforcements that were to be sent into Germany would be provided for? he answered, It was very probable the march of those troops may make our enemies prefer peace before war; if not, I foresee there will be very great difficulties in raising the money necessary for this Campaign.

Orders are given to suspend the building of the frames; the flat-bottomed boats are unrigged; and the Irish and Scotch regiments march into Germany. This proves, better than anything I can say, that all thoughts of an invasion are laid aside; so your Court may take their measures in consequence.

If a peace does not take place, I believe Prince Soubise will command the army of the Lower Rhine. Count Maillebois is here and makes his court to M. Belleisle, who will join him in endeavouring to ruin the Duc de Broglio. . . . If that can be brought about, it is very probable Count Maillebois will have the command of the Duc de Broglio's army.

Orders have been sent to the greater part of the Infantry, to begin their march from their respective garrisons towards Aix-la-Chapelle and Trèves, the beginning of next month; but the cavalry are not yet in a condition to march.

Translated Copies of Original Letter from the King of Prussia to the Chevalier de Froulay. With Answer, and the Duc de Choiseul's Original Observations on the same.

ALSO,

Original Letter and Memorial from the Duc de Choiseul to William Pitt, and Secret Notices from the Spanish and British Ambassadors at Versailles to their respective Courts upon the Family Compact.

Copy of " *The King of Prussia's Letter to the Chevalier de Froulay, Feb. 14th*, 1760. *

" Attribute, Monsieur, but to your respectable character that

----

* *MS. Mus. Brit.* 6844. *Plut. C. L. xix. H.*

In 1759 the King of Prussia wrote to the King of England a letter proposing peace :

" Monsieur mon Frère,

" Nous avons agi avec toute la vigueur possible. Nos succès, loin de leur (les ennemis) donner des sentimens pacifiques, n'ont fait que resserrer les liens qui les unissent," &c. — *Correspondence of the Earl of Chatham, p.* 413, *Vol. i.*

which attracts my confidence towards you. I believe you to be the most fitting of all Frenchmen to whom to make these Overtures, because your Quality of Ambassador *s'y prete mieux*, and because I believe you as attached to your Country as to your Order. It concerns Peace. I speak to you of it without any other Preamble, and as I believe myself to be able to give some certain Notions upon this subject to the King of France and to his Minister, I believe you to be the most suitable Person to fulfil that Object. Since this war, the Interruption of all Correspondence and the Changes so common to the French Nation, have filled Versailles with so many new Personages, that it is difficult to any one who does not daily follow these little Revolutions to know to whom to address one's self. . . . But as I do not know the sort of Prejudices which may reign at that Court, and the *Façon dont les Esprits y sont peutétre prevens*, I leave you to arbitrate upon the Choice of the Channel of which you may serve yourself.*

" . . . . You are informed, without doubt, that the King of England and myself, We have proposed to our Enemies the Session of a Congress, there to terminate the Dissensions which have given place to this War. We know that the Courts of Vienna and of Petersburgh have refused themselves to this, — we at least are in the Persuasion that the King of France does not think the same ; And this Persuasion makes us believe that it would not be impossible to arrive at the End so desirable for humanity. I will not

" Andrew Mitchell informs Mr Pitt that the King asked me, ' But can your Ministers make a peace ? ' . . . . I answered, ' I was sure they wished for Peace.' ' And,' says he, ' I hope I shall not be forgot.' " Ibid. p. 407.

* Letter from political Employés — " Cui Bono, if Prussia be sincere ? "

parade to you the Reasons which may induce the King of France to give his hands to this. I will not tell you that Martinique would be lost, Pondichéry and even Canada" (*de méme*)—" All the Commerce of the Nation ruined. I will not depict to you what you feel better than I do, That, the War continuing, France would play but the Part of Auxiliary, which will not be suitable to Her, ... and that She would be perhaps by consequence carried away by those two Powers into Measures which the Force of conjunctures would oblige her to adopt . . . diametrically in opposition to Her Interests, &c. &c. France can withdraw herself with Honour from the pitiful Situation in which She finds Herself, if She will a separate peace with Ourself, England, and our Allies. If France consent to maintain the Equilibrium of Germany, and oblige her Allies to subscribe to it, in making Common Cause with England, she may expect Conditions much more favourable than she will be able to find under any other case. I pray you to know if these Ideas would possibly find favour in the Country where you live, and what is the *Façon* of thinking on the part of the King and of His Ministry. For myself *Je pais le Volontaire.* I act as volunteer— I fire off a Pistol to find out what will result from it. For, you and the English, you have a Desire to Speak, and Nobody wishes to be the first. Very well, my dear Chevalier, let us be the Lost Children of Politics. Let us work at Concord, and let us see if there will be no means by some strokes of the pen to terminate a Discord so fatal to all Europe. These Propositions are vague, truly. But let them explain themselves . . . . They will serve as *Cannevas* Preliminaries. The first thing is to speak, the principal to agree, and Peace will be a natural Consequence. . . . I feel, Monsieur, that I charge you with a Commission which you did not expect. . . . In quality of a good Frenchman I do not believe that you will act as a bad citizen. And, in quality of Chevalier, you ought to assist one who has fought to excess against Barbarians and Nations who pretend to more polite Denominations."

The answer from the Chevalier de Froulay expresses : "His very Christian Majesty's desire for Peace, Justice, and Tranquillity ;" and reports that the Minister of Foreign Affairs adds to the expression of these pacific inclinations on the part of his very Christian Majesty, "*que le Roy son Maitre pensoit que le Moyen le plus certain pour faire la paix Generale etait de traiter et de conclure Separément la Paix de la France avec l'Angleterre.*"

That this would be the shortest way ("*voye la plus courte) qu'enfin le Roy son Maitre ne pouvoit Sans Manquer a ses Alliés, ou recevoir les propositions de l'Angleterre ou Lui en faire.*" Also : "*Si le Roy de Prusse comme il paroit desirer la Paix et qu'il ait l'Intention de communiquer la Reponse à Sa Lettre aux differentes Cours de l'Europe, il peut prendre la Voye d'Angleterre pour parvenir au But qu'il se propose ; et nous Lui ferons connoitre la bonne Opinion qu'il doit avoir de Notre Probité et de Notre Franchise. Car à la première Apparence de Reussite de Paix avec l'Angleterre autant nous avancerons nous pour conclure un Ouvrage si Salutaire.*"

De Froulay passed on his Prussian Majesty's Letter to the proper Authorities. The official answer to it is :
"From M. le Ministre de Choiseul, by Mons. de Froulay.

1.

"If his Prussian Majesty desire that the opening of the next Campaign do not take place, it is necessary that there be Preliminaries agreed upon or nearly contracted before the Month of June.

2.

" As soon as there may be an appearance of peace with England, France will do her best to conclude the rest.

3.

"The unhappiness of the circumstances does not permit us to explain ourselves in any other way, *et que l'on se serve d'une autre voye.*

4.

" As soon as it may be seen that they trust a little to us, we shall be less measured than we appear to be at present."

Then follows:

From M. Froulay separately.   De M. Froulay à part.

5.

" M. de Choiseul strongly inclined to our Ideas.   He has told me privately, ' You know it is not I who made the Treaty of Vienna.'

6.

" They fear that a bad use might be made of Overtures, that is why they dare not advance more.

7.

" The Courts of Russia and of Vienna have made, the 19th of this month, new Protestations to France to engage her to enter early into the Campaign, and to abandon the Marine entirely, to indemnify herself fully in Germany, where it appears that Fate and Forces will decide this year in favour of the Vows and of the Desires of the Empresses.

8.

" It is a motive the more to engage France to hasten Peace with the proposed Parties, Because her Intention is in no wise to derange the Equilibrium in Germany, and in particular to wear out the King of Prussia (*Le R. de P.*), —(if one may avail one's self of such a term.)

9.

" Russia has engaged to give a Corps of 30m. men to join to that of the Grl. Laudohn, besides the formidable army which she sends into Germany.

10.

" If the K. of P. (King of Prussia) has had enough confidence in you to do you the Honour to charge you with the commission of which you have just acquitted yourself, he will certainly add Faith to that, which you will say to have received in Answer upon this subject.

11.

" We imagine that no Party will gain great things in this war. And we ourselves, although we may have Port Mahon, &c., feel very well that in making Peace we shall lose something just as the others."

———

Translation of " *one from the Duc de Choiseul to Mr Pitt, sent in Lord Bute's most secret letter to Mr Mitchell, the 1st of April,* 1761."

" Most Secret.
" Paris, the 26th of March, 1761.*

" The King, my master, in uniting himself to the senti-

* MS. Mus. Brit.
h 2

ments of his Allies to attain, if possible, to the re-establishment of general Peace, has authorized me to send to your
Excellence the Memorial here joined, which concerns only
the interests of France and of England, relative to the particular war of the two crowns.   The King has cause to
hope that the frank manner with which he proposes to treat
with his Britannic Majesty, will take away all distrust in the
course of the negotiation if it take place, and will engage
his Britannic Majesty to make known to the King his true
sentiments, either on the conclusion of the Peace, or concerning the principles which ought to be operated upon to
procure this benefit to the Two Nations.

"I will add to your Excellence, that I am hereby authorized
to certify that, relatively to the war, which concerns the
King of Prussia, the Allies of the King, my master, are
decided to treat their interests in the future Congress with
the same simplicity and the same frankness which I can
assure to your Excellency on the part of France, and that in
conserving that which is due to their dignities and to their
positions, and to justice, they will carry into the negotiation
all the facilities which their humanity inspires to them for
the general happiness of Europe.

"The King, my master, and his Allies do not doubt but
that they may find the same sentiments in the heart of his
Britannic Majesty and of his Allies.   I regard as a blessing
for my Ministry to have been the organ of sentiments so
happy, which furnish to me the occasion to assure your Excellence of the distinguished consideration with which I have
the honour to be,

                    "Sir,
            "Of your Excellence
        "The very humble and obedient Servant,
                        "de Choiseul."

Y.

Translation of the Original State Memorial (MS.) subjoined to the Duc de Choiseul's Letter, foregoing, dated Paris, the 26th of March, 1761.

" Sir,

"The Most Christian King* desires that the particular

* It is well known that the Marquise in these negotiations between France and England objected to the King of England being styled the titular ' King of France,' whilst Louis XV. was *only* " the Most Christian King."

De Choiseul pleaded : " Louis XIV. yielded to precedent in this dry husk of titles."

" The blood of Bourbons is august," went on Madame, " and do not I know the History of England ? Shall the King of France submit to the successor of Henry VIII. who was the executioner of his Queens ?—To the successor of Mary who overflowed the Island with the blood of Protestants, and of Elizabeth who inundated it with the blood of Catholics, and who chopped off the head of the Queen of Scotland, Mary Stuart, the Dowager Queen of France ? — the successor of Cromwell, the Regicide ? — of William, the usurper of the throne of a legitimate Prince, who, in consequence of such usurpation, was with his family thrown on the royal generosity and bounty of France ? . . . . Is civilization to yield to ferocity ? "

Madame de Pompadour has been repaid by England for this national insult by the foul stigma branded on her memory by English writers. In England, during and after the French Revolution, was propagated such abominations as " *Le Parc aux cerfs, ou l'origine de l'affreux déficit*, 1790." We have seen, in the Narrative, how M. Capefigue's royalist researches have failed to find any Parc aux cerfs at all. It is observable, also, that in the malignant Secret notes of Intelligence, in this Appendix, written by the political employés of England and Prussia (MSS. unadulterated), no mention whatever is made of this abomination. The omission will be welcome to M. Capefigue, whom England to-

Peace of France with England may be united to the general
Peace of Europe, for which His Majesty entertains the most sincere wishes ; but as the nature of the objects which have occa-
sioned the war between France and England is totally foreign
to the contestations of Germany, His most Christian Majesty

day has styled the " Varillas of the 19th century," for his justifica-
tion of humanity in the 18th Century.

M. M. Goncourt, who, as before said, quote largely from revolutionary historians, are frustrated in their search for this den of
kingly iniquity. All they can find in its place, is " *une toute petite
et assez pauvre maison, avec un tout petit Jardin . . . . et qui
semble plutot faite pour une seule, supposition que corroborent les
récits de Madame du Hausset, les récits de Mercier, commissaire
de la guerre qui présida l'éducation de l'Abbé de Bourbon.*" * . . .
. . . . . " *Le Parc aux cerfs n'est pas la propriété de l'Ermitage,
qui aurait été donnée au Roi par Madame de Pompadour. Ce
n'est pas le sérail légendaire des historiens et des romanciers.*"

M. M. Goncourt—19th century enemies of Madame de Pompadour, and scoffers at the 18th century Cabinet in petticoats—
assert that Frederic, when Fortune turned her back upon him after
Kölin, sent an emissary to the Duc de Richelieu, who represented to
that hero that " the reign of the woman who had deranged the
ancient system of diplomacy could not last long ;—that in case of
her death the Dauphin would resume the ancient policy, &c."
" The emissary asked Richelieu if the conqueror of Mahon ought
not to reserve himself for the future, adding, in the name of his
Master,—' Ought three women ' (Maria Theresa, Elizabeth of
Russia,· and Madame de Pompadour) ' to be allowed to destroy the
Edifice reared by the greatest Kings of France ? '

" Carried away, seduced, won over, Richelieu remained tranquil,
respected Magdebourg, and its 3000 or 4000 recruits incapable of resistance, abandoned his own forces to the Prince de Soubise, and
let that favourite general of Madame de Pompadour lose that disastrous battle of Rosbach, ... which for long nights robbed

---

* This *toute petite maison* was probably used as a nursery for the
illegitimate child of Louis XV., called Louis Bourbon. (*See
Autograph Letters of Louis XV., this Appendix. Note 3.*)

has thought that it was necessary to agree with His Britannic Majesty on the principal points which will form the basis of their particular negotiations, to accelerate so much more the general conclusion of the Peace. . . . . The best method of arriving at the end proposed is to discard the embarrassments which may cause an obstacle to it. In the case of a Peace the discussions of Nations upon their reciprocal conquests, the different Opinions upon the utility of the conquests, and the compensations for restitutions, form ordinarily the embarrassing matter of a pacific negotiation. As it is natural that each Nation, upon these different points, seeks to acquire the most advantages possible, Distrust and Interest combat and produce tardiness. To avoid these inconveniences and to prove the frankness of his proceedings, ... the most Christian King proposes to His Britannic Majesty to agree that, relatively to the particular war of France and of England, the two crowns shall remain in possession of that which they have conquered upon the one side and upon the other side, and that the situation in which they shall find themselves on the 1st of September of the year 1761, in the East Indies, on the first of July of the said year in the West Indies and in Africa, and on the first of next May

Madame de Pompadour of rest." "*Goncourt; Les Maitresses de Louis* XV." *Livre* 2. Pub. 1860.

In justice, however to the Duc de Richelieu (for even the devil deserves his due) it is right to add here that M. M. Goncourt found the above statement partly on the *Mémoires de Madame du Hausset (Baudouin,* 1824), the Advertisement prefixed to which so called Mémoires will show how revolutionary pamphleteers quarrelled among themselves over Court offals, and thus robbed themselves of their prey.—M. M. Goncourt also support the above statement by the "*Mems. of the Duc de Richelieu,* 1793," *Enlarged Edition.* (!)

in Europe, shall be the basis to the Treaty which may be negotiated between the two Powers. . . . .

" The most Christian King trusts that the dispositions of
His Britannic Majesty may be as his own."

   " By order, and in the name of the

     " Most Christian King, my Master,

       " Le Duc de Choiseul.

" *Paris, le* 26 *Mars,* 1761."

Replied to with diplomatic courtesy by W. Pitt, 8 Avril,
1761. With what result the Narrative has told.

In a letter to Mr Pitt of the 20th of August, Mr Stanley,
British Envoy, writes from Versailles : " The Duc de Choiseul
said to me the other day, in the warmth of conversation, that
' the Treaty of England had hurt him ;' and certainly the State
of the negotiation has lately been very disadvantageous to
his Excellency in a private light . . . M. Grimaldi" (Spain),
" being an Ambassador *de famille*, has perpetual opportunities
of following the Court: he acts on all occasions with M. de
Stahremberg, who is extremely well with Madame de Pompadour." . . . .

On the 8th of September Mr Stanley writes to Mr Pitt :
" I this day heard, from good authority, that 15 Spanish
ships of war are to sail speedily, in order to convoy home the
fleets which they expect."

On 2nd Sept., in a private letter to Mr Pitt, Mr Stanley
writes :

" I have secretly seen an article drawn up between France
and Spain, in which the former engages to support the interests of the latter equally with her own in the negotiation of
the Peace with England. . . Some of my intelligence is so
secret that I am very apprehensive of the persons being

guessed. . . I have seen some of M. de Bussy's letters; he knows more than he ought."

Again, Stanley writes to Pitt: . . . "The Duc de Choiseul's behaviour this day, though personally very polite to me, was extremely grave, and he appeared full of anxiety . . . . He mentioned to me that if affairs had gone differently upon some points, and if he had seen better hopes of a reconciliation, he would have proposed a meeting with you, and have desired you either to send him a yacht in order to his coming to Dover, or to have given him that opportunity on shipboard between that place and Calais, ... that both should have had the authority of their Sovereigns. . . . "

The Marquis Grimaldi writes to the Count Fuentes this letter in cypher (Extracts).

"Paris, September 13, 1761.

" Choiseul has despatched a messenger to Bussy, with his answer to the ultimation of England. Your Excellency will see that they give up everything here: they only continue firm in regard to their Allies, and consequently the system of this ministry is to remain true to us . . . . I think it should be our aim not to let France make peace without our inclusion; but, at the same, we ought to wish that, *if possible, it should not be said that peace has been made on account of our differences with England.* So I answered Choiseul that it was not hearsay to mention Spain in the memorial, and that it would be sufficient to repeat to Bussy the order of the 10th of August, *not to sign anything* without the *accommodadation of matters with Spain likewise,* according to the stipulation of the Treaty, &c."

This was the treaty afterwards so famous as the Family Compact. The discovery of the existence of this Treaty confirmed Mr Pitt's opinion of the hostile intentions of

Spain.   Considering war with that power on these grounds inevitable he represented to the Council that . . . . " we ought from prudence as well as from spirit to secure to ourselves the first blow " . . . . Warmed by opposition, Mr Pitt declared that " this is the moment for humbling the House of Bourbon ; and if he could not prevail in this instance this should be the last time he would sit in the council." . . . . The King having rejected the written advice of Mr Pitt and Lord Temple, they resigned on the 5th of October. *See* " *Annual Register and History of the Minority*," *p.* 34. *See also,* " *Correspondence of the Earl of Chatham*," *Vol. ii. pp.* 139, 140, 141, 142, 143.

PARIS GOSSIP 100 YEARS AGO.

One touch of sympathy makes even a world at war akin. In 1761, Mr Pitt wrote a letter of homage to Voltaire (the draught in Lady Hester Pitt's handwriting) concerning the works of Corneille, of which Voltaire, at Ferney, was then editing an edition, the profits of which were to be applied to the Grand-niece of Corneille whom Voltaire had adopted. Among the subscribers were Louis XV. for 200 copies, nearly all the princes of the blood, Madame de Pompadour, the Duc de Choiseul, Pitt, and Mr Stanley, English Envoy at Versailles. . . . To the latter Voltaire wrote :

" Monsieur,

"I hear that when you take our settlements, you take subscriptions too.   Corneille belongs to every nation, and especially *to those who greatly think and bravely die ;* had Shakspeare left a grand-daughter I would subscribe for her.

Give me leave to thank you for what you do in favour of Corneille's blood." *

Voltaire's letter (in broken English) to Mr. Pitt is signed,

" Voltaire,
" Gentilhome ord. de la Chambre du Roy."

Voltaire still enjoyed this sinecure at Ferney, although the King's displeasure kept him exiled from Versailles long after Madame de Pompadour's death. Madame de Pompadour before her death forgave even the " Pucelle d'Orléans," in favour of those old days when Voltaire the poet and her friend improvised,

" Pompadour, ton crayon divin
Devait dessiner ton visage
Jamais une plus belle main
N'aurait fait un plus bel ouvrage." †

By the protection and intervention of the Duc de Choiseul, of M. de Malesherbes, and of Madame de Pompadour, the Encyclopédie, under the direction of Diderot and d'Alembert, eventually flourished, although Voltaire (become a territorial *Grand Seigneur*) grew chary of personal risk in the enterprise. The Pompadour and de Choiseul, on the contrary, as already seen, became more enthusiastic in favour of the Encyclopédie as their political power increased. Voltaire had sent back his Cross and his key to Prussia with these verses :

" Je les reçus avec tendresse
Je les renvoie avec douleur,

* See Correspondence of the Earl of Chatham, year 1761, p. 133, Vol. ii. .
† Quoted in " Biographie Universelle."

Comme un amant jaloux dans sa mauvaise humeur,
Rend le portrait de sa maitresse." *

Note 3, to Narrative, p. 97, Vol. ii.   * Although Voltaire revenged himself afterwards by scoffs at Prussian *Poëshies* for the terror Prussian bayonets caused him at Frankfort, he, the philosopher Voltaire, wrote at the time unto the royal Author of the *Poëshies* this Declaration :

"I am dying : I protest before God and before men that being no longer in the service of his Majesty the King of Prussia, I am not the less attached to him, nor less subject to his will, for the little time I have to live. He arrests me at Frankfort for the book of his poetry of which he had made me a present. I remain in prison until such time that the book comes back from Hamburgh. I have restored to the minister of his Prussian Majesty at Frankfort all the letters that I had preserved of his Majesty's, as loved marks of the goodness by which he had honoured me. I will restore at Paris all the other letters that he requires of me." Voltaire concludes, after speaking of a bit of paper which has nothing to do with this history, but seems to have been prized, or feared, by the King of Prussia as a memorial of their intercourse which preceded it years before :

" My niece, who is near me in my illness, engages herself under the same oath to restore it if she find it. In the mean while . . . I declare to lay claim to nothing from his Majesty the King of Prussia, and I expect nothing in the condition in which I am, but the compassion which is due from his greatness of soul to a dying man, who lost all and sacrificed all to attach himself to him, who has served him with zeal, who has been useful to him, who has never personally failed him, and who reckoned on the goodness of his heart. I am obliged to dictate, not being able to write. I sign with the most profound respect, the purest innocence, and the most lively pain,

" Voltaire."

SEMIRAMIS.
Voltaire v. Crébillon.

See Narrative, Vol. ii. p. 86.   The " Semiramis " of Voltaire had been (fifteen years before its publication) treated by him as " Eriphyle." Crébillon had also produced a tragedy,

In 1762 Voltaire wrote to Madame de Pompadour requesting her aid in a work of charity. The Marquise replied:—

" I am charmed, Sir, that you have addressed yourself to me. That confidence imparts to me a little vanity, for it shows you think I have a good heart. Yes, I have, or I believe I have such; and upon this occasion, I will try to merit your esteem, and those who resemble you."

Again: "How can one write with so much fire and genius at your age? . . . A man endeavoured the other day to maintain that you had made injurious verses upon the King and myself. . . . I maintained that they could not have come from you because they were bad, and that I had never done you an injury. . . . See by that what I think of your genius and of your justice! I willingly pardon my enemies, but I do not easily forgive the enemies of the King."

The Pompadour had entreated the King to permit Voltaire's return to Versailles, but this the King refused. He knew that Voltaire was in correspondence with Frederic of Prussia, and Louis regarded Frederic as the sworn enemy of France and of the Catholic Faith.*

called " Semiramis," but that having been forgotten since its birth, it was rather a compliment to Voltaire, at the. expense of Crébillon (that object of Voltaire's jealousy in the Pompadour's favour), to think of "Semiramis" at all. Crébillon died on the 17th of June, 1762, 88 years of age. Louis XV. erected a mausoleum to Crébillon in the Church of St Gervais, where he was buried.

The love of Madame de Pompadour for her friends survived them. It will be remembered how one of her first acts on coming into power was to perpetuate the memory, and to continue the work of Crozat, the friend of her childhood, who had died in 1740.

* Before the expulsion of the Jesuits, some self-called "philosophers" who remained, gagged, in France, were bribed by Frederic of Prussia, equally with those whose talents and treachery were

In the midst even of the general insurrection against the Jesuits their order was traditionally reverenced by Louis XV.

on hire at Potsdam. Their letters were firebrands by which Frederic inflamed England, alarmed Protestantism, and lighted up the seven years' war:—witness the following two or three further extracts:

" Nov. 1756. The Court of France proposes to itself to undertake . . . . a powerful diversion against the States which England possesses in India, ... of which the end is to form the siege of Madras. . . . They contemplate sending a new envoy of troops to Canada, ... who will be embarked from different ports on Merchant ships." *

" Nov. 1756. I have just learned, upon very good authority, that during these past days, an Emissary of the Pretender has appeared at this Court, who has had various conferences with the Duc de Belleisle, and other members of the Council, which creates suspicion . . . . of the project of a diversion against the Britannic Isles."†

" Nov. 1756. The vertigo of the nation" (concerning the Austrian Alliance) " moderates itself; . . . the new system which they have adopted scarcely sustains itself but by the animosity which the King of France appears to have against the King of Prussia." ‡

In war-time Voltaire had boasted that it depended upon him whether France and Prussia should wage war with the pen as fiercely as by the sword.

A Courier, laden with royal Prussian *Poëshies*, had been stopped on his way to Voltaire at Ferney, and the *Poëshies*, insulting to France, had been handed over to the Duc de Choiseul, who said, " We will cut up Prussia by the pen as we hope to do by the sword," although, as Voltaire said, the blame of those *Poëshies* will rest on me,

---

* Secret note of Intelligence enclosed in the K. of Prussia's letter to M. Mitchell, sent in M. Mitchell's secret letter of the 20th Nov. MS. Mus. Brit. 6844. Anon.

† MS. 6844. Mus. Brit. Anon.

‡ Intelligence of Nov. through M. Mitchell to the Earl of Holdernesse. MS. Mus. Brit.

Whilst the decree for their expulsion was suspended,* the 'Very Christian King' wrote to the General of the Jesuits at Rome, to ask if a compromise might not be effected between Church and State. The answer was, "We must be that which we are, or not at all." The Jesuit Father Neuville wrote the following letter (dated January 1762) to Madame * * * at St Germain-en-Laye.

" Madame,

" The night of prejudice is too dark, and the tempest too violent; we shall not escape this shipwreck. I know not if the State will gain much by the destruction of the Society. I hope that religion will lose nothing thereby. It is true that the suffrage of the Bishops has been highly in our favour,* but it will serve us only as an honourable epitaph."

Christopher de Beaumont himself, Archbishop of Paris, of Southern origin, brought up in rigid purity of conduct by his mother, and inflexible in the virtue of a long life (he was 60 years old when the Jesuits were expelled), commands the respect of posterity even by the consistency of his intolerance,

doing me harm with the King of France, and "what is worse, with the Pompadour."

Frederic wrote to the Marquis d'Argens a letter full of hope for the future of philosophy at Potsdam :

" Near Breslau, 27th August, 1760.

" I know not if I shall survive this war, but in that case I am resolved to pass the rest of my days in Retreat in the bosom of Philosophy and of Friendship. . . .

" Adieu, dear Marquis,

" I embrace you." †

* See Narrative, Vol. ii. Two last Chapters.

---

† *Mus. Brit. MS.* 4863.

although he, like all other celebrities, was pasquinaded in his day.

Archbishop Beaumont hoped that the Jesuits and the King's soul might be redeemed after Madame de Pompadour's death. But, unsustained by her influence, the King from that time forth sought distraction from serious affairs, whether of Church or State, in libertinage which compelled his saint-like Queen to kneel continually before heaven and the Church on earth, craving intercession and absolution for the father of her children. The Dauphin, her beloved son, who joined his prayers to hers, died at Fontainebleau in 1765. The Queen and the Dauphiness, his wife and mother, daughters of rival kings, but united by the bonds of earthly love and heavenly hope, kept watch beside the Dauphin. The misfortunes of their country, after the "illustrious brigand's" * invasion of it, helped to draw these two women, princesses of Poland, together. Marie Lecskinska, Queen of France, lived to mourn her father Stanislas, who was burned to death. Marie Lecskinska died after devoted attendance on her son's widow, the Dauphiness, the daughter of her father's usurper, who never recovered the death of that young husband who was so coldly indifferent to her during the first period of her married life. Both these women died from unselfish devotion to one object of their love in life,—a life of dreary pilgrimage to them, uncheered but by hope of heaven. Louis XV. reverenced his Queen as a saint. But after the death of their son, the temptations of his courtiers and of his

---

* " Les violences inhumaines que le Roy de Prusse fait à toute la Saxe sont suffisamment connües. . . . . . Il est pour cet effet très necessaire que vous vous serviez de toutes les occasions pour depeindre bien vivement le procedé barbare et l'inhumanité du Roy de Prusse." — " *Circular letter to Russian Ministers at various Courts from the Empress Elizabeth Petrowna.*" *MS. Mus. Brit.*

century caused Louis to drown remembrance in pleasure, which alternated with remorse, and he saw but little of his Queen, whose earthly crown was exchanged for an aureole of heavenly glory, until she too lay dead before him. Then, as he knelt before her corpse, a passion of love, of grief, and of repentance overtook Louis XV., to be drowned as before in sin, for which his beloved daughter, Louise, the nun of St Denis, henceforth alone rebuked him. The love of Louis XV. for his children, as declared in the narrative, was extreme. This love was even a part of his religion.*

In removing the restrictions enforced by such men as de Beaumont, even Voltaire (who had become territorial possessor at Ferney) dreaded the effect of latitudinarianism on the people. We have elsewhere read Voltaire's letter to the Marquis d'Argens,† showing the necessity of popular religion to public safety. In 1766, Voltaire wrote to another philosophic friend : ‡ " I do not think that we understand each other

---

* In the Bibliothèque Impériale there is a volume in 4to bound in Vellum, containing 456 folios, in two columns—date, the end of the 14th Century. Rebound in red morocco, with the arms of France on the side, and the cypher of Louis XV. at the back. This volume, familiar to his use, is deficient in one leaf of the Psalter, but the first words are preserved thereof in old French, and speak of the hope which, in the case of Louis XV., was overshadowed by a gloomy conscience, and of the love for his children which never failed him in the midst of the sins by which he vainly strove to distract his melancholy . . . " *L'esperance des bons car c'est le commencement de beneurté celeste* . . . . *ausi comme nous benissons les enfans pour leurs bonnes semiles, car por ce nous avons esperance* que en leur *temps benoiz seront.*"

Les Manuscrits François. *Anciens Fonds.*

Fonds de Colbert. No. 3360. No. 7295.

† See this Appendix, Note " French Finance and Philosophy."

‡ Danielaville, who at one time held the seals of Controller-General of Finance.

upon this article of the people, whom you believe so worthy of instruction. By the people I mean the populace which has but its hands to live by. I doubt whether this order will ever have the time or the capacity to instruct itself. If you were worth an estate, as I am, and had ploughs, you would be of my opinion. When the populace begins to reason all is lost." In the mean while, the Marquis de Mirabeau (father of the famous Mirabeau), a political economist and disciple of Du Quesnay, published a pamphlet called "The Friend of Mankind," to inculcate upon the masses the principles of Economy and Production.

But Mirabeau's pamphlet was before its time. Other pamphlets must do their work; the ground must be ploughed by the people's sorrow, and watered with king's blood. Mirabeau's son must do his work before France could understand aright the Principles of Economy and Production. In the mean while Frederic of Prussia rendered a tribute to the interim of Peace which was the work of Madame de Pompadour, as was the liberty of the Press which allowed free course to Opinion. The Count de Ségur, whose father had been one of the heroes of France in the Pompadour's time, went to Potsdam to see the King of Prussia.* Frederic began by declaring that he desired to draw the "bonds of friendship tighter" between Louis XVI. and himself, and by professing his admiration of the French. Afterwards: "I see," said he to de Ségur, "that you wear the decoration of Cincinnatus. You have made war in America. Your youth is always warlike. Nevertheless, since 1763 you might well have forgotten war; so long a peace might enervate. How have you been able, in a country so far, and where civiliza-

---

* Mémoires ou Souvenirs de M. le Comte de Ségur, Tome 2, p. 111. Published, Paris and London, 1826.

tion but begins, to forget Paris, and to do without luxury, balls, perfume, and powder?"

Piqued by these sarcastic words, "I feigned," says de Ségur, "to misunderstand him upon the word *powder*."

"Sire," said I, "we have not unhappily found an opportunity to burn as much as we would: after three short campaigns the English, in shutting themselves up in their fortresses and in resigning themselves to peace, have deprived us too soon of that pleasure."

This boast of a French soldier leads us to look again at the statue of Louis XV. (once upon a time the king of armies) near the Church of the Magdalene; the statue of the King whom the Capuchine Marquise had loved, and for whom de Segur, father and son, had fought. In taking a farewell glance at that statue, its origin and history, briefly told, may not be inappropriate.

In 1748, a statue of Louis XV., the *See Narrative,* idol of his people, was proposed by the civic *Note Z. Last* authorities of Paris. *Chapter.*

In 1748, the Marquise de Pompadour, "sitting at the King's feet at Choisy," fostered her own love by delineating the King as a hero. The King, charmed by her talent, and flattered by her representation of him, submitted the design to Bouchardon, his favourite's protégé. Bouchardon, enchanted with the design as an artist, undertook to execute it for the civic authorities of Paris. Bouchardon died before the statue was finished, and thus the task devolved upon Pigalle, who, loyal to the King, and loving the Marquise (his patroness), eloquently interpreted the design which did honour to both of them. In 1763, the statue was transferred to the Plâce Louis XV., called "*the Place de prédilection*" of the Pompadour. After its erection there, the statue was hidden from the public for two years while completed. It was not, therefore, unveiled to the people until one year after the death of Madame de Pompadour. The pedestal was ornamented by bas-reliefs in bronze representing the battles won by Louis XV. At each angle of this pedestal were four figures— "Virtues;" Strength, Peace, Prudence, Justice. In the reign of Louis XVI. the statue was surrounded by a white marble balustrade. In 1792, this statue of Louis XV. was thrown down, and one of "Liberty" was erected on its pedestal. The *Place de Louis XV.* was then called the *Place de la Révolution.* In 1800 it was decreed that a "National Column" should supplant the statue of Liberty. Lucien Buonaparte, Minister of the Interior, went in great state to lay the first stone of this national column. Then in the earth was found —beneath the former pedestal of the statue of Louis XV.—a cedar-wood box containing coins stamped "1754," and bearing the impress of Louis the King, once "Well-beloved."

The Magdalene Church was converted, for a time, into the "Temple of Mars."

Who, in the Temple of Mars, thought of the penitence the Magdalene Church had been designed to commemorate? Nearly half a century before, the meekest of Christian queens had uttered a bitter satire upon popular favour and popular gratitude. Scarcely was Madame de Pompadour buried than the Queen, Marie Leczinska, wrote to President Hénault: "For the rest there is no longer any question here of the Marquise, who is no more, than if she had never existed. Such is the world,—is it worth the trouble of loving it?"

THE END.

INDEX

OF

A P P E N D I X

TO

VOL. II.

CONTAINING

AUTOGRAPH AND ORIGINAL LETTERS,

&c.

INDEX

OF

APPENDIX TO VOL. II.

Paris Gossip 100 years ago,
concerning
Voltaire,*
The Archbishop of Paris and the Jesuits,
The Queen and the Dauphiness,
The King,
Original Secret Notes of Intelligence,
The Statue of Louis XV.

* Notes to Narrative, 2nd vol. pp. 86, 97, and 332.

JOHN CHILDS AND SON, PRINTERS.

ERRATA.

VOL. I.

Page 48; *for* Tournehaim *read* Tourneheim.
— 82; *for* Our French historian *read* One.
— 100; *for* Marmoutel *read* Marmontel.
— 101; *for* games at chance *read* of chance.
— 268; *for* Encyclopédia *read* Encyclopédie.
— 271; *for* 1000 pounds of rent *read* francs.
— 272; *for* 1000 pounds of rent *read* francs.
— 273; *for* d'Agnesseau *read* d'Aguesseau.
— 281; *for* of which this is *read* of which dedication this is
— 288; *for* Zara *read* Zaïre.
— 289; *for* at the Court of Poland *read* of Stanislas of Poland.
— 293; *for* President Maupeon *read* Maupeou.

VOL. II.

Page 13; *for* Acts *read* Arts.
— 15; *for* Imported in England *read* into England.
— 17; *for* his own use *read* Frederic's own use.
— 22; *for* she as *read* which she intended as.
— 22; *for* the building commenced *read* was commenced.
— 28, *line* 7; *read* proposed to preserve and to unite them.
— 69, *line* 4 from top; *for* Marshal *read* Marshal de Richelieu.
— 76, *line* 16; *for* country *read* home.
— 97; *for* who in his company *read* who was in his company.
— 165; *for* Pauliny d'Argenson *read* Paulmy.
— 226; *for* to incidental questions before peace *read* to incidental questions which separated the enemy during war.
— 273; *for* Folio *read* Volume.

Page 17, Appendix, Vol. ii.; *for* the Marquis d'Argeus *read* d'Argens.

Printed in the United Kingdom
by Lightning Source UK Ltd.
130057UK00002B/70/A

9 781428 627246